Man Against Darkness

MAN
Against
Darkness

and Other
Essays

W. T. Stace

University of Pittsburgh Press

Library of Congress Catalog Card Number: 67-18694

"The Snobbishness of the Learned" Copyright © 1936 by The Atlantic
Monthly Company, Boston, Mass. Reprinted with permission.
"Have Nations Any Morals?" Copyright © 1945 by The Atlantic
Monthly Company, Boston, Mass. Reprinted with permisssion.
"Man Against Darkness" Copyright © 1948 by The Atlantic Monthly
Company, Boston, Mass. Reprinted with permission.
"British Colonialism" Copyright © 1954, Yale University Press. Re-
printed by permission of *The Yale Review.*

Copyright © 1967, University of Pittsburgh Press

Manufactured in the United States of America

Publication of this book has been aided by a grant

from the A. W. Mellon Educational and Charitable Trust

Preface

THE reader may be puzzled by the jump from the apparent irreligion of the first essay, "Man Against Darkness," to something which may fairly be called theism (of a sort) in "The Philosophy of Mysticism." Twelve years elapsed between the writing of the first and the second—an interval long enough to be a partial explanation of a change of opinion. But this is hardly enough. What happened in the interval to cause so great a change? The answer is that the writer had meanwhile made a study of mysticism, of Christian, Hindu, Islamic, Buddhist, and other mystics.

But one must not exaggerate the greatness of the change. Merely the intellect and not the emotions were involved in it. Nothing was altered in the writer's feelings about the world or about religion. Some people have professed to detect a certain religious element in "Man Against Darkness" which, they said, hid itself behind a mask of anti-religion. However that may be, neither at the time of the writing of the first essay, nor of the second, nor at the present day, has the writer ever become involved in the usual practices and feelings of worship by means of which religious minds commonly express their emotions. This is what I mean by saying that the change was only intellectual.

Seven essays in this volume were given as public lectures. The three on values were delivered at the University of Nebraska in 1930, "Imagery and Thought in Poetry" at Wheaton College, Massachusetts in 1956, "Science and Ethics" at Lexington, Kentucky, in 1964, and the two lectures on mysticism at Mount Holyoke, Massachusetts, in 1961. "Snobbishness of the Learned," "Have Nations Any Morals?," and "Man Against Darkness" were published in the *Atlantic* in 1936, 1954, and 1948 respectively. "British Colonialism" appeared in the *Yale Review* in 1954, "The Place of Philosophy in Human Culture," "Science and the Physical World," and "Science and Explanation" in *Philosophy* in 1954, and "Survival After Death" in *The Crane Review* in 1963.

I wish to thank the journals and institutions concerned, including the trustees of the will of M. T. Garvin, for their kind permission to use these articles in the present collection.

W. T. Stace

Contents

I

Concerning Religion

Man Against Darkness

THE Catholic bishops of America once issued a statement in which they said that the chaotic and bewildered state of the modern world is due to man's loss of faith, his abandonment of God and religion. I agree with this statement though I do not accept the religious beliefs of most bishops. It is no doubt an oversimplification to speak of *the* cause of so complex a state of affairs as the tortured condition of the world today. Its causes are doubtless multitudinous. Yet allowing for some element of oversimplification, I say that the bishops' assertion is substantially true.

M. Jean-Paul Sartre, the French existentialist philosopher, labels himself an atheist. Yet his views seem to me plainly to support the statement of the bishops. So long as there was believed to be a God in the sky, he says, men could regard him as the source of their moral ideals. The universe, created and governed by a fatherly God, was a friendly habitation for man. We could be sure that, however great the evil in the world, good in the end would triumph and the forces of evil would be routed. With the disappearance of God from the sky all this has changed. Since the world is not ruled by a spiritual being, but rather by blind forces, there cannot be any ideals, moral or otherwise, in the universe outside us. Our ideals, therefore, must proceed only from our own minds; they are our own inventions. Thus the world which surrounds us is nothing but an immense spiritual emptiness.

It is a dead universe. We do not live in a universe which is on the side of our values. It is completely indifferent to them.

Years ago Mr. Bertrand Russell, in his essay "A Free Man's Worship," said much the same thing.

Such in outline, but even more purposeless, more void of meaning, is the world which Science presents for our belief. Amid such a world, if anywhere, our ideals henceforward must find a home. . . . Blind to good and evil, reckless of destruction, omnipotent matter rolls on its relentless way; for man, condemned today to lose his dearest, tomorrow himself to pass through the gate of darkness, it remains only to cherish, ere yet the blow falls, the lofty thoughts that ennoble his little day; . . . to worship at the shrine his own hands have built; . . . to sustain alone, a weary but unyielding Atlas, the world that his own ideals have fashioned despite the trampling march of unconscious power.

It is true that Mr. Russell's personal attitude to the disappearance of religion is quite different from either that of M. Sartre or the bishops or myself. The bishops think it a calamity. So do I. M. Sartre finds it "very distressing." And he berates as shallow the attitude of those who think that without God the world can go on just the same as before, as if nothing had happened. This creates for mankind, he thinks, a terrible crisis. And in this I agree with him. Mr. Russell, on the other hand, seems to believe that religion has done more harm than good in the world, and that its disappearance will be a blessing. But his picture of the world, and of the modern mind, is the same as that of M. Sartre. He stresses the *purposelessness* of the universe, the facts that man's ideals are his own creations, that the universe outside him in no way supports them, that man is alone and friendless in the world.

Mr. Russell notes that it is science which has produced this situation. There is no doubt that this is correct. But the way in which it has come about is not generally understood. There is a popular belief that some particular scientific discoveries or theories, such as the Darwinian theory of evolution, or the views of geologists about the age of the earth, or a series of such discoveries, have done the damage. It would be foolish to deny that these discoveries have had a great effect in undermining religious dogmas. But this account does not at all go to the root of the matter. Religion can probably outlive any scientific discoveries which could be made. It can accommodate itself to them. The root cause of the decay of faith has not been any particular discovery of science, but rather the general spirit of science and certain basic assumptions upon which modern science, from the seventeenth century onwards, has proceeded.

It was Galileo and Newton—notwithstanding that Newton himself was a deeply religious man—who destroyed the old comfortable picture of a friendly universe governed by spiritual values. And this was effected, not by Newton's discovery of the law of gravitation nor by any of Galileo's brilliant investigations, but by the general picture of the world which these men and others of their time made the basis of the science, not only of their own day, but of all succeeding generations down to the present. That is why the century immediately following Newton, the eighteenth century, was notoriously an age of religious skepticism. Skepticism did not have to wait for the discoveries of Darwin and the geologists in the nineteenth century. It flooded the world immediately after the age of the rise of science. Neither the Copernican hypothesis nor any of Newton's or Galileo's particular discoveries were the real causes. Religious faith might well have accommodated itself to the new astronomy. The real turning point between the medieval age of faith and the modern age of unfaith came when the scientists of the seventeenth century turned their backs upon what used to be called "final causes." The final cause of a thing or event meant the purpose which it was supposed to serve in the universe, its cosmic purpose. What lay back of this was the presupposition that there is a cosmic order or plan and that everything which

5

exists could in the last analysis be explained in terms of its place in this cosmic plan, that is, in terms of its purpose.

Plato and Aristotle believed this, and so did the whole medieval Christian world. For instance, if it were true that the sun and the moon were created and exist for the purpose of giving light to man, then this fact would explain why the sun and the moon exist. We might not be able to discover the purpose of everything, but everything must have a purpose. Belief in final causes thus amounted to a belief that the world is governed by purposes, presumably the purposes of some overruling mind. This belief was not the invention of Christianity. It was basic to the whole of Western civilization, whether in the ancient pagan world or in Christendom, from the time of Socrates to the rise of science in the seventeenth century.

The founders of modern science—for instance, Galileo, Kepler, and Newton—were mostly pious men who did not doubt God's purposes. Nevertheless they took the revolutionary step of consciously and deliberately expelling the idea of purpose as controlling nature from their new science of nature. They did this on the ground that inquiry into purposes is useless for what science aims at: namely, the prediction and control of events. To predict an eclipse, what you have to know is not its purpose but its causes. Hence science from the seventeenth century onwards became exclusively an inquiry into causes. The conception of purpose in the world was ignored and frowned on. This, though silent and almost unnoticed, was the greatest revolution in human history, far outweighing in importance any of the political revolutions whose thunder has reverberated through the world.

For it came about in this way that for the past three hundred years there has been growing up in men's minds, dominated as they are by science, a new imaginative picture of the world. The world, according to this new picture, is purposeless, senseless, meaningless. Nature is nothing but matter in motion. The motions of matter are governed, not by any purpose, but by blind forces and laws. Nature in this view, says Whitehead—to whose writings I am indebted in this part of my essay—is "merely the hurrying of material, endlessly, meaninglessly." You can draw a sharp line across the history of Europe dividing it into two epochs of very unequal length. The line passes through the lifetime of Galileo. European man before Galileo—whether ancient pagan or more recent Christian—thought of the world as controlled by plan and purpose. After Galileo European man thinks of it as utterly purposeless. This is the great revolution of which I spoke.

It is this which has killed religion. Religion could survive the discoveries that the sun, not the earth, is the center; that men are descended from simian ancestors; that the earth is hundreds of millions of years old. These discoveries may render out of date some of the details of older theological dogmas, may force their restatement in new intellectual frameworks. But they do not touch the essence of the religious vision itself, which is the faith that there is plan and purpose in the world, that the world is a moral order, that in the end all things are for the best. This faith may express itself through many different intellectual dogmas, those of Christianity, of Hinduism, of Islam. All and any of these intellectual dogmas may be destroyed without destroying the essential religious spirit. But that spirit cannot survive destruction of belief in a plan and purpose of the world, for that is the very heart of it. Religion can get on with any sort of astronomy, geology, biology, physics. But it cannot get on with a purposeless and meaningless universe. If the scheme of things is purposeless and meaningless, then the life of man is purposeless and meaningless too. Everything is futile, all effort is in the end worthless. A man may, of course, still pursue disconnected ends, money, fame, art, science, and

7

may gain pleasure from them. But his life is hollow at the center. Hence the dissatisfied, disillusioned, restless, spirit of modern man.

The picture of a meaningless world, and a meaningless human life, is, I think, the basic theme of much modern art and literature. Certainly it is the basic theme of modern philosophy. According to the most characteristic philosophies of the modern period from Hume in the eighteenth century to the so-called positivists of today, the world is just what it is, and that is the end of all inquiry. There is no *reason* for its being what it is. Everything might just as well have been quite different, and there would have been no reason for that either. When you have stated what things are, what things the world contains, there is nothing more which could be said, even by an omniscient being. To ask any question about *why* things are thus, or what purpose their being so serves, is to ask a senseless question, because they serve no purpose at all. For instance, there is for modern philosophy no such thing as the ancient problem of evil. For this once famous question presupposes that pain and misery, though they seem so inexplicable and irrational to us, must ultimately subserve some rational purpose, must have their places in the cosmic plan. But this is nonsense. There is no such overruling rationality in the universe. Belief in the ultimate irrationality of everything is the quintessence of what is called the modern mind.

It is true that, parallel with these philosophies which are typical of the modern mind, preaching the meaninglessness of the world, there has run a line of idealistic philosophies whose contention is that the world is after all spiritual in nature and that moral ideals and values are inherent in its structure. But most of these idealisms were simply philosophical expressions of romanticism, which was itself no more than an unsuccessful counterattack of the religious against the scientific view of things. They perished, along with romanticism in literature and art, about the beginning of the present century, though of course they still have a few adherents. At the bottom these idealistic systems of thought were rationalizations of man's wishful thinking. They were born of the refusal of men to admit the cosmic darkness. They were comforting illusions within the warm glow of which the more tender-minded intellectuals sought to shelter themselves from the icy winds of the universe. They lasted a little while. But they are shattered now, and we return once more to the vision of a purposeless world.

Along with the ruin of the religious vision there went the ruin of moral principles and indeed of all values. If there is a cosmic purpose, if there is in the nature of things a drive towards goodness, then our moral systems will derive their validity from this. But if our moral rules do not proceed from something outside us in the nature of the universe—whether we say it is God or simply the universe itself—then they must be our own inventions. Thus it came to be believed that moral rules must be merely an expression of our own likes and dislikes. But likes and dislikes are notoriously variable. What pleases one man, people, or culture displeases another. Therefore morals are wholly relative. This obvious conclusion from the idea of a purposeless world made its appearance in Europe immediately after the rise of science, for instance in the philosophy of Hobbes. Hobbes saw at once that if there is no purpose in the world there are no values either. "Good and evil," he writes, "are names that signify our appetites and aversions; which in different tempers, customs, and doctrines of men are different. . . . Every man calleth that which pleaseth him, good; and that which displeaseth him, evil."

This doctrine of the relativity of morals, though it has recently received an impetus from the studies of anthropologists, was thus really implicit in the whole scientific mentality. It is disastrous for morals because it destroys their entire traditional foundation. That is why philosophers who see the danger signals, from the time at least of Kant, have been

9

trying to give to morals a new foundation, that is, a secular or non-religious foundation. This attempt may very well be intellectually successful. Such a foundation, independent of the religious view of the world, might well be found. But the question is whether it can ever be a *practical* success, that is, whether apart from its logical validity and its influence with intellectuals, it can ever replace among the masses of men the lost religious foundation. On that question hangs perhaps the future of civilization. But meanwhile disaster is overtaking us.

The widespread belief in "ethical relativity" among philosophers, psychologists, ethnologists, and sociologists is the theoretical counterpart of the repudiation of principle which we see all around us, especially in international affairs, the field in which morals have always had the weakest foothold. No one any longer effectively believes in moral principles except as the private prejudices either of individual men or of nations or cultures. This is the inevitable consequence of the doctrine of ethical relativity, which in turn is the inevitable consequence of believing in a purposeless world.

Another characteristic of our spiritual state is loss of belief in the freedom of the will. This also is a fruit of the scientific spirit, though not of any particular scientific discovery. Science has been built up on the basis of determinism, which is the belief that every event is completely determined by a chain of causes and is therefore theoretically predictable beforehand. It is true that recent physics seems to challenge this. But so far as its practical consequences are concerned, the damage has long ago been done. A man's actions, it was argued, are as much events in the natural world as is an eclipse of the sun. It follows that men's actions are as theoretically predictable as an eclipse. But if it is certain now that John Smith will murder Joseph Jones at 2:15 P.M. on January 1, 2000 A.D., what possible meaning can it have to say that when that time comes John Smith will be *free* to choose whether he will commit the murder or not? And if he is not free, how can he be held responsible?

It is true that the whole of this argument can be shown by a competent philosopher to be a tissue of fallacies—or at least I claim that it can. But the point is that the analysis required to show this is much too subtle to be understood by the average entirely unphilosophical man. Because of this, the argument against free will is generally swallowed whole by the unphilosophical. Hence the thought that man is not free, that he is the helpless plaything of forces over which he has no control, has deeply penetrated the modern mind. We hear of economic determinism, cultural determinism, historical determinism. We are not responsible for what we do because our glands control us, or because we are the products of environment or heredity. Not moral self-control, but the doctor, the psychiatrist, the educationist, must save us from doing evil. Pills and injections in the future are to do what Christ and the prophets have failed to do. Of course I do not mean to deny that doctors and educationists can and must help. And I do not mean in any way to belittle their efforts. But I do wish to draw attention to the weakening of moral controls, the greater or less repudiation of personal responsibility which, in the popular thinking of the day, result from these tendencies of thought.

What, then, is to be done? Where are we to look for salvation from the evils of our time? All the remedies I have seen suggested so far are, in my opinion, useless. Let us look at some of them.

Philosophers and intellectuals generally can, I believe, genuinely do something to help. But it is extremely little. What philosophers can do is to show that neither the relativity of morals nor the denial of free will really follows from the grounds which have been supposed to support them. They can also try to discover a genuine secular basis for morals to replace the religious basis which has disappeared. Some of us are trying to do these things. But in the first place philosophers unfortunately are not agreed about these matters, and their disputes are utterly confusing to the non-philosophers. And in the second place their influence is practically negligible because their analyses necessarily take place at a level on which the masses are totally unable to follow them.

The bishops, of course, propose as remedy a return to belief in God and in the doctrines of the Christian religion. Others think that a new religion is what is needed. Those who make these proposals fail to realize that the crisis in man's spiritual condition is something unique in history for which there is no sort of analogy in the past. They are thinking perhaps of the collapse of the ancient Greek and Roman religions. The vacuum then created was easily filled by Christianity, and it might have been filled by Mithraism if Christianity had not appeared. By analogy they think that Christianity might now be replaced by a new religion, or even that Christianity itself, if revivified, might bring back health to men's lives.

But I believe that there is no analogy at all between our present state and that of the European peoples at the time of the fall of paganism. Men had at that time lost their belief only in particular dogmas, particular embodiments of the religious view of the world. It had no doubt become incredible that Zeus and the other gods were living on the top of Mount Olympus. You could go to the top and find no trace of them. But the imaginative picture of a world governed by purpose, a world driving towards the good—which is the inner spirit of religion—had at that time received no serious shock. It had merely to re-embody itself in new dogmas, those of Christianity or some other religion. Religion itself was not dead in the world, only a particular form of it.

But now the situation is quite different. It is not merely that particular dogmas, like that of the virgin birth, are unacceptable to the modern mind. That is true, but it constitutes a very superficial diagnosis of the present situation of religion.

Modern skepticism is of a wholly different order from that of the intellectuals of the ancient world. It has attacked and destroyed not merely the outward forms of the religious spirit, its particularized dogmas, but the very essence of that spirit itself, belief in a meaningful and purposeful world. For the founding of a new religion a new Jesus Christ or Buddha would have to appear, in itself a most unlikely event and one for which in any case we cannot afford to sit and wait. But even if a new prophet and a new religion did appear, we may predict that they would fail in the modern world. No one for long would believe in them, for modern men have lost the vision, basic to all religion, of an ordered plan and purpose of the world. They have before their minds the picture of a purposeless universe, and such a world-picture must be fatal to any religion at all, not merely to Christianity.

We must not be misled by occasional appearances of a revival of the religious spirit. Men, we are told, in their disgust and disillusionment at the emptiness of their lives, are turning once more to religion, or are searching for a new message. It may be so. We must expect such wistful yearnings of the spirit. We must expect men to wish back again the light that is gone, and to try to bring it back. But however they may wish and try, the light will not shine again—not at least in the civilization to which we belong.

Another remedy commonly proposed is that we should turn to science itself, or the scientific spirit, for our salvation. Mr. Russell and Professor Dewey both made this proposal, though in somewhat different ways. Professor Dewey seemed to believe that discoveries in sociology, the application of scientific method to social and political problems, will rescue us. This seems to me to be utterly naïve. It is not likely that science, which is basically the cause of our spiritual troubles, is likely also to produce the cure for them. Also it lies in the nature of science that, though it can teach us the best means for achieving our ends, it can never tell us what ends to pursue.

13

It cannot give us any ideals. And our trouble is about ideals and ends, not about the means for reaching them.

No civilization can live without ideals, or to put it in another way, without a firm faith in moral ideas. Our ideals and moral ideas have in the past been rooted in religion. But the religious basis of our ideals has been undermined, and the superstructure of ideals is plainly tottering. None of the commonly suggested remedies on examination seems likely to succeed. It would therefore look as if the early death of our civilization were inevitable.

Of course we know that it is perfectly possible for individual men, very highly educated men, philosophers, scientists, intellectuals in general, to live moral lives without any religious convictions. But the question is whether a whole civilization, a whole family of peoples, composed almost entirely of relatively uneducated men and women, can do this. It follows, of course, that if we could make the vast majority of men as highly educated as the very few are now, we might save the situation. And we are already moving slowly in that direction through the techniques of mass education. But the critical question seems to concern the time-lag. Perhaps in a hundred years most of the population will, at the present rate, be sufficiently highly educated and civilized to combine high ideals with an absence of religion. But long before we reach any such stage, the collapse of our civilization may have come about. How are we to live through the intervening period?

I am sure that the first thing we have to do is to face the truth, however bleak it may be, and then next we have to learn to live with it. Let me say a word about each of these two points. What I am urging as regards the first is complete honesty. Those who wish to resurrect Christian dogmas are not, of course, consciously dishonest. But they have that kind of unconscious dishonesty which consists in lulling oneself with opiates and dreams. Those who talk of a new religion are merely hoping for a new opiate. Both alike refuse to face the

14

truth that there is, in the universe outside man, no spirituality, no regard for values, no friend in the sky, no help or comfort for man of any sort. To be perfectly honest in the admission of this fact, not to seek shelter in new or old illusions, not to indulge in wishful dreams about this matter, this is the first thing we shall have to do.

I do not urge this course out of any special regard for the sanctity of truth in the abstract. It is not self-evident to me that truth is the supreme value to which all else must be sacrificed. Might not the discoverer of a truth which would be fatal to mankind be justified in suppressing it, even in teaching men a falsehood? Is truth more valuable than goodness and beauty and happiness? To think so is to invent yet another absolute, another religious delusion in which Truth with a capital T is substituted for God. The reason why we must now boldly and honestly face the truth that the universe is non-spiritual and indifferent to goodness, beauty, happiness, or truth is not that it would be wicked to suppress it, but simply that it is too late to do so, so that in the end we cannot do anything else but face it. Yet we stand on the brink, dreading the icy plunge. We need courage. We need honesty.

Now about the other point, the necessity of learning to live with the truth. This means learning to live virtuously and happily, or at least contentedly, without illusions. And this is going to be extremely difficult because what we have now begun dimly to perceive is that human life in the past, or at least human happiness, has almost wholly depended upon illusions. It has been said that man lives by truth, and that the truth will make us free. Nearly the opposite seems to me to be the case. Mankind has managed to live only by means of lies, and the truth may very well destroy us. If one were a Bergsonian one might believe that nature deliberately puts illusions into our souls in order to induce us to go on living.

The illusions by which men have lived seem to be of two kinds. First, there is what one may perhaps call the Great Illusion—I mean the religious illusion that the universe is moral and good, that it follows a wise and noble plan, that it is gradually generating some supreme value, that goodness is bound to triumph in it. Secondly, there is a whole host of minor illusions on which human happiness nourishes itself. How much of human happiness notoriously comes from the illusions of the lover about his beloved? Then again we work and strive because of the illusions connected with fame, glory, power, or money. Banners of all kinds, flags, emblems, insignia, ceremonials, and rituals are invariably symbols of some illusion or other. The British Empire, the connection between mother country and dominions, used to be partly kept going by illusions surrounding the notion of kingship. Or think of the vast amount of human happiness which is derived from the illusion of supposing that if some nonsense syllable, such as "sir" or "count" or "lord" is pronounced in conjunction with our names, we belong to a superior order of people.

There is plenty of evidence that human happiness is almost wholly based upon illusions of one kind or another. But the scientific spirit, or the spirit of truth, is the enemy of illusions and therefore the enemy of human happiness. That is why it is going to be so difficult to live with the truth. There is no reason why we should have to give up the host of minor illusions which render life supportable. There is no reason why the lover should be scientific about the loved one. Even the illusions of fame and glory may persist. But without the Great Illusion, the illusion of a good, kindly, and purposeful universe, we shall *have* to learn to live. And to ask this is really no more than to ask that we become genuinely civilized beings and not merely sham civilized beings.

I can best explain the difference by a reminiscence. I remember a fellow student in my college days, an ardent Christian, who told me that if he did not believe in a future life, in heaven and hell, he would rape, murder, steal, and be a drunkard. That is what I call being a sham civilized being. On the other hand, not only could a Huxley, a John Stuart Mill, a David Hume, live great and fine lives without any religion, but a great many others of us, quite obscure persons, can at least live decent lives without it. To be genuinely civilized means to be able to walk straightly and to live honorably without the props and crutches of one or another of the childish dreams which have so far supported men. That such a life is likely to be ecstatically happy I will not claim. But that it can be lived in quiet content, accepting resignedly what cannot be helped, not expecting the impossible, and being thankful for small mercies, this I would maintain. That it will be difficult for men in general to learn this lesson I do not deny. But that it will be impossible I would not admit since so many have learned it already.

Man has not yet grown up. He is not adult. Like a child he cries for the moon and lives in a world of fantasies. And the race as a whole has perhaps reached the great crisis of its life. Can it grow up as a race in the same sense as individual men grow up? Can man put away childish things and adolescent dreams? Can he grasp the real world as it actually is, stark and bleak, without its romantic or religious halo, and still retain his ideals, striving for great ends and noble achievements? If he can, all may yet be well. If he cannot, he will probably sink back into the savagery and brutality from which he came, taking a humble place once more among the lower animals.

The Psychology of Mysticism

Very few American psychologists have paid any attention to the psychology of mysticism. William James, of course, stands out as an exception. But that was a long time ago. There was also Professor James H. Leuba, who wrote a book called *The Psychology of Religious Mysticism*. J. B. Pratt's writings have some importance, but he was primarily a philosopher, not a psychologist.

This neglect of the subject probably has a number of causes. I shall pick out only two for mention because they happen to impinge upon the treatment I myself want to give the matter. One is perhaps that the subject can hardly be approached except by the method of introspection, which psychologists wish to avoid. Another may be the failure of psychologists to make a clear distinction between psychology and philosophy. There certainly are states of mind which are ordinarily called mystical. To describe, classify, and analyze these states of mind should be the work of the psychologist. But another problem arises here which falls within the area of philosophy and with which the psychologist should not meddle. Mystics nearly always claim that in their mystical experiences they are in touch with a transcendental realm of reality. Is this claim true or false? Are mystical states purely subjective; do they reveal anything about the nature of objective reality? This, I say, is a philosophical problem which lies outside the science of psychology. Perhaps because psychologists, quite rightly from their point of view, do not wish to get mixed up with metaphysical or transcendental problems, or are at any rate skeptical about them, they steer clear of mysticism altogether. But this is a pity. If they would deal only with the psychology of mysticism and leave the philosophical side of it alone, they could, I am sure, do valuable work.

It is usually a good idea to bear in mind the distinction between philosophy and an empirical science such as psychology. I once received a valuable lesson in this. A very distinguished astronomer visited the Department of Philosophy in Princeton and gave us a lecture entitled "An Astronomer's Philosophy." We philosophers were delighted. And I in my enthusiasm offered to reciprocate by giving a lecture to the astronomers which was to be entitled "A Philosopher's Astronomy." But this proposal was received by the astronomers with marked coldness.

At this point I may be asked why, in these circumstances, I now propose to write on the psychology of mysticism. Why don't I, being a philosopher and not a psychologist, take my own advice and stick to my own subject? My excuse is that I only venture to write about the psychology of mysticism because no one else does it. When the professional psychologists take the subject out of my amateur hands, then I will stop.

The other matter to be discussed was the method of introspection, which psychologists do not like. Some psychologists go so far as to say that there is no such thing as an inner consciousness to be introspected. But this view is so absurd that only very learned men can believe it. Hence many psychologists today think that consciousness exists but they say that bodily behavior is publicly verifiable whereas the inner life of consciousness is not. This distinction is rather dubious.

However, the psychologist is perfectly right in insisting that introspective reports are very inferior to extrospective reports in respect of reliability. They are right to concentrate on behavior rather than on inner conscious states whenever possible. Apart from the question of verifiability there are other good reasons for this, chief among which I think are the following: It is far easier to give an exact and accurate description of the pattern of a butterfly's wing than it is to give an accurate description of one's inner feelings or mental states. This has nothing to do with one's being public, the other private. It is because inner mental events are dim, fleeting, and evanescent, and also without the sharp and definite boundaries which external things have. Physical things may remain unchanged for long periods of time. The same thing, say a mountain, can be observed and reobserved an indefinite number of times. But no mental state, no feeling, emotion, or idea remains unchanged in a man's mind for more than a few instants. Also the markings on a butterfly's wing or on a leaf have sharp boundaries. But the mental life tends to be blurred and smudgy, everything merging imperceptibly into everything else. The external world is bright and vivid, the mental world is dim and faint. Introspection is like describing objects which loom only vaguely and momentarily through a fog and then disappear altogether. Above all, physical states can be measured, mental states cannot.

But these same considerations also show that introspection should not be rejected altogether. And in the field of mysticism no other method of study is possible. Hence it is foolish to refuse to study a very important part of human life merely because the only means of studying it are introspective. We have in each case to use whatever methods of study are available. If the best methods cannot be used, then we have to make use of methods which may be less good but are not wholly worthless. We must agree then to study mysticism by the method of introspection. And I will proceed to give an account and analysis of the introspective reports which mystics themselves have given.

There are at least two species of mystical consciousness,

which I call the extrovertive and the introvertive, but in this essay I can examine only one. I choose the introvertive type because it is by far the more important.

William James wrote, "Our normal consciousness, rational consciousness as we call it, is but one special type of consciousness, while all about it, parted from it by the filmiest of screens, lie potential forms of consciousness entirely different." James was thinking of the mystical consciousness, and was right in stating that it is entirely different from ordinary consciousness. Our ordinary consciousness may be compared to a house with three stories. The ground floor consists of physical sensations, colors, smells, sounds. The second floor consists of images, pictures painted in the imagination. We often think in pictures. Images, more vivid or more dim, are continually floating through our minds. They are, in some sense, mental copies of sensations or combinations of such copies. They are, therefore, sensuous in character. The third floor of our normal consciousness is the intellect. It consists of conceptual thoughts, abstract ideas, processes of reasoning, and the like. The two lower floors are sensuous, the top floor abstract and intellectual. We may therefore characterize our normal consciousness as the *sensory-intellectual consciousness*.

When we say that the mystical consciousness is entirely different we mean this quite literally. It is neither sensuous nor intellectual. All three floors of our ordinary consciousness are absent from it. In other words, there are in it no sensations, no images, and no thoughts. I do not mean merely that it has different kinds of sensations and thoughts. I believe there are animals which see infra-red or ultra-violet colors. But these, though they are sensations presumably quite different from ours, are still sensations. But the mystical consciousness possesses no sensations at all, neither like nor unlike our normal ones. And since it contains no sensations, neither can it contain those mental copies of sensations which we call images, and neither does it contain any conceptual thinking.

For this reason too it must be pointed out that what are called visions are not mystical experiences, for a vision is a sensuous phenomenon consisting of imagery. For instance, a vision of a man or woman will have color and shape, which are sensuous characteristics. That visions are not mystical experiences is recognized by all mystics. For example, St. John of the Cross, the Spanish mystic of the sixteenth century, writes about "discursive mental activity by means of images, forms, and figures that are produced imaginatively . . . as happens for example when we picture in our imagination Christ crucified . . . or our imagination sees God seated upon a throne with great majesty." And he goes on to say, "Now the soul must be emptied of all these imagined forms, figures and images if it is to attain to the Divine Union."

So far all I have said is negative. The mystical consciousness is *not* like the sensory-intellectual consciousness. It does *not* contain sensations, images, or thoughts. Very shortly I shall have to try to say something positive about it, to say what it *is*. But let me postpone this for a moment in order to ask another question. How does a man set about getting rid of his sensory-intellectual consciousness, this being the necessary preliminary to the mystical consciousness? It does not matter who or where the man is, whether he is a monk in a Catholic monastery, or a Hindu monk, or a Zen Buddhist monk in Japan, or anyone else. The process may differ in detail from culture to culture, but certain basic features of it are nearly always the same. The man must struggle and fight to empty his mind of all sensations, images, and thoughts, to get rid of them entirely from his consciousness. This is an enormously difficult task, in which a man can, as a rule, only succeed after intensive training in mind-control over a long period of time. It may take ten years in effort, or half a lifetime. It is true that there are occasional cases of mystical consciousness which seem to arise unsought and without effort. But in most cases, years of effort are needed. Ordinary people have almost no control of their minds. Try the experiment of ridding your consciousness of all images and thoughts. You will find that unless you fall asleep you will keep on thinking about one thing or another, and at least faint images will keep floating in and out of your mind.

Since it is so difficult to stop completely the flow of sensations, images, and thoughts, many mystics adopt techniques which are designed to reduce the stream of consciousness from a broadly flowing river to the thinnest possible trickle. They do this by concentrating their consciousness on one single point or object to the exclusion of everything else. It does not seem to matter *what* thing you concentrate on. An easy thing is the stream of one's own breath. This is the essence of what are called breathing exercises. You breathe in a regular rhythmic way, concentrate on that, and keep everything else out of your consciousness. Another technique is to concentrate on some short formula of words. You keep silently repeating the words to yourself—any words will do, perhaps even nonsense words—over and over again till the words lose all meaning to you. It is necessary to get rid of all meaning, because meaning is thought, and you have to get rid of thought. The words have to become nothing more than a monotonous sound-image, and this single monotonous sound-image must occupy your whole consciousness. I don't know whether it is true that in India Yogis sit and stare at their navels. But if they do, we have merely another example of the same technique of concentration on a single thing.

What is the object of this process? It is well known that consciousness, our ordinary consciousness, depends on contrast or difference. In order to retain your consciousness you must have in it more than one thing, two at least, I suppose, to be discriminated from one another and to keep the mind actively in motion from one to the other. Therefore, if you reduce your consciousness to one point, there is no contrast, no distinction to discriminate, and therefore this last point of consciousness will also disappear, and therefore all consciousness of the ordinary kind will disappear.

You would, of course, expect the result to be unconsciousness, perhaps sleep. But this, as those who have traveled this road tell us, is not what happens. You have gotten rid of your sensory-intellectual consciousness, but what happens then is that another kind of consciousness emerges, the mystical consciousness. Perhaps this mystical consciousness underlies our ordinary consciousness all the time, so that when the ordinary consciousness is peeled off, the mysictal consciousness is revealed.

The techniques of concentration on a single point or thing will no doubt remind one of hypnosis, which can also be induced by concentration on a single point. There is no doubt a connection between hypnosis and the mystical consciousness, but they nevertheless are not the same. In deep hypnosis there is no consciousness. But the mystic can and does remember and describe his mystical consciousness after he has returned to his ordinary consciousness; and it is certainly nothing like what the hypnotized person might experience, if he experiences anything. The outer symptoms may appear the same but the inner consciousness is quite different.

This brings us back to the question of what the positive characteristics of the mystical consciousness are. In trying to say what they are, I will begin with an example, which is found in one of the Upanishads. The Upanishads are documents which were composed by unknown Hindu mystics somewhere between 2,500 and 3,000 years ago. They are among the supremely great spiritual documents of the world. The following is from the Mandukya Upanishad: The mystical consciousness, it says, "is beyond the senses, beyond the understanding. It is the pure unitary consciousness wherein awareness of the world and of multiplicity is completely obliterated. It is ineffable peace. It is the Supreme good. It is One without a second. It is the Self." I will now examine these sentences in detail. This consciousness, the Upanishad first says, is "beyond the senses"—in other words it is non-sensuous, and there are no sensations or images in it. This we have already seen. Next it says that it is "beyond the understanding." The understanding means the intellect, the faculty of concepts, or thoughts. So "beyond the understanding" means that there are no thoughts or concepts in it. So these two phrases mean only that it is totally different from the sensory-intellectual consciousness. After this negative statement we find some positive ones. The passage goes on—"It is the pure unitary consciousness wherein awareness of the world and of multiplicity has been completely obliterated. . . . It is One without a second." The words *unitary* and *one* mean, of course, the same thing. What this sentence tells us is that the mystical consciousness is a pure unity without any multiplicity in it. What has happened is this. The mind of any one of us is a unity which holds together a multiplicity of sensations, images, and thoughts. It is essential to note that in our ordinary consciousness there is not only this multiplicity but also the unity. Your consciousness is one single consciousness, a unity in which are held together the multitude of your ideas, sensations, images, and so on. There are, of course, abnormal cases in which we find a dual or split consciousness, two consciousnesses in the same body, but the normal consciousness is single. Now what the passage we are discussing says is that when you have expelled the multiplicity of sensations, images, and thoughts, the pure unity will be left. This is also called pure consciousness, the word *pure* meaning empty of contents.

All of this may be summed up by saying that the essence of the mystical consciousness is an "undifferentiated unity." An ordinary consciousness is a unity differentiated into a multitude of images, ideas, and so on—in other words a multitude of objects. Here, however, the multiplicity of ideas and objects has gone, and therefore the unity is now undifferentiated. This is the essence of the mystical consciousness everywhere in the world, not only in the Upanishads, but in Plotinus, in Christian mysticism, in Islamic mysticism, and in Buddhism. The phrase *undifferentiated unity* is useful but it means no more than we said before. Our one consciousness is usually differentiated into the multitude of particular contents. When you get rid of these, the one consciousness, the unity of it is, of course, undifferentiated.

But now we naturally ask the following question. What is this new kind of consciousness conscious of? What are its objects? We have gotten rid of all the ordinary contents of consciousness, so if consciousness is still left what is it conscious of? Does some new object emerge in it? The answer is, no. No new object emerges. The new consciousness just *has* no object. It is completely empty. It is pure consciousness, completely undifferentiated, completely empty of all objects. Thus it is negative in the sense that it is empty, but positive in the sense that it is consciousness, not unconsciousness.

This statement that you can have a consciousness which is not conscious *of* anything at all is so completely paradoxical, so extraordinary, that I am sure the immediate normal, healthy reaction of anyone hearing it for the first time is likely to be disbelief. No such consciousness, empty of all objects, can possibly exist—this is what will be said. This is what I should certainly say myself if I were not aware of the fact that the evidence of its existence is worldwide and overwhelming. Evidence can be collected from everywhere— Europe, Asia, America, from all ages, from all highly developed cultures, and the evidence is unanimous. It is obviously impossible that I should in this essay be able to lay before you all this vast amount of evidence so as to convince you. All I can do is to give the testimony of a few persons picked from different cultures, ages, and countries. I have already given the evidence of the ancient Indian mystic incorporated in the Upanishads. Let me now, as my second example, quote a famous Christian mystic of the thirteenth century, Jan Van

Ruysbroeck. This is what he wrote: "The God-seeing man"—
that is his phrase for the mystic—"his spirit is undifferentiated
and without distinction, and therefore he feels only the
unity." The very words are almost the same as those of the
Upanishads.

The same is true of Meister Eckhart, who was a contemporary of Ruysbroeck but about thirty years older. Eckhart
writes that if you are to attain this experience, "you must
depart from the agents of the soul and their activities: memory, understanding, and will in all their diversifications. You
must leave them all: sense perception, imagination, and all
that you discover in the self." What he is saying in this passage
is that to attain the experience you have to "depart from," in
other words get rid of, all the activities of imagination, sense
perception, understanding or intellect, and so on. What will
be left? Eckhart's phrase for what is left is "God's undifferentiated essence." Being a Christian, Eckhart interprets the
experience in terms of the concept of God.

My next witness will be Plotinus, the third-century Greco-
Roman mystic. He writes, "In this seeing we neither distinguish, nor are there two. The beholder has become the
unity, having no diversity either in relation to himself or
anything else." I have space for only one more witness, so
I will choose a man of our own time, well known to all—
Martin Buber. He writes this: "From my own unforgettable
experience I know well that there is a state in which . . . we
experience an undivided unity . . . . this basic unity of my own
soul is . . . beyond the reach of all the multiplicity it has
hitherto received from life."

But it could be suggested that, although we may think
that these witnesses sincerely believed what they said, they
might well have been mistaken. This, after all, is the great
danger of introspection. The inner life is dim and vague and
the best attempts to describe it may go astray. We may believe that the mystics reduced the flow of sensations, images,

and thoughts to the minimum possible. But we may think there must have been at least faint images floating about in their minds, perhaps so faint that they were not noticed.

There happens to be a little experimental evidence about this. Professor Pierre Janet made a study of a modern mystic, a woman named Madeleine, whom he was able to keep under observation when she was in a condition of mystical trance. He writes of her as follows: "Madeleine," he says, "supposes that she does not breathe at all during her ecstasy, but if one measures the respiration one finds it slight indeed, but sufficiently normal. . . . Observations show us that sensation is also not suppressed. . . . Madeleine perceives very well the objects which I place in her hand . . . she recognizes them, and she hears and sees if she consents to open her eyes."

We must all welcome empirical evidence in the matter. But I am afraid that in the present case the evidence is wholly indecisive. The remarks about breathing are not relevant because the issue is not whether Madeleine actually breathed but whether she was *conscious* of breathing. The fact that Madeleine is breathing, but is not aware of it, tends rather to support the claim that sensation is obliterated from consciousness than to disprove it. Then we have the observation that Madeleine hears and sees and recognizes objects put in her hand, but this does not show that she is *conscious* of these objects. The somnambulist avoids bumping against the pieces of furniture amid which he walks, but is he really conscious of them? In hypnosis a man must in some sense "hear" the suggestions of the operator, but I do not know of any evidence that he is conscious of them. When the trance is over he acts on the hypnotist's suggestions apparently in the belief that they emerge spontaneously out of his own consciousness. He seems unaware that he ever heard them. Even in everyday affairs in our normal waking states it would appear that in some way we often act intelligently without the thought having appeared in consciousness. This happens in the case of actions performed out of habit and as a result of practice. All Professor Janet shows is that Madeleine recognizes objects, but not that she is conscious of them. I hope it may someday prove possible for the experimental psychologist to put the introspective reports of the mystics to the test. But it has not been done so far.

We must therefore fall back on the evidence of the introspective mystics themselves. And I repeat that the volume of this evidence is overwhelming and comes from sources in many different cultures, quite independently of one another. For instance, the evidence of Eckhart is quite independent of the evidence of the Upanishads, of which Eckhart presumably had never heard.

What we have seen so far is that the mystical consciousness is a completely empty unity without any object or content. But now at this point I think someone will say: Surely this consciousness has an object, namely, what the mystic, rightly or wrongly, calls God. Do not all mystics say that their experience is a direct and immediate consciousness of God? It is true that some say this. Others say that the mystical consciousness is not a consciousness *of* God, but that it is simply identical with God. But there are atheistic or at least agnostic mystics who do not believe in a Supreme Being at all and who would never say that God is the object of their consciousness. This is quite likely to be the case in our own modern, Western civilization, where religious skepticism is rife, for the mystical consciousness—the undifferentiated unity of empty consciousness—may come to any human being, whatever he believes or disbelieves. But, of course, the classical example of an atheistic or agnostic mystic is the Buddha. The Buddha was perhaps the greatest mystic who ever lived in the world. But he did not accept the belief in what we call God, and therefore we cannot say that God is the object of the Buddhist mystical consciousness, although that consciousness is the same undifferentiated unity as that of the Christians. So I return to the statement that this consciousness is not a consciousness *of* anything. It is completely empty of objects. It is true that the Christian mystic sometimes says that this emptiness *is* God, or the Godhead, and that the Buddhist mystic says that it is what he calls Nirvana, which is a state of ultimate peace and blessedness. But when the mystic says that his empty consciousness is God, or is Nirvana, we must say that *he is going beyond the psychological description of his consciousness and indulging in metaphysical interpretation and speculation.* The Buddhist I believe has the same experience as the Christian, but he gives it a different interpretation. Whether either interpretation is correct is a philosophical, not a psychological, question. So far as psychology is concerned we must reiterate that the experience is a pure, empty consciousness, an undifferentiated unity, without objects, without internal multiplicity. That human beings do sometimes have this kind of pure consciousness is simply a fact. To deny this fact is impossible unless you ignore the evidence. But the allegation that the experience constitutes union with God is an opinion, not a mere description of fact. It may be either true or not true. In this essay I am discussing only the psychological facts.

But now, I must turn to a second characteristic of the mystical consciousness which we have not so far mentioned. An aspect of the experience is a feeling of what I will call the dissolution of individuality. Each of us in our ordinary consciousness thinks of himself as an individual person. We use the word *I* to express this individuality. If we prefer to use a Latin word, we perhaps call it the ego. Now in the introvertive mystical consciousness the "I" is felt to disappear, to dissolve, or fade away into the Infinite. This is so in all cultures and I will give you some examples taken from cultures widely separated in space and time.

We may begin with a quite modern example. The English poet Tennyson, from youth up, experienced frequent onsets of mystical consciousness. He had not achieved this by any long training in Yogic or other exercises or techniques. It came to him spontaneously, although he could induce it at will by the simple process of repeating his own name to himself. Apparently this was an example of concentration on a word or set of words, which I mentioned earlier. Tennyson's account of the matter is as follows: "A kind of waking trance —this for lack of a better word—I have frequently had, quite up from boyhood, when I have been quite alone. . . . All at once, as it were out of the intensity of the consciousness of individuality, *individuality itself seemed to dissolve and fade away into boundless being,* and this was not a confused state, but the clearest, the surest of the sure, utterly beyond words . . . *the loss of personality,* (if so it were) *seeming no extinction but the only true life"* (my italics).

We see that the essence of this experience was that the "I," the individuality, was felt to fade away into "boundless being." We must notice also the paradoxical fact that, although the "I" seems to disappear, this is not its extinction but "the only true life." The paradox is that the "I" experiences its own disappearance so that, as it were, it ceases to be "I" while yet somehow not being extinguished but remaining "I." We shall find that this phase of the experience is quite universal. And it is curious how the words *fade away* or *melt away* or *pass away* keep reappearing in the descriptions we gather from all over the world, which are for the most part quite independent of one another, so that they are not to be explained by copying. I will now give a number of other examples.

We will begin with the Upanishads, which are surely far away enough in space and time, and in culture characteristics, from Tennyson. One of the Upanishads says: "As a lump of salt thrown into the water melts away . . . even so the individual soul, dissolved, is the Eternal. . . . With the disappearance of consciousness of the many, in divine illumination, individuality disappears."

31

Henry Suso, a Christian mystic of the thirteenth century, says: "The spirit is set free from its individual properties. . . . It passes away into God. In this merging of itself in God, the spirit passes away."

What Tennyson called "boundless being," Suso, being of course a Christian, calls "God." Tennyson too I believe was a Christian in some sense or other, but he probably speaks only of "boundless being" because he is aware that "God" is an interpretation and because he wishes to stick to psychological description.

My next example is Meister Eckhart. There are in his writings large numbers of descriptions of the dissolution of individuality of which I here quote only one: "In this exalted state," says Eckhart, "the soul has lost her proper self and is flowing full-flood into the unity of the divine nature."

One finds many examples of the same aspect of the experience in the writings of Islamic mystics, or Sufis. For instance, Al Junayd, who lived in the twelfth century, writes: "The saint is submerged in the ocean of unity by passing away from himself. He leaves behind his own feelings and actions as he passes away into the life of God."

So far we have the testimony of Tennyson, and an ancient Hindu of long pre-Christian times, of two Christian, and one Islamic mystic. These are surely wide enough apart culturally. But I will quote one more instance, this time from a present-day Buddhist, the well-known authority on Zen Buddhism, D. T. Suzuki. He is speaking of *satori*, which is the Zen word for enlightenment or mystical consciousness. He says, "The individual shell in which my personality is so solidly encased explodes at the moment of satori. Not necessarily that I get unified with a greater being than myself. But my individuality, which I found rigidly held together and kept separate from other individual existences, melts away into something indescribable, something which is of a quite different order from that which I am accustomed to."

We may note Suzuki's remark that this does not necessarily mean that "I get unified with a being greater than myself." I presume he writes this in order to differentiate the non-theistic Buddhist interpretation from the Christian interpretation as "union with God." We see then that the feeling of the dissolution of individuality is experienced by the mystics of quite different cultures and ages.

A third characteristic of the mystical consciousness is that it carries with it extreme feelings of peace, blessedness, joy, bliss, and so on. You can call this "euphoria" if you prefer jargon words to English. But this adds nothing to what is said by the ordinary English words *peace, blessedness, joy,* and so on. In fact with the jargon word you obliterate the fine distinctions of meaning which the English words carry. For instance, *peace* and *bliss* are not identical, and *blessedness* is different from either of them because it carries religious overtones which are absent from the other two.

A fourth feature of the mystic's psychology is that it nearly always includes an unshakable conviction that his experience is not merely a subjective mental state, but that it is objective in the sense that it constitutes a revelation of some transcendental reality. He may call this reality God or Nirvana or the Absolute, but the point is that no mystic will ever admit that his experience is merely a subjective state of his own consciousness, and no more.

If the mystic is asked why he believes this, he will as a rule have no reason in the sense of either argument or evidence to offer. He will simply assert that he has a sense of assurance, and that he knows, and is absolutely certain. It is possible that one of the more philosophical mystics, such as Plotinus or Meister Eckhart, might argue and give reasons, but this would be only as a concession to their questioner, not because they would feel the need of any reasons themselves. For their own part they would rely on their own inner sense of certainty.

This feeling of conviction may in different cases be stronger or weaker, or at least more strongly expressed or less strongly. Or the mystic may not trouble to put it in words at all. But it is always present in his mind. Nor can it as a rule be shaken even in after years, not even many years after the experience has ceased. Once he has had the experience he will possess throughout the rest of his life the solid conviction that the experience was a revelation of reality. I believe there is no case known of a mystic who ever came to doubt this. It might be well to quote an example. R. M. Bucke, a Canadian physician contemporary with William James, had in his life only one single mystical experience, which came to him unsought and quite spontaneously around the age of thirty. He describes this experience and then says: "The vision lasted a few seconds and was gone, but the memory of it and the *sense of reality* it left has remained during the quarter of a century which has since elapsed. I *knew* that what the vision showed was true. That conviction has never been lost." For this conviction Bucke, who was a highly educated man and himself a psychiatrist, gives no reason or evidence at all. He simply feels that he *knew* it. This is a well-marked characteristic of the psychology of the mystic.

Fifthly and finally, I think it is fair to note, under the heading of psychology, the effects of the mystical experience on human life and character. Experiences of trance of a non-mystical kind, for example cataleptic trance, tend to be symptoms of mental disease. Such trances cannot possibly result in any benefit, but rather tend towards the degeneration of the sufferer. Hypnosis apparently does no one any harm but neither does it do any good. Good actions or effects of one kind or another may possibly result from suggestions fed into a patient during hypnosis. But the state of hypnosis in itself seems to be neither good nor bad.

The mystical consciousness, however, is remote from this state of affairs. All the evidence is that, in the first place, the sense of peace and joy which is felt during the experience may last for an indefinite time afterwards, and even throughout life. The effects on character are not merely beneficial but often are beneficial to the extent of revolutionizing the life of the man. It is the universal testimony of those who know, that mystical experience transforms human life often from the squalid and mean to the noble and selfless. The ennobling effects of a single mystical experience, which perhaps lasted half a minute, may be felt throughout the rest of a long life. Or again, a wretched and unhappy life, a life which is felt to be without meaning and without purpose, may suddenly take on meaning and purpose. The mystic interprets his experience as being a revelation of God, or of the Infinite, the Eternal, and the Divine. We may or may not accept his claims in this respect. So far as he believes himself to be experiencing the divine being, the skeptic will no doubt regard him as suffering from delusions. But this makes no difference. The effect on his life is the same. We will behave *as if* he had in fact had an experience of the Divine; he will behave *as if* he had seen God. There is no trace of a diseased mind here. Nor is it, as is sometimes charged against it, a mere device of escape from the hard realities and duties of daily life. No doubt it *can* be used as an escape, and sometimes has been. For instance, Plotinus writes that the mystic life is "a liberation from the alien that besets us here, a life taking no pleasure in the things of earth—a *flight* of the alone to the Alone." Again the accusation which the Mahayana Buddhists made against the Hinayana Buddhists, namely that they sought each his own private Nirvana, not caring about the masses of men who were left outside Nirvana—this amounted in fact to a charge of escapism. Hence, the Mahayana Buddhists rejected this view and created instead the idea of the bodhisattva, who swore that he would not himself enter Nirvana until all other men had achieved it. Plotinus and the Hinayana Buddhists are about the only historical instances I can think of where the accusation of the mystical experience being nothing but an escape could *perhaps* reasonably be charged.

Now let me sum up what we have found out about the psychology of the mystic. We have not discussed the type of mysticism which is called extrovertive, but only that which is reached by introversion. In this state the mystic has expelled all sensations, images, and conceptual thoughts from his consciousness. He has reached the fundamental unity of consciousness without its differentiations. Its psychological essence, therefore, is an undifferentiated unity. This is accompanied by a feeling of the dissolution of individuality, the melting away of the individual person into what he feels to be the Infinite. There is a powerful feeling that this is the revelation of a transcendental reality. The emotional coloring of the experience is a sense of blessedness and peace. And finally the aftereffects are a certain serenity, a change of attitude which may in certain cases amount to a complete transformation of the personal life, a turning away from that which is mean and evil towards that which is fine and noble. And these aftereffects are not as a rule transient but may last indefinitely.

The Philosophy of Mysticism

In the previous essay I distinguished between the psychology of mysticism and the philosophy of mysticism. To the field of psychology belongs the task of describing and analyzing the mental processes of the mystic, leaving on one side the question of whether those processes are purely subjective or objective; also, whether, that is to say, they indicate or reveal the existence of anything in the real world outside the mystic's mind; whether they are subjective like a dream, or objective like our perception of the real world. This question arises because mystics themselves always passionately affirm that in their experience they have a revelation, or a direct perception of God, or of Nirvana, or of the Absolute, or of some transcendental and eternal existence or being. To try to decide whether this claim, or any claim like it, is true is no part of the function of psychology. Whose business, then, is it? The mystic himself is likely to say that no one can pronounce on this question except himself. He has within himself a sense of absolute certainty that his experience is objective, that it is a revelation of the Absolute and Ultimate Being, and that neither the psychologist nor the philosopher can judge of this. If the philosopher and the psychologist do not themselves have the mystical experience what can they know about it?

Now it is all very fine for the mystic to talk in this way. But what are the rest of us to do if we have no mystical experience of our own? We surely have a right to try to make up our minds. The mystic or the prophet has a message for mankind. He cannot expect us to accept it blindly without any attempt to examine and test what he says. If we are to accept it, we must have some sort of reason for doing so beyond the mystic's own dogmatic statement. And this can only mean that we must search out reasons for ourselves, even if the mystic refuses to give us any. And if we then ask whose business it is to do this, I think it is reasonable to say that, while any human being has the right to make up his own mind, it is perhaps in a special sense the business of the philosopher.

This, then, is the question which I propose to discuss here. Is the mystic's vision really, as he claims, the revelation of some transcendental and eternal reality, or is it merely a subjective illusion or hallucination? Even if we think it is only subjective, however, this does not mean that it is something worthless, an unfortunate aberration of the mind to be gotten rid of as a superstition. On the contrary, the mystical consciousness is enormously beneficial; it is a way to health, serenity, happiness, and peace of mind. It is not a diseased state of mind. It is, we said, the way, or *a* way of salvation, using the word *salvation* in a humanistic and non-superstitious sense.

As I pointed out in the previous essay, on the psychology of mysticism, the mystical consciousness is reached by completely emptying the mind of all sensations, images, and thoughts. What is left is the empty unity of consciousness, which is an undifferentiated unity. It is nevertheless a positive state of consciousness although it is not a consciousness *of* any objects. Another aspect of it is that it includes the dissolution of individuality. The individual experiences a sense of infinite expansion; he feels that his individuality is melting away into "boundless being," as Tennyson expressed it, so that his own finite personality or individuality disappears and is swallowed up in this greater being. A third aspect is that there is in this experience a sense of profound bliss, peace, serenity, blessedness. Fourthly, the effects of the experience usually last through the rest of the man's life. Serenity and peace and an increase of nobility and life-value may continue to the end. Finally, he feels an unshakable conviction that his experience was no dream, but an immediate apprehension of the divine or of some eternal reality.

And now, after these preliminaries, let us try to face squarely the question of objectivity. I will begin by examining further the passage from the Upanishads quoted in the chapter above. The mystical consciousness, it says, "is beyond the senses, beyond the understanding; it is the pure unitary consciousness wherein awareness of the world and of multiplicity is completely obliterated. It is ineffable peace. It is the Supreme good. It is One without a second. It is the Self." All of this was discussed above except for one sentence, the last little sentence of four words: "It is the Self." Now these four one-syllable words are the key to the understanding of the problem before us. "It is the Self." *What* is the "it" which is the Self? If we read the passage we see that *it* refers to the mystical consciousness. So we may say that, according to the Upanishads, the mystical consciousness *is the Self*. What, however, is meant by this? We can say if we like that *self* is another word for what used to be called the soul. We may say this if we don't mind using old-fashioned language. But just to use another word does not help us much. For now we have to ask, "What is the soul or self?"

The answer which the mystics have in mind is that the self or the soul is simply the *unity* of consciousness as distinct from the *multiplicity* of its contents or objects. The consciousness of a normal man is a unity, it is one single consciousness, but its objects are many. At this moment I am aware of a multitude of objects, chairs, windows, the human beings in front of me, and so on. Now the unity of this consciousness, taken by itself and apart from the multiplicity of its contents or objects, is considered by the mystics to be what we mean when we speak of the self or the soul. The ego or "I" simply is this unity. What then will happen when the mystic empties his consciousness of the entire multiplicity of its objects, of all sensations, images, and thoughts? What will be left is just the bare unity which is the self or "I." After all, this is a quite natural conclusion. Consider your own case as you sit there. You call yourself "I" and this I is your self or soul. This self of yours, which you call "I," holds within it the awareness of many objects. You say, "I see the clock and the chairs and the windows." Suppose you could, as the mystic does, empty your mind, your self, of all its objects, what would be left? Surely the I, the self itself. But what is left is nothing but an undifferentiated unity. Therefore the undifferentiated unity *is* the self. That is the meaning of the last sentence of our quotation from the Upanishad. The mystical consciousness which is the undifferentiated unity is identical with the soul or self. This is exactly what the Upanishad says. To quote its words once more, "It is the pure unitary consciousness wherein . . . multiplicity is completely obliterated. . . . It is the Self."

If we accept this conclusion we have taken one step in our examination of the problem of objectivity. Now we must go on to the second step, and it is of crucial importance. So far, the self which we have reached in the mystical experience is the finite self of this or that particular individual. It is the ego of you or me or some other individual. But at this point the mystic of the Upanishads makes a sudden and tremendous and almost incredible leap. He jumps straight from the finite individual self to the universal self of the world, the cosmic self, the infinite Self, Brahman, God. He says that when the mystic has emptied himself of all objects, all sensations, images, and thoughts, and reached his own self, then in reality what he has reached is not merely his own self but the infinite Self. He identifies his own self with the infinite. If this is true, then of course the mystical consciousness is a revelation of the universal or cosmic Self. We have been discussing this matter in terms of Hindu mysticism. The Christian mystic however makes exactly the same tremendous leap from his individual self to the universal Self of the world, which he calls God and with which he believes his individual self to be "in union," as he expresses it.

Now suppose we ask the mystic *why* he thinks this, why he believes that his individual self, as he reaches it in the mystical consciousness, is identical with or in union with, the universal Self of the world. We shall find that he usually gives no reason at all. He simply tells us that he *knows* it, he feels absolutely certain of it within himself and he requires no further reason, and can give us none. Nevertheless, I think we can dig out for ourselves some of the reasons for this sense of certainty.

You notice that I am distinguishing psychological causes from logical reasons. The question we are asking just at the moment is not what *arguments* can be found for believing what the mystic says, but what, as a matter of bare psychological fact, *causes* him to believe it. To give the causes of a belief has no bearing on its truth. A psychosis may cause you to believe that you are the emperor of the Sahara. But to give valid logical reasons for a belief is to prove it true. At present I am inquiring only into the psychological causes of the mystic's belief that his individual self is identical with the universal Self.

There are three such causes, I think. First, there is the experience of the dissolution of individuality, which I fully described in the previous essay. We remember Tennyson's mystical experience. "Out of the intensity of the consciousness of individuality," he says, "individuality itself seemed to dissolve and fade away into boundless being." And we remember that Suzuki, the Buddhist mystic, says, "My individuality . . . explodes at the moment of satori and melts away into something of quite a different order." And we remember that Christian mystics have the same experience of what seems to them to be the melting away of the finite individuality into the infinite.

Now I believe this experience is the primary psychological cause of the leap from the individual self to the infinite Self. The mystic might say—though he usually does not analyze his state of mind—that his belief that he has reached union with the infinite being is not a mere theory or opinion of his, but something which he has actually experienced. We must always distinguish an experience of any kind, whether it is a sense experience or a mystical experience, from the interpretation which our intellect puts upon it. The experience itself is certain and cannot be doubted. The intellect's interpretation can always be doubted and is at most only a probable opinion. For instance: Suppose three men are walking alone in a dark forest at night. They see something glimmering white through the trees. One may suppose it is a ghost, another that it is a white rock, the third that it is a sheet hung out on a clothesline. In this case the experience itself is just a white glimmer. This is absolutely certain. It cannot be doubted that they did experience a white glimmer. But they make three different interpretations of it. All three interpretations are mere opinions, and any or all of them may be false. Now in just this same way the mystic feels that his loss of individuality, its passing away into "boundless being" or the infinite, is what he actually experienced and is therefore as certain as the white glimmer in our illustration. It is not his *opinion* that his individuality melted away into "boundless being." He *experienced* this fact. Therefore it is certain. This, I think, is the main cause which explains his leap from the individual self to the world Self.

It thus becomes clear why the mystic believes that his experience is not merely subjective. The skeptical critic says that the mystic's experience, however inspiring, however beautiful, however valuable it may be, is like a beautiful dream, something which exists only in the mind of the mystic and does not reveal anything outside him. But the mystic feels that his experience is one which in itself, and apart from any interpretation, transcends subjectivity. The experience, therefore, is a direct experience of the infinite and it is natural to identify this infinite being with God. It is natural at any rate for a theist who believes in God. The Buddhist, who does not believe in God, has the same experience and makes the same leap to the infinite. But he calls this infinite existence Nirvana, not God, and Nirvana is not a self or a personal being, but a transcendental plane of existence.

The second cause of the mystic's feeling of certainty that he has received a transcendental revelation, is, I believe, that he feels his experience to be outside space and outside time, and therefore transcendent of the world which is in space and time. His experience, he might explain—if he were sufficiently vocal and philosophical—must necessarily be admitted to be non-spatial and non-temporal. For space and time are differentiated, space into points or positions, time into moments. Space and time are, in fact, the very principles in terms of which we differentiate all other things. For instance, two billiard balls which are exactly alike are differentiated only by the spatial distance between them. Therefore since the mystical experience is undifferentiated it clearly has nothing to do with space and time, but is non-spatial and non-temporal. It therefore clearly transcends not only the subjectivity of the individual but the whole world of nature. Since it is non-temporal it is eternal. The mystic therefore believes that he is experiencing the eternal, and in a theistic culture it is natural to interpret the eternal as God. Accordingly Meister Eckhart says, over and over again, that the experience is what he calls "the eternal now," in which there is neither past, nor present, nor future.

There is a third reason for the mystic's belief that he is in touch with a Divine reality. This consists in the feelings of utter bliss, peace, blessedness—one may also have the feeling of sacredness or holiness—which invariably accompany the experience. It is the peace which passeth all understanding.

These then are the psychological factors which impel the mystic to feel certain that he has received a revelation of a transcendental reality, and has not been merely shut up in his own subjectivity.

Now, although we must always carefully distinguish a psychological cause from a logical reason, we must point out that sometimes the two coincide so that the psychological cause is *also* a logical reason. For instance, I believe that if the three sides of a triangle are equal then its three angles must also be equal. I believe this because it has been proven by logic. And so far as I know there was never any psychological process in my mind which made me believe this except the logical proof. Or, again, I believe that 3,472 plus 4,394 make 7,866. I believe this because I have added them and the arithmetical process of addition constitutes logical proof. And in this case too there is nothing which makes me believe this except the proof. The logical proof is itself the psychological cause of my belief.

It is therefore possible that the psychological factors which make the mystic feel certain of the revelatory character of his experience may also constitute logical arguments which we should have to accept. And we have now to ask whether this is so. The first question is whether the mystic's feeling of the melting away of his individuality into the infinite is a good logical argument for his belief in a revelation. Now, although it is the psychological cause of his feeling of certainty, I am afraid it cannot by itself be considered a good logical reason for it. The mystic actually experiences the fading away of his individuality into boundless being. But it must be pointed out that no factor of any experience, when that experience is considered by itself, can ever show that the experience is objective. Proof of objectivity always involves comparison of experiences and a fitting of them together in a consistent pattern. What I experience inwardly, however intensely I feel it, may nevertheless be false outwardly, unless I have some reason which is drawn from other sources and is independent of the experience itself. If this is obscure, let me give a few instances of what I mean. I may in a state of extreme giddiness have a feeling that I am falling through space. This feeling might be so intense as to cause me to believe that I am really falling when as a matter of fact I may be lying on the ground. Mystical literature is full of examples of what is called "levitation." St. Teresa of Avila when in a state of ecstasy had a feeling that she was being lifted off the ground and was floating unsupported in the air. She believed that this was true. And although we hear of the same phenomenon in India and elsewhere, you will perhaps agree with me in thinking that no mystic ever does really leave the ground and float unsupported in the air. We may also give the example of dreaming. In a dream one may have the experience of falling off a cliff or flying through space. And note that this is actually a part of the dream experience, and not an interpretation. Nevertheless it is false, as we find out when we test it by reference to the rest of our experience. In the same way the fact that the mystic feels that he is melting away into infinity does not in itself prove that he is so. His experience which he thus describes may be only subjective although it may be a fact that he does have the actual experience of melting away into the infinite and that this is not an interpretation. For these reasons I fear we have to conclude that we have so far failed to discover any valid reasons for believing in the objectivity of his experience.

It follows that a valid reason, if one exists, must be such that, although of course it takes the mystic's inner feelings into account and regards them as part of the evidence, it will also subject these feelings to some sort of objective test by checking them with factors which are outside and independent of the experience. Suppose I have the experience of killing a lion. Outside observers testify that I was in bed all the time. I conclude that it was a dream. But if they testified that they too saw me kill this lion, I should conclude that I was awake and that my experience of killing the lion was objective. The question which therefore arises is this. Are there any arguments for the objectivity of the mystic's experience which rely not merely on his own inward experience but on independent and outside checking? The answer is that there do exist such arguments.

One such argument bases itself on the fact that mystics all over the world, in all ages, countries, and cultures, say the same thing, agree in their accounts of the mystical experience. Thus one mystic's experience is supported by the evidence of other mystics. For instance they all say, in one set of words or another, that the core of their experience is an undifferentiated unity, that it is spaceless and timeless, and that it brings peace and blessedness. And there are various other points on which they agree.

The argument then is that there could hardly be this unanimous testimony if it were not true. We are not here relying on the internal characters of any one single experience. It is true that we are not going outside the mystical experience altogether. But we are going outside any individual experience to compare it with all others. This is entirely parallel to going outside one sense experience of killing a lion to the sense experiences of other people who also see it. This argument has frequently been appealed to as regards mystical experience. Even William James treated it with respect, though he did not commit himself so far as to say that he was convinced by it. I will quote a version of it which is found in R. M. Bucke's book *Cosmic Consciousness*. According to him, the only way one can know that any experience, even an ordinary sense perception, is objective is that other persons have or can have the same experience. Bucke's version of the argument we are considering runs as follows: "You know that the tree is real and not an hallucination because all other persons having the sense of sight . . . also see it, while if it were an hallucination it would be visible only to yourself. By the same method of reasoning do we establish the objective reality of the universe tallying cosmic consciousness. Each person who has the faculty is made aware of essentially the same facts."

We must now examine this argument. The agreement of mystics all over the world about the essentials of their experience is a most impressive fact and does, I think, prove something of great importance. But taken by itself it is not sufficient to prove the objectivity of the experience. We can see this at once if we note that there are illusions of sense which are quite universal and which all normal humans will have if they put themselves in the appropriate situation. For instance, the mirage of water in the desert will be seen by all persons who look in the right direction, yet the water, of course, is not objective. Here is another simpler example. Anybody who pushes his eye on one side with his finger will see everything doubled. This is a universal experience of everyone. But this doubling of things is not objective. It is an illusion. What then is the important fact which the mystics' unanimity concerning their experiences does prove? It does not prove that the experience is objective. What it proves, I believe, is that the capacity for mystical experience is universal among men and is independent of country, or period, or culture. It points to a common element in human nature but does not in itself prove objectivity.

Perhaps we shall have more success if we try another line of thought. The problem is one regarding the objectivity of the experience. Would it not be wise if we began by asking what are the criteria of the objectivity of any experience? Bucke gave agreement of everyone in having the same experience as the criterion. But this, we have found, is not enough. Let us begin again. Let us take a dream as a typical example of subjective experience, and a true perception, for example my perception of this desk, as a typical example of an objective experience. What is the difference? If we can answer that question we shall thereby discover the criteria of objectivity. We may be inclined to say that the dream is only subjective because it is private, whereas the true perception is objective because it is public. But this is just what Bucke said and which proved to be incorrect or at least insufficient. This is also what is meant by the misleading phrase "publicly verifiable." A mirage in the desert is publicly verifiable, yet is subjective. I do not doubt that being publicly verifiable is *part* of the criterion and is very useful as a rough test. But it is not the whole of the criterion. Something is missing. What is it?

My belief is that this missing factor is what I will call *orderliness,* by which I mean obedience to the laws of nature. The ultimate criterion of objectivity is orderliness in this sense. And the ultimate criterion of subjectivity, of dream, and hallucination, and illusion, is disorderliness, disobedience to the laws of nature. Let us take a few examples. Why is the desert mirage of water subjective, although it is publicly verifiable? Because when I walk right up to the spot where the water was seen I find it disappears and there is only sand. It is contrary to the laws of nature that water should disappear and turn into sand. But if, when I walk up to what appears to be water, I still see the water and can touch and drink it, and, if I cannot find any breach of the laws of nature, I conclude that the water is objective.

Another example. Suppose I dreamed last night that I was in London. Then I suddenly find myself in bed in America. I conclude that my visit to London was a dream because otherwise I should have to think that I had been in London one moment and the next moment I was in America, and that I had traveled from London to America instantaneously and without crossing the ocean in a ship or plane. And this would involve various breaches of the laws of nature.

In the end we think that an experience is objective if it can be fitted into the natural order—the one order of events past and future which constitute that regular sequence of causes and effects we call nature. If it cannot be so fitted into the order of nature we call it subjective. Thus the criterion of objectivity is order, and that of subjectivity is disorder.

Can the criterion of objectivity which we have discovered, namely orderliness, be applied to mystical experience so as to show it objective? In order that this might be so, it would have to be the case that within the experience there are orderly patterns of events. And this means that you must have a multiplicity of events within it to constitute an objective order. But within the mystical experience there is no multiplicity of events. There is no multiplicity at all, but only unity. Therefore it follows that since the experience does not exemplify the criteria of objectivity it is not objective.

But let not the skeptic too hastily exult. For now comes a surprise. The very same criteria which show that mystical experience cannot be objective also show that it cannot be subjective either. For what is the criterion of subjectivity? The subjective, we showed, is the disorderly. It consists in experiencing events which infringe the laws of nature. Now mystical experience is not disorderly. Just as there is in it no multiplicity of items to be orderly, so there is no multiplicity of items to be disorderly. In a pure undifferentiated unity there can be neither order nor disorder. And therefore that experience can be neither subjective nor objective.

Now this conclusion, that mystical experience is neither subjective nor objective, may seem extraordinary, but as a matter of fact it is not at all surprising, and it is in fact what the mystics themselves often say, as in the description of mystical experience from the Mandukya Upanishad which I quoted above. That very passage, which is given only in part, contains also these words: "It is not subjective experience, nor objective experience, nor experience intermediate between the two." The composers of the Upanishads were, of course,

Hindus. But we find Christian mystics saying exactly the same thing. Dionysius the Areopagite, the earliest, or one of the earliest, of the Christian mystics—he lived somewhere around the fifth century—says of the Supreme Being: "It belongs neither to the category of existence, nor to that of non-existence." What this really means is simply this—the distinction between subjective and objective is a pragmatic one, a very useful one in daily life, but it is not an ultimate distinction. It does not apply to ultimate reality. A theist should not say, properly speaking, that God—his name for ultimate reality—is objective, or exists. God, he should say, transcends altogether the common distinction between subjective and objective. He is neither. It means the same thing to say he is neither existent nor non-existent. These terms, these distinctions of objective and subjective, are valid within the finite world but they apply only to finite things, not to the infinite. The infinite is, as it were, greater than anything which is merely subjective. Of course in common speech we speak, if we are theists, of the *existence* of God. We also say that he is a person, that he is good, and just, and loving. I am no theologian. But I think most theologians would agree that all these words we use of God cannot be literally true. St. Thomas Aquinas supposed that they are only analogies of the truth. Therefore when we say that the mystical experience is neither objective nor subjective we are not saying anything so outrageous as might at first appear. I will use the word *trans-subjective* to mean the status of mystical experience as being neither subjective nor objective. I say we have given valid reasons for believing that the mystical consciousness is trans-subjective.

There is another way of expressing this truth. If we say that God exists we cannot mean that he exists in the same sense as a cow or a mountain exists. To say of cows and mountains that they exist, or are objective, is just another way of saying that they are parts of the world of nature. Now a transcendent reality of any kind, whether it is conceived as God or Nirvana or in any other way, cannot of course be a part of nature. For to say that it is transcendent means that it transcends nature. Therefore it cannot be said to exist in the way natural objects exist. The category of the trans-subjective to which we have decided that the ultimate reality must belong is not something less than existence. It is something greater than existence. There is, therefore, a transcendental reality, although the word *is* does not mean the same as the word *exist.*

There is also another line of approach which leads to the same conclusion. It depends upon the Leibnizian principle of the identity of indiscernibles. Suppose that two persons, *A* and *B*, expel all empirical content from their minds so as to reach the unity of pure consciousness. We incline to say that what we have left is two pure egos. But if these egos are distinct and separate, there must be some principle of individuation which makes them two distinct beings. What is the individuating principle or fact? There is, in the first place, no difference of empirical content to distinguish *A* from *B*, for both *A* and *B* have expelled all empirical content. Nor is there any spatial division, for we are here talking about minds, not physical bodies. Mental phenomena do not appear to occupy space. It makes no sense, for instance, to ask whether my belief in God is to the left or right of my belief in the existence of matter; nor whether my feeling of anger is north or south of my feeling of joy. Nor, if we suppose that *A* and *B* are simultaneously reaching the mystical consciousness, can time be a differentiating principle. There is in fact no difference whatever between pure ego *A* and pure ego *B*. Therefore, by the principle of the identity of indiscernibles, they are in fact identical, and this conclusion may be extended from these two individuals to all individuals in the world. There are in the universe not a multitude of pure egos, but only one. For the difference between one mind and another is solely a difference of content; and if we abstract from the content, there is no difference. Hence there is ultimately only one ego, which is in all men but above all individuals; it may reasonably be called a super-ego, or universal Self, or God.

My conclusion then is that the mystics really have a direct experience of something beyond the world of space and time, something which has given rise to the world's religious, something which we may if we like call an infinite and eternal Mind or Self, or, if the reader so desires, God.

Survival After Death

THOSE who believe in the survival of the conscious person after the death of his body have to meet certain preliminary objections and difficulties having to do with the physiological connection of consciousness with the physical brain. Consciousness in all known cases exists only in connection with a brain and a nervous system. Moreover, the quality of consciousness varies with the age and condition of the body. In an infant body we find an infant consciousness. The maturing of the body brings the maturing of consciousness, and with old age the quality of consciousness declines with the decline of the body. When an old man dies, what kind of consciousness is supposed to survive? Is it his consciousness as it was just before death, which may perhaps have become imbecile? Or is it the consciousness of his mature middle age? Or is it the infant mind that he had when he was a baby? The point of these questions is not that we do not know the answers to them. The point is that all possible answers are equally senseless. Suppose we suggest that it is the mature consciousness which will survive because it is the best. Then will the old man who dies suddenly revert to his middle years after death? And will the infant who dies suddenly become mature? The dependence of the mind on the body appears further in the fact that an injury to the brain may produce a mental life disordered or insane.

The theory of evolution also creates difficulties for the concept of survival. Human consciousness presumably evolved out of animal consciousness. At what point in the continuous development from trilobite to man was an immortal soul suddenly introduced? Does man have an immortal existence, but not *pithecanthropus erectus*? Was the miracle of the creation of an immortal soul suddenly performed when the first man appeared on the planet? Does it even make sense to talk about a first man in the light of modern biology? Plainly the belief that men are immortal, but that the lower animals are not, is a survival from pre-evolutionary times when man was regarded as a special creation unrelated to "the beasts of the field." The alternative to the view that men alone are immortal, while other animals are not, is the view that all animals have immortal souls. Since it is impossible to draw the line anywhere, this will mean, I think, that lobsters, flies, mosquitoes, centipedes, spiders, worms, fleas, bedbugs, beetles, wasps, earwigs, and all the rest have immortal souls. This seems difficult to believe.

These arguments against the survival of man after death are merely probable and empirical, not certain, and are therefore theoretically capable of being rebutted by evidence on the other side. We certainly ought to hear the other side. Is there then any positive evidence in favor of survival? There is, of course, the endless mass of statements of belief in survival to be found in the religious literatures of the different world religions. But, with whatever reverent awe we may rightly regard these scriptures, it has to be said that they rarely or never produce any positive evidence which can be weighed and evaluated. They rely on revelation and inspiration. So far as I know, the only evidence which can be weighed and found either strong or weak is in the area of psychical research. Unfortunately, I have made no study of this evidence so as to be able to give a first-hand opinion on it. There is a great deal of uniformed prejudice against it. Like all prejudice, this should be rejected by rational men, and the evidence should be studied with impartiality and without presuppositions. Since I cannot offer an opinion myself, I can only quote from one whom I regard as the most enlightened, careful, and reliable philosopher who has made a lifelong study of it. I refer to Professor C. D. Broad of Cambridge, England. He tells us that, after excluding the numerous cases of fraudulent mediumship, there remain cases where a surviving person seems to take control of the medium's body and to speak in his own characteristic voice and manner through the medium's lips. Professor Broad thinks that this evidence of survival is strong, but he refuses to rule out the possibility that the phenomena may be explained in some other way which is not at present known. Thus we are left in doubt at the end.

Taking into account all these considerations regarding the apparent dependence of consciousness on the physical brain, the facts of evolution, and the evidence of psychical research, I think it is fair to conclude that we do not know whether survival and immortality are realities or not, and that, while they cannot be proved, neither can they be ruled out by science or philosophy. Since on the available evidence we cannot decide definitely whether the human spirit is immortal or not, I propose in the remainder of this essay to discuss what the different cultures and world religions have to tell us about the nature of the life hereafter and the quality of immortality. We do not know if what any of the world religions say about this is true or not. But we shall find that to examine, classify, and discuss their views will raise questions which are not without profit and interest.

The more important world religions may be regarded as falling into two distinct groups, the Western and the Eastern. Under the head of Western religions I include Christianity, Islam, and Judaism. And under the head of Eastern religions I include Hinduism and Buddhism. This classification is no doubt open to criticism on various grounds. It may be said, for example, that there is a sense in which all five religions are in reality Eastern, and none of them Western, for Palestine, where both Christianity and Judaism originated, belongs to the Middle East and not to the West. But we can afford to ignore these objections. Whatever the experts on geography may say, our classification will prove convenient for our purposes, and that is its sufficient justification.

The chief difference between the Western and the Eastern religions in regard to the life after death is that Hinduism and Buddhism accept the doctrine of reincarnation, whereas the Western religions do not. I have seen it stated that reincarnation, though not asserted by Christianity, is not repugnant to it and not heretical. This may be true. There may be Christians who believe in reincarnation and can do so without being declared heretics. But reincarnation is no part of the essential creeds of any of the Western religions, whereas it is essential both to Hinduism and Buddhism. The ordinary belief of Westerners, if they believe in any afterlife at all, is that after death the spirit of man becomes discarnate, becomes a disembodied soul. It is true that this is not the official creed of Christendom. The Apostles' Creed confirms belief in "the resurrection of the body and the life everlasting." And the Athanasian Creed states that men shall rise again at the day of judgment "with their bodies." I doubt, however, whether the belief that not only the soul, but the body also, enjoys a future life is any longer effective among any except a few fundamentalist theological sticklers. And I suggest that most people in the West who believe in a future life think they will be simply disembodied spirits.

There is another important difference between Eastern and Western views of immortality. The Western religions think that the personal identity of each individual will persist forever. John Smith will be John Smith through all eternity, and Bill Jones will be Bill Jones. They may of course undergo development and no doubt improvement, or even attain moral perfection, during the ages, but they will still always remain the same identical persons. Eastern beliefs are different. Both Hinduism and Buddhism maintain that the individual retains his personal identity throughout all his subsequent reincarnations, which may run through millions of years, but in the end, after the last reincarnation, there comes something like the dissolution and absorption of individuality in the infinite life of the universe.

There is really nothing more to say about Western views of immortality. They are, of course, essentially vague and imprecise, but so far as they can be captured in any one formula they seem to suggest two things. First, the soul will be naked and disembodied after death—although this is contrary, as we noted, to the orthodox Christian creeds; and second, the individual will remain the same individual, will retain his personal identity indefinitely into the future.

We may now turn to the views of the Oriental religions, which cannot be summed up in any such simple terms as can the Western creeds, with the result that we shall have to spend the rest of this essay examining them.

We will begin with a discussion of reincarnation, which is common to both Indian religions. Since they both assume that between incarnations there is a lapse of time during which the spirit is discarnate, we have all the same difficulties we found in the theories of Western religions. And in addition reincarnation is beset by special difficulties of its own. It almost inevitably involves belief in pre-existence. There is no reason to suppose that this present life is our first incarnation. But if we have already lived through many previous lives, we naturally ask when and how the series of our reincarnations began. The Buddha when questioned about this gave the following answer: "This round of existence," he said, "is without known starting point; and of beings who course and roll along from birth to birth, blinded by ignorance and fettered by desire, there is no beginning discernible." The question when and why we began to reincarnate then shows itself as unanswerable. Perhaps, however, it is not fair to fasten this as an objection to Hindu and Buddhist views, because Western religions are equally incapable of answering questions about the origination of our immortal souls.

The more serious difficulties about the theory of reincarnation turn upon the question of personal identity. The question is: Does the personal identity of each individual persist through all these innumerable reincarnations? The natural answer is: Yes, for this is implied in the very word *re*incarnation. If the word means anything, it must mean that I existed in a former incarnation, and that the same "I" exists again in this present life, and in my next life, and in all future incarnations of me. And this is undoubtedly what the very concept of reincarnation, as accepted both by Hinduism and Buddhism, means. But the main difficulty in believing this is that we do not remember our past lives. Suppose it is asserted that in my previous existence I was the philosopher Descartes. I am, of course, very much flattered by this identification, but since I do not remember being Descartes I do not see how my identity with him can be asserted or established.

One possible reply to this objection is that there exists within each one of us something which we may call an ego, or a self, or a soul, which persists and remains the same throughout all changes of consciousness, and even where there is complete loss of memory. It is true that my consciousness is a flux of changing mental states. Sensations come and go, and so do thoughts, feelings, and volitions. But I remain the same "I" throughout all these mental changes, although I do not remember many of my past experiences. There have no doubt been days and perhaps weeks in my life, all memory of which has now been entirely blotted out. And yet I am now the same person as I was during those days or weeks, because it was the same ego or self which persisted through them all. Personal identity, in this view, is located not in the stream of consciousness itself but in a soul or ego which, as it were, lies behind consciousness and, so to speak, owns it. If this is so, we can easily believe that I am the same person throughout all my reincarnations, although I do not remember any of them. I think this view, or something like it, can be attributed to most Hindu thinkers.

Buddhism, however, presents a quite different view. Buddha himself apparently, and certainly all the schools of Buddhism, flatly and emphatically denied that there exists any such thing as a soul, or a self, or an ego. Yet Buddhism continues to believe in reincarnation. And Buddhism faces, therefore, the interesting question: How can there be reincarnation without any soul to be reincarnated? It is worth examining the Buddhist views on these matters in some detail.

Let us begin by asking what is the reason given by Buddhism for denying the existence of an ego, which most of us in the West are perhaps inclined to take for granted. In the first place the non-existence of an ego which persists through the changes of consciousness follows from one of the basic tenets of Buddhism, namely that everything in the universe is constantly changing and that nothing is permanent. Like the Greek philosopher Heraclitus, Buddha held that "all things flow." There is nothing to be found in the world but flux, and therefore there cannot be any such thing as an ego which continues the same from one day to another, much less from one incarnation to another. Indeed, so radical is the Buddhist theory of flux that there cannot be, it says, any existence which remains the same even from one moment to another. Here is a quotation from one of the Buddhist scriptures: "Strictly speaking, the duration of the life of a living being is exceedingly brief, lasting only while a thought lasts. . . . The life of a living being lasts only for the period of one thought. As soon as that thought has ceased, the being is said to have ceased."

Buddhism has also another argument for denying the existence of an ego. In its essential logic it is the same as the argument used in the eighteenth century by the Scottish philosopher David Hume. We shall understand it most easily if we state it first in Hume's words, and then we can go on to see that Buddha was saying the same thing in slightly different terms. Hume put the argument as follows: "When I enter most intimately into what I call *myself* at any time, I always stumble on some particular perception or other, of heat or cold, love or hate, pleasure or pain. I never can catch *myself* at any time, and can never observe anything but the perceptions."

You can repeat Hume's psychological experiment if you like. Look introspectively into your own mind. What do you find? You find thoughts, sensations, emotions, wishes, etc. These are all changing constantly. You cannot introspectively discover anything else, anything permanent. You say, "I have a color sensation." You can observe the color, but not the "I." You say, "I think." You can observe your thought but not the thinker. You cannot observe the so-called ego. You therefore have no right to postulate its existence. That is Hume's argument. Buddha used the same argument except that the details of his psychology were different, and no doubt more primitive. He lists five elements which make up the human being. The first is the physical body, and the other four are what we would call mental—sensations, perceptions, predispositions, and consciousness. These are the only things which we can observe in a human mind, says Buddha. We cannot observe an ego, and we have no right to postulate its existence.

It should be noted that it makes no difference to the argument whether the account given of the observable contents of the mind, either by Hume or Buddha, are correct or not. Hume says we can observe only what he calls perceptions, by which he means thoughts, sensations, emotions. Buddha says we can observe only sensations, perceptions, predispositions, and consciousness. What they both mean is that we can observe only the flux of mental states, never the unchanging ego.

Next we have to inquire how, according to Buddhism, this

can be made consistent with reincarnation. How can there be reincarnation if there is no ego to be reincarnated? The answer which we get in the Buddhist books is that although there is nothing but a fleeting consciousness, it does constitute a single continuous series of mental states, which can be traced through our lives and also from one reincarnation to another. A river is an example of a flux which constitutes a single continuous series, or a fire which spreads from one part of the country to another. In the same way the mental states of each person constitute a single series, whether in this reincarnation or the next.

We may well object that this account is not acceptable unless memory is brought into it. It is memory which constitutes your stream of consciousness, or mine, a single continuous series. Memory is the thread on which the successive items of consciousness are strung. If I *remembered* being Descartes, writing his books, and so forth, there would be a continuity between my consciousness and his. But since I remember none of his experiences, where is the continuity between his consciousness and mine?

Buddhist philosophy admits this point. But it says that in a sufficiently developed person there *is* memory of his past reincarnations. The Buddha is said to have remembered his, and so did many of his disciples. The reason you and I cannot remember ours is that we are spiritually immature. We shall all of us develop in spirituality as we proceed from one reincarnation to another, and someday we shall arrive at such an exalted level that we shall remember our past lives. Perhaps we shall not evolve to that level for several million years, but a million years is but the winking of an eye.

But reincarnations, even if they continue over millions of years, do not amount to immortality. We must now ask: What have Hinduism and Buddhism to say about immortality proper? Do they mean that our reincarnations will continue forever? Is that their conception of immortality? The answer is: No; they both believe that we shall someday, when we have evolved into perfect beings, pass beyond all reincarnations into a true, blessed, and final immortality. In the Hindu view we shall be reabsorbed into the infinite being, Brahman, from whence we and all the worlds originally came. According to Buddhism we shall pass into Nirvana. And what, we must now ask, is Nirvana?

Let me quote part of a conversation which Buddha is said to have had with a skeptic named Vaccha.

"Where," asks Vaccha, "will the saint exist who has attained to this deliverance of his mind?"

"Vaccha," replies the Buddha, "to say that the saint will exist does not fit the case."

"Then does Buddha say that the saint will not exist after death?" asks Vaccha.

"Vaccha," replies Buddha, "to say that the saint will not exist does not fit the case."

Thereupon Vaccha becomes exasperated. Either the saint must exist or not exist, he says.

And Buddha replies, "Enough, O Vaccha. Profound is this doctrine, and not to be reached *by mere reasoning*."

The point is that Vaccha has been trying to understand Nirvana by logic, whereas its nature cannot be grasped by any kind of intellectual or conceptual thinking. To make a long story short, what is required here is not the logical intellect but mystical experience. Nirvana just *is* the mystical consciousness. If we know what this is, we know what Nirvana is.

I want now to compare our Western conceptions of immortality with these Eastern views. When we compare them, or rather contrast them, what we find is this. The Western concept of immortality may be defined as the continuous persistence of the personal identity of each individual through infinite future time. As we said before, Smith will always be Smith, and Jones Jones forever. Moreover each will maintain his ordinary, everyday kind of consciousness, the kind of consciousness with which we are all familiar in our everyday lives. There is no mention of a mystical state of mind. But according to Indian ideas, immortality will consist in the eternity of the mystical consciousness.

But there is another very important contrast. Whereas in the West the personal identity of each individual is believed to be immortal, in the Eastern mystical conception personal identity disappears in Nirvana. This is because the dissolution of individuality is a prominent characteristic of the mystical consciousness even in the present life. This is true of the mystics both of the East and of the West. This means that when you pass suddenly from your normal consciousness into a mystical state, whatever religion you happen to profess, whether it is Western or Eastern, when you have a mystical experience, you necessarily have as part of it a feeling that your individuality, your little personal finite self, is dissolving, fading away into something infinite.

Now it may seem that these statements contain a hidden paradox. They say that in the mystical consciousness "I," this finite "I," this individual person, disappears, fades away into the Infinite, or into God, or into Nirvana. But this amounts to saying that "I" experience my own disappearance, my own fading away. How can "I" experience this dissolution of my individuality unless "I" continue to exist while I experience it? I experience the disappearance of "I" and apparently I am still there when "I" have disappeared. This is the paradox.

All I can do by way of resolving the paradox is to quote again what the English poet Tennyson says about his own mystical experiences, which he frequently had from the time he was a boy. He uses these words in his description: "All at once," he says, "as it were, out of the intensity of the consciousness of individuality, individuality itself seemed to dissolve, and fade away into boundless being, and this was not a confused state, but the clearest of the clear, *the loss of personality (if so it were) seeming no extinction, but the only true life.*"

You notice here two things. First Tennyson says that the

loss of individuality is not its extinction. Somehow or other "I" continue to exist and to experience my own loss of individuality. Secondly, he says that this seems to be "the only true life." I suppose that by this rather curious phrase, "the only true life," Tennyson means just about the same thing as Oriental writers mean by the word Nirvana.

This then is what we have to say of Nirvana. Tennyson and the others I have quoted each experienced, while still in the body, a momentary glimpse of Nirvana, just as Buddha, while still on earth, is declared by all the Buddhist books to have attained Nirvana. And according to Indian conceptions a human being after many reincarnations may reach a stage of spiritual development when he may pass finally into Nirvana, never to return to this earth, never to inhabit another body.

It is natural for us who live in time to say that those who have passed into eternity will live forever. For instance, if the Buddha died in the sixth century B.C., we naturally say that he passed into his final Nirvana then. He will have been in Nirvana for about twenty-four centuries. But this is to describe the matter from our point of view because we are still in time. Those who have finally passed into Nirvana will know nothing of time, which for them no longer exists. And while the West still thinks of immortality as continuance through never-ending time, the Buddhist and the Hindu thinks of it as timelessness.

I will end by quoting a description of Nirvana said to have been given by the Buddha to an assemblage of Buddhist monks:

There is, monks, a plane where there is neither extension nor motion, neither this world nor another, neither the sun nor the moon. Here, monks, I say there is no coming or going or remaining or deceasing or uprising, for this is itself without support, without continuance, without mental object. And this, monks, is itself the end of suffering.

II

Values

Values in General

WHAT is meant by the common English word *wisdom*? It is difficult to define. Though it plainly has to do with the practical living of life, it is not on a par with the common practical virtues, such as truthfulness, honesty, sobriety, or even justice. For although the man who is truthful, honest, sober, and just is certainly wise to be so, what we mean by the wise man goes beyond these virtues. Wisdom is the characteristic of sages, and being truthful, honest, and sober is not the same as being a sage. Evidently wisdom, though concerned with practical life, has in it some intellectual element, some element of knowledge. Yet on the other hand it is not a branch of pure knowledge like history, mathematics, science, or philosophy.

To attempt a rough definition, I will say that wisdom is the knowledge of values, or more explicitly the knowledge of the comparative values of the different ends, purposes, and goals which men may pursue in life. The word *knowledge* allows for the intellectual factor, and the emphasis on the values of life allows for the practical factor.

It is important to realize that what is implied here is the notion of a *scale* of values. Wisdom is not merely the knowledge of what is good or bad, right or wrong—as if all things were painted either black or white. To know that honesty is good and dishonesty bad is an elementary wisdom to which most people attain and for which the intellect and experience of a sage are not required. The idea of a scale of values means not merely that there are good and bad human purposes, but that among the good ones there are shades of better and better still, and among the bad ones shades of worse and worse still. If all possible human purposes could be precisely evaluated, placed in a scale which would show exactly which is higher or lower than which, we should have an exact science of wisdom.

No such science is now, or ever will be, possible, for the exactitude, precision, and measurement which science demands are not possible in regard to values. Indeed all truly human things, and this means all the most important things in man's life, escape the net of scientific concepts, and the attempt to apply scientific method to them produces only pseudo-scientific jargon.

The impossibility of a science of comparative values is due not only to the fact that the most valuable things cannot be measured. It is due also to the complexity of life. We speak of two different men having at different times the same purposes, or doing the same actions. If this were true, if actions and purposes repeated themselves constantly, we might come to know by experience, with a fair degree of accuracy, where they should be placed in a scale of values. But in fact no two purposes or acts are ever the same; they are always altered by the context of circumstances in which they arise. I perform an action today and you might try to repeat it tomorrow. But it would not be the same, because the circumstances in which it was done would be different. Therefore your act would have a different value, better or worse, than my act. The study of values is in this respect like the study of history. Science can deal only with the repeatable items of the universe, and because history never repeats itself there can never be a real science of history. And because human situations never repeat themselves, there cannot be a science of the values embedded in them.

This is one of the facts which lend some plausibility to the views of those who say that all values are relative. It seems to mean that what is good for one man or one culture may be bad, or less good, for another. It looks as if anybody's valuations are as good as anybody else's. And if values were all thus chaotic and relative, there could not be any knowledge of them at all; that is to say there could not be any wisdom. But this cannot be the case. There certainly have been wise men, universally recognized as such by the overwhelming consensus of men's intuitive appraisals. I think that all the great moral teachers of the world—Buddha, Confucius, Christ, the Hebrew prophets—have been essentially concerned with this problem of a scale of values. What they spoke of was not merely the values within their own cultures, much less merely the values of individual men on particular occasions. Their insights were not merely local or regional. It cannot reasonably be denied that they said many things about the values of human life which are profoundly important and true for us now in America or for any men in any culture which is ever likely to exist for many thousands of years to come. When Socrates rebuked the Athenians for heaping up the greatest amount of money and caring so little for what he called "wisdom and truth and the greatest improvement of the soul," he was saying something about a scale of values, about the superiority of "wisdom and truth and the greatest improvement of the soul" to the pursuit of money, which was valid not only for himself, not only for Greek culture, but for all cultures everywhere—for Americans, and Chinese, and Frenchmen, and Peruvians. Hence, while admitting that values are bedeviled by relativity, we must find what are the limits to it. And, while admitting that there cannot be a science of values, we must refuse to admit that there can be no knowledge of them at all. What knowledge, then, can we have?

First of all, we must distinguish between particular value-judgments and general value-judgments.

I mean by particular value-judgments those which only

claim to be true either about a single human being or about a restricted number, those for instance in a particular culture or country. I might say to one man, "Celibacy will be better for you than marriage." To another I might say, "Marriage will be better for you than celibacy." Again I might say, "Monogamy is the best marriage system for America, but polygamy may be better in a country where females greatly outnumber males." These are particular value-judgments.

By general value-judgments I mean those which may claim to be valid for mankind in general. I do not think that it is sensible to claim that there are value-truths which are absolute, in the sense of being valid for every single human being. I think we shall have to be content with general truths which will be valid for all normal men in all normal cases. These can very well be important guides in life.

Now when I talk about a scale of values, I mean a set of general value-judgments telling us what things are better or worse, higher or lower, in human life generally. For this is all that we can discuss. We cannot discuss particular cases without knowing the particular individuals or cultures involved and their particular circumstances. Socrates in speaking as he did to the Athenians was evidently laying down principles which he thought valid for human life in general. The same is true of all the great moralists in all ages.

One of the most interesting and instructive attempts to set up a scale of general values was that made by Plato in the eighth and ninth books of the *Republic*. Of course it could be argued that this was meant to apply only to Greeks, but I do not think this would be correct. Plato recognizes a hierarchy of five kinds of value, one above the other. The highest value, according to Plato, is knowledge. In this he includes the knowledge of values, that is to say, wisdom. But he also includes science and mathematics, though he regards them as ancillary to wisdom. For him, then, the philosopher-scientist is the highest kind of man. The second value in

Plato's scale is honor; and one may also use here such words as ambition, reputation, prestige, position, fame, glory. The military man is Plato's special example. The third value is money, exemplified by the money-getter or the businessman. Fourth comes the sort of life purpose which aims at pleasure, counting all pleasures as of equal value. The corresponding type is what we should call the man of pleasure, or perhaps the sensualist. The last and lowest goal is that of the man who, his entire life dominated completely by some single sensuous pleasure or passion, aims at that and nothing else. The drunkard, the drug addict, and the sex maniac are examples. Thus the main values of life in order of merit are knowledge, honor, money, pleasure, and the satisfaction of some single overpowering sensuous appetite.

Plato thinks that we can largely appraise or evaluate both individual men and civilizations (or at least states) by this scale. The question to ask in each case is: This being the ideal scale, which of these five kinds of purpose does the man, or the civilization, put at the top of his, or its, own scale of values? Plato is not, of course, contending that all men, or even all Greeks, actually accept his ideal scale. Different men have, in fact, different scales of value. Thus the philosopher and the scientist are those who put knowledge at the top. The sensualist puts sensuous pleasure at the top. And you can both classify and judge a man's or a society's real worth by discovering which of these five values that man or society ranks highest. Tell me, says Plato, what a man values most and I will tell you what sort of man he is, and where he is to be ranked in the true scale of values. For a man's philosophy of life, or even his character, may be said to be identical with his scale of values. The man whose main aim in life is money —we know him by that fact, by the fact that in his actual life (whatever he may say in theory) he places wealth highest in his scale, above knowledge and learning, above honor and prestige and fame, above mere sensuous pleasure, above everything. We know the mainspring of his character and at least roughly the things he will do. We also know, according to Plato, his intrinsic worth as a man. He is inferior to the philosopher, the scientist, the knowledge-seeker. He is inferior to the seeker after glory. But he is superior to the sensualist and the man of pleasure, and of course to the man dominated by some evil passion such as drugs or drink.

Societies are to be judged in the same way. Athens, he thinks, is the highest of his time because its dominant ideals are intellectual—love of learning and knowledge. The military state of Sparta, seeking honor and glory, but negligent of the things of the mind, takes a lower but still a high place. Love of money he attributes to the Phoenicians and Egyptians as their dominant aim. I think Hitlerite Germany would have been placed by Plato along with Sparta in the second category, and I am afraid he might have classed America with its dominant love of money in the third category, below Hitlerite Germany and along with the Phoenicians and Egyptians, who in his opinion were barbarians. This is a dreadful thought.

Evidently Plato's scale has serious defects and omissions, but also it contains important insights. I will mention first some of its defects and omissions. It of course involves a vast oversimplification. And it is in some respects very artificial. First among its omissions we may note the total absence of any reference to religious values. In the procession of the five types of men, from the philosopher down to the drunkard and the drug addict, where do the saint and the mystic come? Nowhere. But is not the love of God even higher than the love of knowledge? In view of the facts that Plato was himself a man of profoundly religious feelings and that there is a definite mystical trend in his philosophy, this omission may seem the more surprising. No doubt it is to be explained by the characteristics of Greek religion. Plato thought very poorly of the gods of Olympus and their doings. And his own deeper religion probably appeared to him as a part of philosophy, so that he would see no need for a separate place for it in his scale.

Another omission is the absence of any reference to the values of love, charity, compassion, sympathy, self-sacrifice. But these values were, of course, to be emphasized afterwards by Christianity.

A third serious omission is aesthetic value. The love of power as a predominant human motive is also left out, but perhaps Plato would have associated it with honor and glory in his second category.

From the defects I will pass to some of the valuable insights in Plato's scheme. In spite of the artificiality and the over-simplification, Plato's classification of human types is, I think, very shrewd. If you try it on your friends, you will be surprised how well most of them seem to fit into one or other of his five compartments. For instance, the scholar who remains a pure scholar presumably loves knowledge more than honor or position. But the one who becomes a dean loves position more than knowledge and is therefore inferior in the scale of virtues. We know them well, these human types: the intellectual, the seeker after titles, position, and reputation, the money-grubber, the sensualist, and the completely degraded slave of some passion. Are these not the dominant motivations of a vast majority of human beings—either knowledge, or fame, or money, or pleasure—and may they not be rated perhaps in something like that order of value?

Secondly, it is a really important insight that a man's philosophy of life, and even his character, can be simply identified with the answer to the question, what does he in his actual life, as distinct from what he says about himself, value most? To ask that question is to brush aside inessentials and camouflage and hypocrisy and to get to the root of what the man really is.

I must comment on the fact that Plato places knowledge at the top of his scale as the supreme value of life. Of course it is the intrinsic value of knowledge, knowledge for its own sake, that he has in mind, not its usefulness as a means to other ends. We shall probably think that Plato, being a Greek, over-valued pure intellect. We should not agree that it is the highest conceivable value. Nevertheless we owe to Plato and the Greeks in general the fact that we value knowledge for its own sake at all, and that many of us do give it at least an honored place among our ideals. It is the ideal which is the life-blood of universities, and it has also been the dominant motive of most scientific discoveries. It is certain that if we were all practical minded, if there were never any people who out of mere curiosity wanted to know things without caring at all whether what they discovered had any practical applications or not, there would never have been anything worth calling science. There never has been any civilization which held this ideal in high esteem except the Greeks and those who (like ourselves) have inherited it from them. In India knowledge was never sought except for the practical purpose of one's personal salvation. The Chinese have always esteemed scholars but apparently have not cultivated the right kind of pure curiosity. Scholarship was valued mainly for social ends. Hence these countries did not produce science. Only Greek-minded civilizations, valuing pure knowledge, have produced it. Other civilizations were too practical.

Though Plato may have over-rated this value, it is questionable whether we in America do not under-rate it, although we do, as I have just been saying, give it a place. I think it is less esteemed in America than in Europe; that is, Europeans place it higher in their scale of values than we do. Einstein, being asked by a student why he wanted to know about relativity, of what practical use this knowledge is, remarked that no student in Europe would ever have asked such a question. I believe most Americans think of science as technology, as the producer of telephones and electric lights, and value it for this almost entirely. And the most famous of American philosophies, pragmatism, has for its message precisely the idea that the only value of knowledge is instrumental and utilitarian. We are in danger of being too practical, of placing pure knowledge too low in our scale of values, just as the Greeks placed it too high. For if we think of it as only instrumental to material comforts and goods, this is in fact to place material wealth, money as Plato would express it, above it in our scale.

The second place in Plato's scale is given to honor or prestige. When the Greeks at the Olympic games gave the victor not money but a wreath of leaves, they were exhibiting the fact that, in their scale of values, honor stood very high, higher than money, in agreement with Plato's scheme. This also appears in our ideal of amateur sportsmanship. I think that many foreign nations, such as the British, express the same idea when they bestow titles. They reward high services to the state by affixing a meaningless word to a man's name. The whole point of a title is that it is worthless, commercially speaking, like the Greek wreath of leaves. We speak of "empty" titles and affect to despise them accordingly. This is rather foolish, because their emptiness of anything except honor is precisely their merit. And if it is a fact that men in Britain can be got to put out tremendous efforts in the public service for the sake of a mere title, what this shows is that their scale of values is in this respect like Plato's. They place honor above money. The same is true of those Americans who, without even a title and only for the sake of the honor itself, fill high positions in the government when they could earn much greater incomes in business. America was doubtless right in abolishing titles because of their abuses. Yet the idea of a title was in itself a good one. It symbolized the thought that honor is a higher value than money. And in abolishing titles America ran the risk of teaching its citizens to contend for money rather than for honor.

Plato, it will be noticed, places the pursuit of wealth and worldly possessions third in his list. It is inferior to knowledge and honor but superior to the pursuit of mere pleasure. In his comparatively low evaluation of material wealth, Plato is in agreement with all the great moralists of the world. This has become, in fact, a moral platitude. This means that almost everyone agrees to it in theory, but of course it does not mean that we act on it. Plato clearly recognizes the higher value of the things of the mind and the spirit over the things of the body and the senses. The things of the mind he places at the top, while the lower three grades—wealth, pleasure, and addiction to one dominant passion—have to do with material and sensuous aims in a descending order of values. This also may sound platitudinous, but it is important to realize that the superiority of the things of the mind (spiritual things as we call them) over the things of the body is one of universal moral intuitions of civilized mankind. It is not confined to any one culture. It is Greek, but not merely Greek. It suffuses all Christian culture. And it is not even confined to Western civilizations. You will find it even more strongly stressed in Hinduism and Buddhism, and I think you would find it in the thought of Confucius and other Chinese seers, though my ignorance of Chinese culture prevents me from quoting sources. The exaggeration of this tendency is what is called asceticism, which is neither Greek, nor Christian, nor Buddhist, though it finds a place in some Hindu thought.

It must be understood that I am using these phrases, *the things of the mind or spirit* and *the things of the body*, merely as convenient labels. I do not mean to imply any particular psychology or theory of human personality, such as a dualism of body and mind. And I do not want to be told by some learned and scientific person that the distinction between body and mind is an ancient superstition now happily got rid of by our scientific age. For I do not believe that any substantial part of the ancient wisdom of man will ever be got rid of by any clever man tinkering in a psychological laboratory. I am not talking metaphysics, or asserting, like

Descartes, that there are two different entities, body and mind, different in nature and substance, although this opinion too may well have more truth in it than our modern enlightenment is inclined to admit. The point is that I do not care what opinion you hold about that. I do not care if you tell me that the mind is made of atoms, or of movements of the legs or larynx. It may be so. You can preach any sort of psychology you like. You can be a materialist or a behaviorist. But even so, you will have to distinguish, if you are to have any wisdom or sense of values, between what I call, using these labels, the things of the mind and the things of the body. All I am saying is that art is not the same thing as eating and that science, philosophy, and religion are not the same thing as having sexual intercourse. And my point now is that according to the unanimous agreement of all the world's wise men, including Socrates, Plato, Buddha, Christ, Sankara, Confucius, Marcus Aurelius, Epictetus, Isaiah, and the rest of the Hebrew prophets, the former kind of things, which I am calling the things of the mind, are nobler, higher, better—that is, higher in the scale of values—than the latter kind of things which I am calling the things of the body. You can call this a platitude if you like. But platitudes may be important truths which the majority of men choose to ignore or despise.

Now at this point you will quite rightly ask some questions which it is very difficult to answer. How can one ever possibly "prove" that the things of the mind are "higher" than the things of the body? How, for that matter, can one ever prove that any one thing is higher or better than any other? Indeed, quite apart from proving the truth of such assertions, one may be asked the even more difficult question: What do such words as *higher* and *lower* mean? Is it not all a matter of personal preference? What one man likes more he calls better, and what he likes less he calls worse. And what pleases one man is not the same as what pleases another. How can anything be, in itself, intrinsically or objectively, higher or lower than anything else? Here we come up again against the old bugbear of relativity.

I shall say at once that I do not know for certain how to answer these most embarrassing questions, although I have some opinions about them. Suppose we consult Plato again. We have to ask him two questions. First, what does he *mean* by saying that knowledge is a higher purpose than honor, honor than wealth, wealth than pleasure? And second, how does he propose to prove that these statements are true?

As to the first point, one of the things that Plato meant (I do not say it was the only thing) was that a value is "higher" when it contributes more to human happiness, "lower" when it contributes less. For instance, he means that the wise man, the philosopher, the sage, the man who cultivates the things of the mind, has in him a greater source of happiness than the man whose chief ends are the pursuit of prestige or wealth can ever find in those things. He means that the pursuit of money, though he does not deny that it can give some real satisfaction, will yield a man less return in dividends of happiness than will the pursuit of knowledge, or even honor. He means again that the life of mere pleasure and amusement, the fourth in his scale, yields an even lower dividend of happiness than does the pursuit of money. And finally he certainly thinks that the life of the drunkard and the drug addict yields only dividends of misery.

We may sum up all this by saying that the meaning of "higher," in Plato, is "contributing more to human happiness," and the meaning of "lower" is "contributing less." But in the phrase *human happiness*, which I have foisted upon Plato and which he did not himself use, there are ambiguities. *Whose* happiness does Plato have in mind? Does he, in placing knowledge highest, mean that the philosopher-scientist who pursues it obtains the best happiness for *himself*? Or does he mean that he contributes most to the happiness of other people? Well, so far as Plato's own argument went, there is no doubt that he meant the former. He was thinking of the man's own happiness, not that of other people. He meant that the knowledge-lover is *himself* a happier man than the money-lover. But I think it is quite reasonable for us to give, for our purposes, a broader meaning to Plato's language than he did. And I rather think that he would approve of this. So let us give this meaning to higher and lower values, that they mean those values which respectively contribute more or less happiness, in the first instance to the man who cultivates them, but derivatively to the rest of the world.

In spite of the lapse of over two thousand years, I do not think that anyone since Plato has given a better statement of what could be meant by the terms *higher* and *lower*. Of course there are plenty of philosophers who would disagree with all this. Above all, there are plenty who have pointed out that *happiness* is a terribly ambiguous, nebulous word. When you try to analyze what is meant by *happiness*, you will find the difficulties apparently insurmountable. I do not think that any philosopher has ever given a satisfactory analysis of the matter. And so it has come about that any professional philosopher who nowadays talks of happiness as the chief end of human endeavor, and as the measure of values, is apt to be considered naïve and looked at askance by his fellow professionals. But it is a characteristic mistake of professional philosophers to believe that concepts which are vague because we do not know their exact analysis thereby lose their respectability and ought to be kept out of discourse. Almost all our concepts, including scientific concepts, are vague, and their proper analysis is unknown, yet they are used with success. For instance, a scientist can perfectly well discuss the cause of a phenomenon, although no one knows exactly what the word *cause* means. Therefore I shall spend no time on philosophical technicalities about what *happiness* means. These are no more than professional disputes of the philosophers. In practical life we all know what we mean by being happy or unhappy, or at least we know when we are happy and when we are not. We know quite well what it means to work for the happiness of other people. And if we had to wait before engaging in such activities until the professional philosophers finished their analysis of what the word means, we should wait forever and no social, humanitarian, or reform work would ever be done.

Now I come to the second question we were to discuss. Having given some sort of meaning, however vague, to the terms *higher* and *lower*, how can we ever "prove" that any one thing actually *is* higher or lower than another? And this means how can we prove, for example, that the pursuit of the things of the mind contributes more to human happiness than the pursuit of the things of the body? Here we shall have to desert Plato and try to find an answer of our own. For although Plato was keenly alive to the problem and did attempt several "proofs," they are all, in my opinion, fallacious.

I should say something like this. Civilized races have existed on the earth for thousands of years. During this time many billions of men have lived and died, each one pursuing a great variety of purposes, ends, and goals, through which he hoped and tried to achieve his own happiness, and sometimes, in some cases, to improve the happiness of a few other people as well. There is thus a vast store of experience in what we may call the art of living, which means the art of trying to live happily. Men have made countless mistakes, doing things which they thought would bring them happiness but which in fact brought unhappiness. Occasionally they made mistakes of the opposite kind. That is, they felt impelled, through some queer motive of pity or sympathy, to do things which they thought would decrease their own happiness, such as giving up something they badly wanted for themselves to some less fortunate person who needed it more. And then, perhaps to their surprise, they may have found that they themselves felt happier for having done so. Men gradually learned by all these mistakes. They accumulated over the centuries this great store of experience, recorded as it were in the memory of the race.

It was found, of course, that the teachings of experience gave different, and sometimes contradictory, answers. What suited one person or nation or culture did not suit another. A purpose or goal which seemed to add to the happiness of some was the very thing which detracted from the happiness of others, so that the thing which some called good others called bad. Amid all this "relativity" it was very difficult to generalize in any way, to state any truths about the art of living which would be true for everybody, or even for the majority of people. When you tried to generalize, to say, "This sort of thing always produces happiness," you were sure to find someone, or perhaps a whole body of people, of whom this did not seem to be true. Nevertheless, a few rather weak and shaky generalizations did gradually emerge, things which could be said about the art of living and about human happiness which, even if one could not be sure that they would always be absolutely true of everybody, at all times and places, in all cultures, would at least be so nearly true of everybody everywhere that they could at least be taken as fairly good guides to living for humanity at large. These generalizations became moral precepts, standards of value, accepted value judgments, more or less admitted scales of value. Plato's views of the comparative values of the main human purposes are really generalizations of this sort, and so are the insights of all the other great moral geniuses of the world. And the only "proof" that can be given of them is the accumulated experience of the human race. Thus, if it is said, for example, that intellectual satisfactions are nobler and finer than bodily satisfactions, this means that, however it may be in some exceptional cases, by and large they have been found to conduce more to happiness; and the only possible proof that can be given is that the accumulated experience of humanity, crystallized in the sayings of its great men, has found that on the whole it is so.

Several things follow from this account. First, general moral truths will be extremely few. Humanity is so variable in its make-up that there are very few things which can be said about men's happiness with any hope of their being anywhere near universally true. Secondly, these few things are likely to be extremely vague and flexible. Moral truths can indicate only the best general attitudes and directions, never details. You can say in general that men should be more unselfish than they are, but if you try to say exactly how unselfish, and even more if you try to say exactly in what ways they should be unselfish, you run into the fact that different prescriptions suit different people; in short you run into the area of relativity. In this way we can now see the limits of relativity. In all matters of detail we shall have relativity. Monogamy may be the best marriage system in one place, polygamy in another. But the relativist is mistaken if he says that there are absolutely no value truths which are generally applicable to humanity at large. Some few generalizations are possible. And these constitute the limits of relativity. But even so the generalizations will not be absolute. They will only be true in such a vast majority of cases that a man, if he disregards them, does so at his peril.

As will be evident from my account, the evidence for the truth of general value principles is of the sort which logicians call inductive. But there is nothing that could possibly be called "scientific" about them. They have been reached for the most part intuitively and unconsciously, and certainly with no scientific controls. When I called them weak and shaky generalizations, I believe I said all there is to be said about this, The point to fasten on, however, is that these generalizations, meager in themselves, weak in their logical grounds, *are all we have to go on in life*. We are therefore foolish if we disregard or despise them. They tell you, shall we say, that too great a love of money is a bad thing. Prove this, you say to me, or I will not believe it. I can only say, "This has been the general experience of mankind. Admittedly this proof is weak. But give me a better proof if you can." And as to your not believing it because the proof is so poor, what I will say to you then is, "You choose to discard the only sort of guidance we have about values. Very well, then, try something else. Invent a new scale of values of your own. But in doing this you are setting yourself up as a moral genius superior to Buddha, Socrates, and Jesus Christ. And you are proposing to rely solely on your own experience, the experience of one single human being, and to ignore and contradict the experience of billions of human beings who lived before you. This seems to me the height of folly."

My admissions that our moral knowledge is so small and that its proofs are quite unscientific may prompt you to inquire whether we may not hope that by the application of more scientific methods we may in the future acquire more, and better grounded, ethical knowledge. In the past we have relied on the unsifted and mostly unrecorded experience of billions of undenominated human beings and on the haphazard intuitions of a few moral geniuses. So long as men did this in other areas of knowledge, they remained steeped in ignorance and superstition. But when the techniques of science were applied, the light dawned and knowledge increased. Why should not the same thing happen in regard to moral knowledge?

I believe there are a great many people who think that something of this sort may happen. They look in particular to the infant sciences of psychology and sociology.

I am somewhat skeptical of this program, and I will try to make the grounds of my skepticism clear. I am not at all sure that, however little our knowledge of values may be, there is very much more for us to know. This may seem a very odd statement. But I make it because, as I have already tried to show, very few generalizations about the art of living—statements, that is to say, which will be true of humanity at large—are possible. And it is extremely likely that by now they are practically all known. I may know Mr. Jones and his particular circumstances well. After carefully considering all the facts I may give him a piece of advice. I may say to him, "Celibacy is the best state of life for you." To another man, after studying the facts of his case, I might say, "You would be happier if you were married." Obviously I cannot generalize either judgment. I cannot say either that all men ought to be married or that all ought to be celibates. For the same reason I cannot say either that all societies ought to be monogamous or that all ought to be polygamous. I can say, I believe, that hatred always produces unhappiness, and that affection and love almost always produce happiness, and that this a valid truth for all men. This is the very simple generalization on which Christian morality is mostly founded. My point is that the very few generalizations which are possible have probably already been made. And if so, there will be none left for science, which is essentially concerned with general principles and laws, to discover; and when we come down to individual cases, infected as they are by relativity, science cannot operate. As I said before, the knowledge of values is like the knowledge of history. Neither can be a science, and for the same reasons in each case. As history never repeats itself, so life situations, which are the locus of values, never repeat themselves. There can be only a very few generalizations about value for the same reasons that there can be few, if any, general laws of history.

After all, this only amounts to saying that it does not seem very likely that anyone, by scientific techniques, will ever improve on the Sermon on the Mount, that there is, on those very general matters of which that sermon treats, not much more to be said. The truths which it contains may have been reached by the haphazard intuitions of a moral genius. But

I must say that I would sooner trust these than the pronouncements of any psychology professor.

Does this mean that psychology and sociology cannot help the human race in its problems of conduct? Far from it. I am not at all sure what their functions can be here. But with very great hesitation and diffidence I would make the following suggestions. We distinguished between general truths about values and particular truths which have to do either with individuals or restricted groups of individuals, not with the whole human race. I think that in the area of general truths, if there is anything more to be known—if, that is to say, the ideals of a Buddha, or a Christ, could ever be replaced by yet better or clearer ideals—such a revelation would have to come from an inspired man, a saint, a mystic, a prophet, and not from a scientific laboratory. But it may well be that in the areas of the individual or the social group, in the matter of what I called particular truths about value, the psychologist and the sociologist may give important advice. This is already being done in the matter of the individual. This is the field of psychiatry and clinical psychology. The discovery, within the framework of our general moral values, of what particular purposes will bring the most satisfaction and mental health to this or that individual is their special skill. All such questions are concerned with particular value-truths. Thus the techniques for ascertaining for what occupations— that of doctor, lawyer, salesman, manual laborer—an individual is best fitted, plainly have to do with his values. They mean that for this individual one aim should be placed higher in his scale; while for another individual another, and perhaps opposite, aim should be given top place. Whether the sociologist will ever be able to give similar advice to whole social groups is a question for the future. There is no reason in the nature of things why he should not.

Democratic Values

In the previous essay I discussed values in general. In this one I wish to come a little nearer to our actual daily thinking by discussing the specific kind of values which we associate with the word *democracy*. If we were asked what value or values in particular we attribute to what we call the "democratic way of life," the word most likely to spring to our lips at once would be *freedom*. We certainly think it is a better thing to be free than unfree—whatever this may mean. This is certainly not the only value we associate with democracy, but it is perhaps the most important.

Now before going on to discuss the values of democracy in detail, I want to relate this topic to what I said earlier. We distinguished between quite general value-principles, meaning principles which we think to be valid, if not absolutely for all human beings, at least for the great majority of men in all ages, times, and cultures; we distinguished between these general principles of value and value-judgments about particular cases. It might be the case, we saw, that a certain thing, or purpose, or end, though not of universal value, might be valuable to a particular people, or in a particular age, or even to one particular person only. Polygamy might be a good thing for a particular culture though it may not be for us. That would be a value-judgment about a particular culture. If we want examples of value-judgments which apply only to an individual person, or a few persons, we find that they abound. If you say to a man, "You are the kind of person who would make a good doctor," you are suggesting to him a purpose or goal which you think would be good in his life, but you certainly do not mean that this is a purpose or a goal for which everybody ought to aim. These are examples of particular value-judgments. On the other hand, when Socrates recommended that men should rate wisdom and knowledge higher than money, this advice would appear to be directed to human beings generally. It claims to be just as true in modern France or America as it was in ancient Greece. It is what I call a general value-judgment.

Under which of these two heads, general or particular, should we class the values of democracy? I think our first impulse is to reply that it is only a particular value. It is good in some cultures and not in others. But I believe that on reflection we may come to the conclusion that this is the wrong answer, that freedom and the other democratic values which are associated with it are really universal in their scope, that they are good for all men. They are human, and not merely American, or Western European, values.

Of course I am aware that this is a debatable issue, and that perhaps there are many people whom I shall not convince. The question is a difficult one, and much depends on it. For instance, on this issue depends whether we are right to go around the world as we do trying to convert other peoples to democracy, or whether we ought not rather leave them to their own ideas of government. Is this a case of relativity, or is there any universal human value involved here?

I will run over briefly the things which tend to make us think that democracy is only a particular value. One is that there may very likely be peoples in the world to whom democracy is not suited at present. There are still plenty of primitive peoples for whom some kind of benevolent autocracy may be the best form of government. But do we not think, in all such cases, that these peoples would be better off if they could be brought to that level of culture at which they could become democratic? The British used to say a hundred years ago, or even less, that Indians were incapable of democracy. But then they always added that they were trying to train them for democracy. These protestations may have been open to criticism on the ground that the British in their ideas of leading the Indians on towards democracy were much too slow, or even that they were insincere and hypocritical. I am not concerned with the justice of these charges. The point is that what was implicit in the British statements was the thought that democracy would be just as much a good for the inhabitants of India as for the inhabitants of Britain, but that—according to British assertions—they were not mature enough for it.

To deny that democracy is a general human value, to assert that it is merely a particular value, on the ground that some peoples are not yet mature enough for it, is like denying that philosophy and art and science are general human values on the ground that infants and even older children are not yet mature enough to understand them. I do not of course offer Shakespeare to a five-year-old. I do not even expect the common values of honesty and truthfulness to be much appreciated by a three-year-old. Yet I certainly believe that they are universal human values, not limited to a particular time, place, and culture. When we say that some value is universal, when we say, for example, that universally the values of wisdom, art, religion, philosophy, and in general the things of the mind, are "higher" than the values of sensuous pleasure, we do not *mean* that every human being is actually now ready to receive their benefits. Young children are not. There may be whole races which are not. Among ourselves there are plenty of people, perhaps indeed the majority, who are quite incapable of appreciating Beethoven or Shakespeare or Einstein. What we mean by saying that these are universal human values is that *if* any human being can be brought, trained, educated, up to a level where he can appreciate these things, then his life will be better, richer, happier, fuller of good things than it would be if he remained always on the level of understanding and appreciating nothing except the pleasures of eating and drinking and sex.

If we apply this to the case of democracy, we see at once that the mere fact that there are said to be peoples who are at present incapable of democracy is not an argument against the view that democracy is a universal human value. And we see also that this belief that it is a universal human value is implicit in those very judgments of ours which assert that some peoples are not yet fitted for it. The British showed this when they talked as they did about training the Indians for democracy. We also showed it when we spoke of trying to educate the Russians for democracy, and when we have said that perhaps someday even the Chinese may see the light. Of course it may be argued that we only want to change the Russians and the Chinese for our own advantage, because the world would then be undivided ideologically and there might be peace. Undoubtedly there is truth in this. We have wanted to convert the Russians and Chinese in order that our own country may be safe. But that is certainly not the whole story. And if it were, there would be no hope for the peace of the world, for we could never successfully foist democracy on a people for whom it would not be, and never could be, a good. Our hope and our belief evidently is that if we could induce these peoples to try democracy, they would some day find it good, good for themselves, that is; just as when you try to induce your philistine teenager to try reading Shakespeare, your hope and your belief is that he will in the end find it good.

Nor is the fact that we are in great danger of trying to go too fast in the process of trying to democratize the world any argument against what I am saying. We probably are trying to force democracy on new nations too fast. And this could spell disaster. But we may also force Greek or mathematics too fast upon our boy, which does not show that Greek or mathematics are not good for him.

A second argument often used against our view is that many cultures and peoples, though they may be quite mature enough for democracy, nevertheless reject it on the ground that they do *not* think it a good. My previous point was that, if primitive and untutored peoples reject democratic values, this does not refute the claim that they are nevertheless universal human values. But now the question is: Does not the fact that there are fully developed and cultured peoples, like the Chinese and Russians, who reject our values, refute our claim? For we cannot in this case use the comparison with children who are not sufficiently mature to appreciate Shakespeare. These people are mature and still they reject our values. To this our answer must be, I think, somewhat as follows. When we say of something that it is a universal human value, we do not mean that every human being, even every mature human being, will agree with us. We are entirely aware that whole cultures, even quite mature cultures, will disagree. What we mean is that *if* these people could be induced to try our way, they would themselves in the end actually come to find it better and come to agree with us.

Of course we may be quite wrong in this. Our belief that democracy is good may quite possibly be mistaken. The Russians may be quite right in their views. These are intellectual possibilities. But what we *mean* by our belief that democracy is a universal human good is not that all people now think it to be so, but that *if* other people would try our way they would find it good, even if they do not think so now. And it must be noted that the Russians also think this of their system; they think their system is a universal human good, as is shown by the fact that they try to convert the whole world to it. They know quite well that we think their system bad. But they nevertheless assert that it is a universal human good, meaning not that everyone agrees with them, but that everyone would come to agree if they would give it a fair trial. Of course here again, as with us, all sorts of other personal and selfish ends are involved. Just as we want to convert them for the sake of our own skins, so doubtless their motives are their own security and no doubt also the lust for power and world dominion. But I think we must also credit them with really believing that their system is good and that we would find it so if we tried it out.

Thus what I am at the moment asserting is not that democracy _is_ a universal human value—although of course I certainly believe that it is—but merely that, if it is a universal human value, this is not at all refuted by pointing out that a whole culture, and a mature culture such as that of Russia, does not think so. If the proposition, "Democratic freedom is a universal human value," meant that all mature peoples agree that it is, then this proposition would be refuted by merely pointing out that there are mature peoples, such as the Russians and Chinese, who disagree with it. But if the meaning of it is, on the contrary, that all peoples who, being educated up to it, gave it a fair trial _would_ find it good, then it is not refuted by the existence of peoples like the Chinese or Russians.

It will be said that, in this case, our proposition is very difficult to prove or verify since it only asserts that something _would_ be the case if certain conditions were fulfilled. To this I agree. It _is_ very difficult to prove. But I must point out that exactly the same is true of any universal human values. For instance the prophets and sages tell us that money is an end inferior to, say, wisdom or knowledge, and that this is universally true of man. But this does not mean that everyone thinks so. If everyone did think so, there would be no need for the prophets and seers to be always pointing it out. It is obvious that the greater part of the world does not believe it today. And when the saint tells us that the religious life is the only true happiness, and that this is true of all men, he does not mean that all men know and believe this. He knows, on the contrary, that practically no one believes it. What he means is: Every man who really and truly tries it will find that it is so. And certainly all propositions of this kind are very difficult to prove. In the previous essay I discussed the nature of this proof. And here, too, I shall try to show that there are good reasons on which we can base our opinion that democratic values are universal to human beings, not merely regional, and this is not a mere prejudice based on nothing but our personal predilections.

I have now explained what I mean by saying that the values of democracy, whatever they may be, claim to be universal human values and not merely particular values. This brings the subject of democracy into line with our general subject, for I did not wish in these essays to discuss what is good only in particular times or countries or cultures or for particular people, but what is good for man at all times and in all places. I hesitate to use the phrase *the eternal verities* because, to tell the truth, I do not think that anything, at any rate anything human, is really *quite* eternal. Yet, if you will allow for some exaggeration inherent in the phrase, I think there is no harm in my saying that I want to discuss some of those things which used to be called eternal verities. And it is my belief that the democratic way of life is an attempt to realize at least some of these—though of course not all. Let us go on to discuss then, what these verities, these values, which democracy aims to realize, are.

First of all, I shall state what I understand democracy to be. I think that in essence it means that our lives should be governed by *reason* and not by *force*. The Greeks, who were the inventors of democracy—however much their democracies differed from ours—asked themselves this question: What is the difference between men and brutes? And they answered: The difference lies in the fact that men possess reason, which the brutes do not. It is from the Greeks that we get the common, but now often decried, definition: Man is a rational animal. The Greek idea was that men share with animals most of their faculties, for example, sense perception, the appetites of hunger, thirst, and sex, the basic emotions such as anger and fear; that wherein man rises above the brute is that he is a rational being. Other differences of course there are. Man alone has speech, lights fires, invents tools, wears clothes, possesses moral ideas, creates works of art. Man also is the only animal which laughs. But all these differences, even the gift of laughter, will be found ultimately to depend upon the fact that man alone, among all animals, possesses what we call reason. Reason, the Greeks thought, is the divine element in man. "Live in the light of reason" was the Greek message to the world, just as "Live in the light of love" was the Christian message. And those two messages are not incompatible, but complementary. We can follow them both.

Before I go any further, I had better try to protect myself against the volley of objections and protests which, even at this stage, are certain to rain down upon me. My philosopher friends will object that the word *reason* is utterly vague and ambiguous. It has been used, and misused, in all sorts of ways. I know some philosophers who are so sensitive about this that they are allergic to any mention of reason at all and will show signs of extreme anguish if you so much as use the word at all in their presence. I am painfully aware of the ambiguities of the word and the mischief that has been done by it in philosophy. But I think that a sensible account of it can be given. I must not go too deeply into this, because to do so would lead us into philosophical technicalities, but I think the essence of the matter can be put quite simply.

I think the essence of reason is the power of abstract thought. If you think about *this* man, or *this* circular wheel, you are thinking about concrete or individual things. But if you think about man in general or circles in general, you are thinking abstractly. That is why geometry is an abstract subject. It never discusses this circle or this triangle, but always

93

the circle or the triangle in general, or, as we say, in the abstract.

Now it is certain that animals do not possess this power of abstract thought, but that men do. This is why animals cannot speak, because words, apart from proper names, always stand for abstract ideas. This is also why, although you can, I expect, condition a dog to distinguish between a particular circle and a particular triangle—to wag his tail, shall we say, when he sees a circle and to bark when he sees a triangle, for there is no end to the wonderful things which modern experimental psychologists can do—although you can teach the dog to do this, the fact remains that you can never teach him geometry. The reason is that to distinguish between this circle here before your eyes and this triangle here before your eyes, all you require is the gift of physical vision. You require eyes, nothing more. But to learn geometry, you must be capable of abstract thought, and of this the dog is incapable. I do not deny of course that the doctrine of evolution requires us to suppose that abstract thinking has somehow or other developed out of potentialities in the animal mind. But it also requires us to believe that animals with eyes have somehow developed from animals which had no eyes. And just as we have eyes now and other organisms do not, so too we have reason now and the animals from which we developed it do not.

I have very little doubt that all the other capacities which man possesses and an animal lacks, such as speaking, lighting fires, inventing tools, wearing clothes, possessing moral ideas, and the like, can be shown to be the result of his capacity for abstract thought. But to show this in any detail would require us to become very technical. I will say only that "reasoning," in the sense of arguing, proving, passing from a set of premises to a conclusion, depends entirely on the use of abstract thought. And if these things are true, I think they justify my statement that abstract thought is the essence of reason or intelligence. They also justify the Greek belief that it is essentially reason which distinguishes us from the brutes, for all the other important differences flow from this.

Another set of objections to all I am saying will come from those who keep on telling us nowadays that man is *not* a rational animal. Emphasis on irrationalism is a characteristic mark of our age. We have had Freud, and the psychoanalysts, and the pragmatists, and other voluntarists, all dinning into our ears what a very irrational creature man is. What governs man, they tell us, is passion, desire, the will, unconscious sex, the Oedipus complex, and all that. Reason is nothing but a cork tossed helplessly about on the top of the dark ocean of desire. We deceive ourselves if we imagine that we are governed by reason.

I will make an offer to these people who keep telling us these things. Abraham said to the Lord, "If there be fifty righteous people in Sodom, will you hold your hand and not destroy the city?" And Jehovah agreed. Then Abraham, who was a businessman, beat Jehovah down from fifty to forty, to thirty, to twenty, and ultimately to only ten people. If there were even ten righteous people in Sodom, God would not destroy it. I should like to strike a similar bargain with the irrationalists. If I admit that man is 95 per cent governed by these dark unconscious forces: the Oedipus complex, the Electra complex, the superiority complex, the inferiority complex, and the whole complex of complexes; if I admit that man is the whole frightful psychological mess that you say he is, will you admit on your side that he is 5 per cent rational? No? Well, will you give me 3 per cent? No? Well, will you give me even 1 per cent? You surely cannot refuse that. Well, if you give me that, I will accept that bargain, and I will go on. I will rephrase my previous remarks as follows. When I define man as a rational animal, I *mean* that he is 1 per cent rational, and that the brutes are zero per cent. When I say that the Greeks thought men ought to try to live more rationally, and that the life of reason is the good life, and that I agree with this, then I will claim that what I and the Greeks mean is that we ought to try to be 2 per cent rational. And when I say man's reason is the cause of his speech, his tool-making, his morals, his art, and his civilization, I mean that this 1 per cent is the cause of these things. Have I said enough about this kind of objection? And can I now go on?

Well, the next point is this. If reason is what distinguishes us from the brutes, if it is what is divine in man, then what is the proper life for man? Plato answered this question in the *Republic*. The proper life for man is the life governed by the highest part of man, his reason. Because the brute lacks reason you can rule him only by *force*. But because man is a rational being, the only government which is consistent with his nature is that he be ruled by *reason*. This great insight of Plato's has been, along with the Christian ideal of the rule of love, the guiding light of Western civilization; and I say that it is the essence of democratic philosophy, although it is true that Plato himself did not at all understand democracy in this way.

Before I explain this further, let me add one more thought. If it is true that reason is what raises man above the brute, and if it is also true, as I affirm, that government by reason is the essence of democracy, then we have here a proof of what I alleged earlier—that the values of democracy are universal human values, not merely particular values. For if man is a rational animal, if reason is of his essence, this means that reason is a common element of all men. It means that all men are rational. It is true that there are insane people—freaks and exceptions from the human rule—just as there are freaks and exceptions born with three legs or none at all, instead of two. But the existence of insane or otherwise totally irrational people will not prevent me from saying that all men, that is all normal men, are rational, and that rationality is of the essence of man, any more than the existence of freaks with three legs will prevent me from saying that two-leggedness is an essential character of the human animal. Now if reason is a universal human character and democracy is justified because it is government by man's highest part, his reason, it will follow that democracy is the ideal government for all men and not merely for Americans, or Britishers, or Frenchmen. This is the proof that the values of democracy are universal values. But of course it depends upon the assertion that democracy is, as I said, government by reason. And this is what we now have to show. We have to ask: *Is* government by reason the essence of democracy?

We have two opposite possibilities of government—government by force, which is the way to deal with animals, and government by reason, which is the way to deal with men. The former I am asserting is the way of totalitarianism or any autocratic government. The latter is the way of democracy. In order to see this let us ask ourselves what, in any state, is the relation between the rulers and the ruled. In a totalitarian state the rulers impose their will by force upon the ruled. In a democracy the rulers, whether they be a president and congress, or a parliament and prime minister, have to *persuade the people by rational argument* that the measures they propose are the best. And if they cannot do this they have to get out and make way for others who can. They have to use the instrument of *persuasion*, not the instrument of force. That, in bold outline, is what I mean by saying that democracy simply means government by reason. Stalin or Hitler simply compelled their subjects to do as they willed. Force was the principle of their government. The President and Congress do not compel us against our will. They have to *persuade* us that the measures they propose are right. Persuasion is the principle of democratic governments. They have to use rational means to persuade us as rational men.

I foresee an obvious criticism of this. It is true, you will say, that a democratic government has to persuade its citizens, but it is quite untrue that they persuade them by reason, by rational arguments. It is notorious that our politicians almost never appeal to reason. They appeal to the ignorance, the prejudice, the self-interest of the electorate. Sometimes they appeal to the basest passions. Sometimes they use unworthy tricks and even deceit and lies and false promises to persuade the people. And where is reason to be found in all this?

The charge, of course, is perfectly true. The facts are as stated. But these facts do not show that I am wrong in saying that the essence of the democratic ideal is government by reason. What they show is that actual democracies fall far short of the essential ideal of democracy, that they are not what they ought to be, that they are not truly democratic. They point to the abuses of democracy, not to the ideal of democracy in which alone, of course, democratic values would perfectly flower. And it is about democratic values that we are talking, not about human failures to reach them. An ideal democracy would be a government in which the people and the rulers "reasoned together," in which the rulers would have to persuade the people by rational means that their policy was good, and in which the people would refuse to be misled by prejudice, passion, and ignorance. That is the real ideal of democracy, not the mass of selfish grabbing, vote-catching, and corruption which actual democracies unfortunately are. We are accustomed to saying that there are some peoples who are not yet fit for democracy. And we self-righteously plume ourselves that we are not among them. The truth is that there is no nation in the world yet fit for democracy, and perhaps there never will be.

Democracy is an ideal, not a fact. But it is an ideal we can strive for. The facts we are discussing—the corruption, the greed, the base deceit, and lying, and false promises which are found in existing democracies—these are the very facts which are seized upon by our enemies in criticism of democracy. Look, they say, how the self-styled democratic countries are actually governed—by falsehood, ignorance, and shameless greed. Is it not better to be ruled by a man, or by a few men, who are above the necessity of sinking to these levels, who can do what they know to be best without having to count the votes of the base and foolish mob? It is a clever argument. But it means the utter abandonment of the ideals of reason. And the answer to it is that it is better to struggle upwards towards the light of reason, badly as we do it, than to lower our standards and to admit once and for all that we are only animals for whom the proper government is by force.

We do not usually think of rationality as the main value of democracy. We think of freedom, equality, and individualism. We shall find, however, that these really depend on the central notion of rationality. They flow from it and are its corollaries. Freedom, equality, and individualism are values only because they are required by the rationality of man. Let us take them in order and examine them. Then we shall find that this is true.

First, freedom. What does it mean? The word, of course, is very ambiguous, and the thing itself has been variously conceived. I cannot hope to distinguish all possible meanings or to offer an accurate definition. But to get rid of at least one ambiguity, I will say that I do not think that what we call political freedom has anything at all to do with the controversy about free will. I think that a determinist, who denies the existence of what philosophers call free will, can perfectly well believe in political freedom, for his point is merely that all human actions are determined by causes, that there is no such thing as an uncaused action. The believer in democratic freedom need not deny this because his creed is, as I shall try to show, merely that reason, not force, should govern men's actions. In other words, what a man does should be caused by the rational motives which proceed from within himself, not by forces applied to him externally. It is true that there is supposed to be a difficulty as to how reason can cause a man to act, since it is said that only desires cause action. I will not go into the technicalities of that matter. But there is no real difficulty. It is obvious that if a man is acting wildly and we ask him to be "controlled by reason," what we mean is simply that he ought to consider all the evidence, all the facts relevant to his action, its consequences both to himself and to other people, and not be led by some single blind passion or desire which is in him. And it is obvious that in this sense there cannot be any psychological difficulty in being "controlled by reason," since sensible people commonly are so controlled in greater or less degree. Thus liberty as a political ideal has nothing at all to do with free will in the metaphysical sense.

Next we have of course to follow the common practice in distinguishing liberty from license. License means lawlessness, doing whatever you please and being controlled by no law at all. Liberty means being controlled by a law, but a law which you impose on yourself, or which the people in a democracy impose on themselves, and which is not merely imposed on them by an alien or external force.

The essence of the matter seems to be that that man is free who is able to decide for himself, by the use of his own reason, what he should do. We may, if we like, define freedom simply as acting from one's own internal motives, uncompelled by any external force. We need not mention reason at all. In that case an animal too is free in so far as he roams about unconstrained. But if we do this, we leave out the notions of freedom as a right and freedom as a value. You can, if you like, allow very young children and insane people to do exactly as they please without any external control. And they are then no doubt in a sense "free." But they have not the right to their freedom, nor is it a value. For the *right* of freedom flows from rationality, and those who have not yet gained, or have lost, rationality, do not have the right of freedom and have to be controlled externally. It is only because, and if, I am a rational being that I have a right to decide, by the use of my own reason, what I shall do. And it is only if I do act rationally that my freedom has any value. Thus the value we call freedom is an offshoot of man's rational nature.

We see the same thing in the ideals of freedom of speech, press, assembly, religion, and the like. The freedoms of speech, press, and assembly mean only the rights of people to use their own reasoning powers to decide what they will think and say. It is the same with freedom of religion. Why was it wrong to imprison Galileo for believing that the earth revolves round the sun? Why would it be wrong to burn someone alive for denying the doctrine of the Trinity? Of course I know that merely pragmatic and utilitarian reasons are commonly given. We are more likely to reach truth, it is said, if everyone is free to give his own version of it. Error is best refuted, not by force, but by giving it free reign so that it will ultimately refute itself. All this is perfectly true. But we may take higher ground. The ultimate basis for denying to the state or the church the power to coerce me in my religious beliefs is that I, as a rational being, have the right to use my reason to decide for myself.

If the right and value of democratic freedom flows from the right and value of rationality, the same is true of democratic equality. What does such equality mean? It obviously does not mean that all men are equally clever, good, or wise. Equality of opportunity comes nearer the target but does not quite hit it. Democratic equality means, I think, that every rational being has, just because he is rational, a right, equally with all others, to develop his capacities and potentialities from within himself as he thinks best without external coercion. External coercion need not take the form of actual violence. It may be exercised by the pressure of public opinion, by taboos, or simply by unreasonable customs. For instance, if a man of great potential powers is prevented by social barriers of caste or birth from realizing them, from becoming what he is capable of becoming, he is being coerced. And this is the same thing as denying his equality with other men. And this again is the same thing as denying his freedom. For freedom and equality are ultimately the same thing, or two aspects of the same thing. Freedom means the right to act from my own internal resources, and not from compulsion, so long as I do this rationally. And equality means that all men equally have this right, and that they must not be deprived of it by class and other social barriers.

Lastly we come to the democratic value of individualism. This again is no more than another expression of the same ideal of rationality. It means the right to be myself, and not to have other people's personalities forced upon me. It means the right to develop my own individuality in whatever way seems reasonable to me. This depends on my *being* reasonable. An irrational being, for instance an insane person, has no right to develop his insane individuality as he pleases. He has to be coerced. Likewise children cannot be granted an unlimited right of individualism. The tendency of modern educational theory has been to grant them more and more the right of individualism. And this may be a good thing. A child is a potentially rational being, and rationality develops in him as he grows older. Therefore he ought to be given the right of expressing his own individuality in exact proportion to the rationality he has developed, no more and no less. It is a matter of degree. Whether former educational theory granted too little individualism to the child, and whether we are now granting him the right amount or too much, I will not try to determine. It may be added that when women were formerly kept in control, it must have been on the theory that they are less rational than men. And their present equality with men must be based on the view that they are just as rational as men. As to whether this is true or not, I shall leave you to decide.

It follows that there is a true and a false individualism. That kind of individualism, sometimes called "rugged," which consists in selfishly grabbing everything you can, trampling on other people's rights, and destroying their happiness, is the false kind, and is no part of democratic theory. For although it asserts my own rights of individuality, it destroys those of others. Individualism should rather be thought of as a duty than as a right. It means the duty to recognize that all men, and not merely I, are, as rational beings, entitled to realize their personalities to the utmost. It means that the emphasis is on the other man's right, not on mine. The democratic ideal of individualism is that every man and woman in the community should develop his inner resources to their most perfect flowering so as to contribute most to the richness of the life of the whole community. And this is precisely what is denied by that false individualism which is merely a euphemism for selfishness and anti-social behavior.

Thus these three concepts—freedom, equality, and individualism—are all based upon, or flow from, the central concept of the rationality of man. It was not an accident that the people whose philosophers defined man as the rational animal and who insisted above all upon the value of reason, thought, knowledge, learning, science, contemplation, and who in fact coined and circulated these values for the Western world down to our own times, were also the people whose statesmen —corrupt demagogues though many of them were—invented democracy. It is not an accident that those vast portions of the globe which, however highly cultured in some respects they may be, have not inherited the Greek tradition of the supremacy of reason, have also never developed a democracy of their own, never had any—except perhaps in village institutions—until it was brought to them from the West. That democracy is an expression of the rational nature of man is the basic philosophical justification of democracy. Its justification is that it arises out of the very nature of man. Some people think that the issue of totalitarianism or democracy is a mere matter of taste, of whether a particular people or culture happens to like the one or the other. I do not agree. I say that democracy is founded in the rational nature of man and therefore is the only government fit for men. Government by force, totalitarian or merely autocratic, is a government proper only to animals.

I will now briefly summarize the rather long and intricate argument of this essay. My main contention has been that the democratic values—freedom, equality, and individualism —are universal human values, not particular values valid only for our West European and American culture. On this question depends the issue whether we have any right to try to democratize other peoples, and also whether there is any chance of our succeeding. In order to support this view we had to discover what this proposition that "the democratic way of life is universally a good for man, that is, for all men" *means*. We saw that it does not mean that all men actually agree with it. For if it did it would be refuted by the mere existence of cultures which do not accept it. What it does mean is that we believe all peoples *would* accept democracy as a good for them on two conditions: (1) that they are sufficiently matured in their civilization, and (2) that they would give it a proper trial.

In this respect democratic values are like any other universal human values. If we say that love and charity are universally goods for all men and that hate and enmity are universally evils, we do not mean that all men accept this code of morals. We mean that if they were mature enough, and if they would give the Christian virtues of love and charity a fair trial in their lives, they would find universally that they would be happier people for doing so, far happier than those who base their lives on hate and enmity. We admitted that propositions of this sort are very difficult to prove. But in the case of democratic values we tried to show that we have good reason for believing them to be universal in this sense by the following argument. Democracy, we argued, is based on the rational nature of man, which is universal. It is not based upon, it is not an expression of, the cultural peculiarities of certain peoples, such as Americans, British, or Frenchmen. It expresses the essential nature of human kind, their rational nature, which distinguishes them from the lower animals. Animals can be governed only by force, which is the principle of totalitarianism. But democracy is government by reason and is therefore the only good government for all rational beings. Also the characteristic values of the democratic way of life—freedom, equality, and individualism—are likewise only expressions of man's rational nature. The democratic way of life is the good life for man because it grows out of the nature of man. And this is not a mere particular, local, or regional truth, but a universal truth about man as man. Ultimately, to be human is to be rational, and to be rational is to be democratic.

Why Do We Fail?

In the first essay in this section on values I discussed general or universal values with the emphasis mostly on those which are of importance in the lives of individuals, the values of the ends which individual men and women pursue, such as money, honor, knowledge, or the pleasures of the senses. These are questions of what we generally call moral values. In the second I discussed certain values which, I tried to show, are still universal human values but have to do with the lives of men living in groups and societies and states. These are generally called political and social values. There is no basic difference between the two types. Values of any kind are universal if they are rooted in the nature of man as man, whereas they are particular when they are rooted only in the idiosyncrasies of individuals or cultures. Thus universal values, whether moral or political, are at bottom the same in that they are those things, or those ends, which are good for human beings everywhere. The division into moral and political has merely to do with whether the emphasis is on the private purposes pursued by individuals or on the purposes pursued in common by the society as a whole.

What I should like to do here is to take a rapid survey of some of the tendencies of our American culture as it exists today and compare them with the conclusions reached earlier about the things that are valuable in life, or more or less valuable, and so to take stock of where our civilization stands on that ladder of values which, we may say, leads upwards from the worse to the better things.

Naturally I cannot make a complete survey. I am afraid that I cannot even be systematic. All I can do here is to throw out a few more or less disconnected and random remarks about what I will call the state of our souls in this America in this year of grace, 1967.

Also I shall not choose to dwell on those aspects of our civilization on which we might reasonably congratulate ourselves—and there are doubtless many—but rather on those of which we have no cause to be proud. I believe it to be true that America now stands as the greatest champion of human freedom in the world. I believe it to be true that Americans, both personally and as a nation, are great hearted and generous. But there are plenty of people who go around, in their conversations, speeches, books, telling the world how great and fine and noble we are, how America is the greatest nation that ever appeared on the earth, how we are leading the world to a brighter day, how idealistic we are. You can always be popular and gather behind you a great following if you do this. But I think it more healthy that, instead of bragging and blowing our trumpets, we should look at some of the dark places in our lives and see where we go astray. And of course to do this is not likely to be a popular way of proceeding.

For convenience, I will divide what I have to say under two heads: political and moral. And I will begin with the political.

Some few conclusions, which are fairly obvious, follow automatically from the considerations I adduced in the last chapter. First we saw that the essence of the democratic ideal is government by reason, and this means that our rulers, in persuading us to choose them and to approve the measures they propose, ought only to use rational arguments and that we on our side ought to listen to nothing except reason. But in fact we obviously fall far short of this democratic ideal because our rulers, both during election periods and at other times, seek to persuade us to their policies by low and un-worthy appeals to base emotions, to prejudices, and to self-interest, instead of by rational considerations and rational arguments. And we allow ourselves to be persuaded. This makes us the target of criticisms which totalitarian rulers and thinkers quite rightly level at us. They say that our vaunted democracy is nothing much better than mob rule, that it is the scene of a shameless race for high places and political favors to be got by any means, honest or dishonest. It is ob-vious that a wise ruler ought to propose policies and measures for no other reason than that he believes they will be good for the body politic; and if this would mean that he would often have to do unpopular things, he ought not to care. He ought to be ready to lose his office rather than do what he knows to be bad for the state. How many such men of prin-ciple are there in our government? There are, I believe, some, but very few. But we take it for granted that even our best politicians will propose steps and do things which are not in themselves good or wise, simply because they will catch the votes of this or that group—the farmers, the industrialists, the Jews, the Negroes, the workers—and so get them into office and keep them in office. I think it is no exaggeration to say that in order to keep themselves in office many of our rulers will not hesitate to ruin innocent men. We think this is all quite natural and part of the game. We laugh at it rather than condemn it. But this is because our political standards are despicably low. All this stems from the fact that our democracy, as our enemies say, is largely ruled by greed and self-interest instead of by reason, from the fact that we allow ourselves to be persuaded by appeals to passion and prejudice instead of by reasoned considerations. The only remedy for this that I know of—apart from a higher moral standard—is a much higher level of general education. On the whole the object of education is to teach men to use their reason, to apply it to the affairs of life, and to act from it. I shall say no more about this because to urge a higher level of education is to urge a platitude. And we are already pressing forward along that road as best we can.

A second way in which we fall short of democratic ideals is in our treatment of Jews, Negroes, and other unpopular minorities. It is obvious that when we criticize the Russians for their sins we ought first to think of the beam which is in our own eye. It is obvious that when they attack us for our undemocratic treatment of Negroes they are right, though much of this discrimination is not open but hidden behind a veil of hypocrisy. For instance, there are many institutions and organizations which have no rule against Negroes on their books, but everyone knows that a Negro will not get in, that he will be rejected on one excuse or another. This matter of undemocratic discrimination against Jews, Negroes, Indians, and others requires no long explanation from me. Everyone knows about it, though we conveniently forget it when we brag about our great American democracy and when we accuse the Russians of being undemocratic. I will only say that I place myself solidly on the side of those who think that our way of treating these our brothers and fellowmen is a scandal, a shame, and a national sin.

The third thing I want to say is that I do not think our democracy has solved the problem of the proper balance between individualism and discipline. The very word *discipline* jars in the ears of many. They think it is undemocratic to be disciplined. This is a very grave error. Any society, if it is efficiently to achieve its ends, whether they be the warlike ends of a fascist state or the peaceful ends of a democratic state, must have discipline. Perhaps if I substitute for the unpopular word *discipline* another phrase which is less unpopular, although it means exactly the same thing, I may succeed in making my point better. Instead of discipline, then, let us say "respect for law and order." This, I say, is necessary for a democracy; but that it is not highly developed in our American society is something which, I think, nearly everyone admits.

I think you can see the absence of a proper sense of discipline operating from the very beginning of our lives. It begins with the nursery and continues through school. There is insufficient discipline in our elementary schools and in our homes. The same is true of universities. In the universities students are encouraged to think, and they do think, that they know better than their teachers what courses and what books will be good for them. I have constantly had to complain that I cannot introduce into a course of mine some book which I know to be basic to the subject and essential to anyone who wants to understand the subject, because the students will consider it dull, as if their object were entertainment rather than education.

This lack of a fundamental sense of discipline in our people made itself evident in the armed services in and at the end of World War II. Directly after the actual fighting was over, discipline broke down. Everyone wanted to throw up the job and run home. A naval officer during the war assured me —he told me to keep it under my hat then, but I think most people know it now—that there were no fighting services in the world so given to looting as the American. Also women abroad, in countries where there were large bodies of American troops, were far more frightened of them than they were of the soldiers of any other nationality, except perhaps the Russians and the Japanese. Several years ago three American sailors were nearly lynched in Cuba for wantonly insulting a Cuban national hero when drunk. Murder, rape, and looting are the terrible fruit which grow from the tree of indiscipline planted in childhood years.

Why is all this? Of course it has historical causes. We can speak of the survival of the frontier spirit and give other such excuses. But there is, so to speak, also a philosophical reason. All this happens because from the very beginning of our lives, from our days in the nursery, we are brought up largely on a false philosophy which resents any sort of control as undemocratic. There is among us a false understanding of the democratic ideal of individualism. True individualism, as I said, does not mean that everyone does what he likes without restraint. It does not mean "rugged" individualism. It does not mean that every man seizes what he can for himself and the devil take the hindmost. This false conception of individualism is what leads to indiscipline and lawlessness. True individualism means that every individual's rights are to be respected, because every individual is a rational being entitled to respect as such. That is the democratic ideal. And this will lead, in a true democracy, to a genuine discipline—that is, self-discipline—and therefore to a deep respect for law and order.

Now there is much more that might be said about our political values, or lack of values. We boast that our constitution is the best in the world. But it is very far from perfect. It is full of abuses. The machinery of the senate and congress is old, and it creaks. I should say it needs a thorough overhauling. One need only mention the device of filibustering, which is a device by which a few bad or greedy or self-interested men can undemocratically obstruct the will of the majority, and which is a national scandal. But I will leave these matters to the constitutional lawyers and political philosophers, and will pass to a consideration of that other branch of universal values which we called moral as distinguished from political, and will try to see how our society stands in regard to them.

In a previous chapter I discussed the idea of a scale of values, and in particular I drew attention to Plato's insight that men and societies could be approximately classified by the things that they value most, by the things that they placed at the top of their scale of values. Approximately speaking, a man's philosophy of life and his way of life are identical with the answer to the question: What purposes does he place at the top of his scale of values? Does he value money most, or pleasure, or learning, or perhaps the love of God? The truly religious man is he who thinks the love of God more important to him than wealth or prestige or even science and learning, and who shows that this is really so by acting on his belief, so that although he may perhaps value these other things too and want to have them, he will at once throw them overboard, if it is necessary, in pursuit of his highest objective. The sensualist is he who thinks sensual pleasure better than anything else and who acts accordingly. Consider the man who inherits a fortune and wastes it on women and drink and gambling and becomes a pauper, although he might have remained rich. We may say that such a man places the pleasures and excitements of the senses higher in his scale of values than money, not to mention that he places them higher than the values of religion, or learning, or prestige. That he places pleasure at the top and all these other things, including money, below it, is *his* scale of values, his philosophy of life. And this philosophy of life determines his actual way of life. Likewise there are men who seek power above all things and make it their chief end. And this determines their scale of values, their practical philosophy of life.

Now if we want to know in this way what a man's scale of values is, we must look at what he does, not at what he says. If a man says that what he values most in life is the love of God, but we see that though he pays lip-service to religious or moral values, in his life he plainly pursues money as his chief end, then we may fairly say that, in his philosophy of life, money and not the love of God is put at the top of his scale of values. For on the whole men act as they believe and believe as they act. Of course there are exceptions to this. There is the man who earnestly, truly, and sincerely sets before himself a high aim but in his life falls far below it. The spirit is willing but the flesh is weak. But such disparities between belief and action usually end in one of two ways. Either the man will gradually bring his actions up to somewhere near his high aims, or he will gradually lose his ideals and lower them to suit his actions. For a permanent disparity between belief and action means a painful inward conflict of the man with himself, which he will always seek to heal in the one way or the other. Thus we can generally judge a man's beliefs by his acts.

One other general remark I must make before I begin to apply these principles to our own civilization. It follows more or less obviously from what I have said that when there is something wrong with a personality, when it is warped or distorted, this fact can very often be traced to a wrong philosophy of life. His scale of values is wrong. Of course this is not always true. Personality defects may come from all sorts of causes. But at least a common cause is a mistaken view of life. And this mistaken philosophy may always be expressed in Plato's language. The man is putting higher a value which is really lower, and lower a value which is really higher. Therefore your scale of values, or a nation's scale of values, is one of the most important things about it. And a good psychiatrist, I am sure, will always have this in mind. He will aim first at giving those whom he treats true beliefs about what is important in life and what is not. It may be the case that some psychiatrists try to build on the false beliefs already in the man's mind, or, worse still, to inject false beliefs which they think will temporarily prop up the man's morale. If so, they are doing bad work, which will never last.

Now what about our national scale of values, if one may speak of such a thing? What sort of a scale is it? We know that Oriental peoples and especially Indians always accuse the West in general, but America in particular, of what they call materialism. Mr. Vincent Sheean in his book, *Lead Kindly Light*, which he wrote after a visit to India during which he was present at the assassination of Mr. Gandhi, repeated this charge of materialism against us. He even said that the materialism of the West is the main cause of its constant wars, and that the only road to peace is to alter our philosophy in this respect. These are not words which we can afford to neglect, if we really want peace, if we really want an end of those holocausts in which our sons are blown to pieces. So we want to know whether this charge of materialism against us is true or false.

First of all, what does materialism mean? It does not, when it is made an accusation against us, have anything to do with what is technically called materialism by writers on philosophy. This philosophic materialism is the belief that everything in the world is made of matter, that there are no non-material things, that everything, including our thoughts and minds, is really composed of material atoms. What we are accused of has nothing to do with any such scientific or metaphysical hypothesis. It has to do with our scale of values. And I think I can give a fairly good rough definition of it. A materialist, in this moral sense, is a man who places money and material things generally at the top of his scale of values. To use our old phrase from the earlier essay, he puts the things of the body above the things of the spirit. Or to use once again the phrase of Socrates, materialism means "heaping up the greatest amount of money and not caring about wisdom and truth and the greatest improvement of the soul."

Now we might try to defend ourselves by saying that this charge of materialism is true of the masses of men everywhere and not especially truer of the West than of the East. This would be a poor defense, since it would consist in saying only that other people are as bad as we are. But apart from that, I am afraid we cannot say even that this defense is true. If we look at India, from whence in particular the accusation proceeds, we shall not find it to be true. The Indian scale of values has never been at all like ours. On the whole it is true to say that in India the love of God has always been put above the love of material things. India is a civilization based on religion, while ours is a civilization based on wealth. Of course I know that such generalizations as this are always suspect. And rightly. It is difficult to say even what they mean, not to mention the question of how to prove them true. Do we mean, when we make such statements, that a majority of the population in India, say more than 50 per cent, care more for religion than for material goods, and that in the United States the state of affairs is the reverse? This seems, to say the least, a very crude interpretation to give to the kind of thing we are saying. It is not so easy, so simple as that. Yet even this crude meaning is not wholly wide of the mark.

One way of judging the main values of a civilization is to look at its great men and especially at the men whom it most admires. To know what kind of man a nation most admires will give us a key to the things it thinks valuable. Another way is to look at its fruits, to ask what notable things it has contributed to the world. For instance, it seems fair to say that the Greeks placed the things of the mind and spirit, such as philosophy, science, mathematics, and art, very high in their scale of values, much higher than most other peoples have ever done, and certainly much higher than we in America do now. For art and science and philosophy are the most notable things they contributed to the world. And their great men were mostly artists, poets, philosophers, and scientists. We might still try to argue that this tells us only about their extremely few great men, the very cream of Greek society, and that we learn nothing from it about the values of those vast masses of Greek humanity who just lived and married and had children and died, leaving no record, so that we know nothing of them. That Sophocles and Aeschylus and Euripides were great poets shows only, we might say, that Sophocles and Aeschylus and Euripides were great poets. It shows nothing at all about the struggling masses of hundreds of thousands of contemporary Greeks whose names are not even known.

But I do not think this is at all true. The great men of a nation on the whole are men representative of the nation. They are of one blood and stock with the masses from whom they spring, and the values cherished in the whole society, both by leaders and by the obscure, are likely to be fundamentally similar. On the whole a nation will tend to produce what it admires most, and what it does not admire will not flourish in it.

In India it is certainly true that the kind of man its vast population has always admired most is the saint, the religious man. And this fact lets us at once into the secret of its scale of values. Also any historian could easily show that most Indian institutions, including those of which we are inclined to dis-approve, such as caste, have a religious basis. I cannot of course go into that. I am only trying to say what I mean, and how I would try to show, if I had time, that India is not materialistic in the way they say we are, and that Indian culture does actually place spiritual values, not material values, at the top of its scale.

It may well be retorted that we certainly do not want to be like India with its grinding poverty, its oppression of the poor, its absence of all democratic values (until recently), its caste system, its gross superstitions, its diseases, its attitudes of pessimism, resignation, and stagnation. But this is really be-side the point. We do not want to copy the bad things of India, but we might want to copy the good things. Even for what we in the West choose to call bad things, there might be much to be said. It is by no means certain (to me at least) that resignation and pessimism are attitudes inferior to blind energism, the itch to keep altering things, and the shallow optimism of a chimerical ideal of progress. And as regards the poverty of India, perhaps it comes as much from a religious spirit which prefers spiritual to material goods as it does from the inefficiency and ignorance to which we attribute it. But the main point is that whatever we may think about these matters, the Indian scale of values which places the love of God at the top of the scale and the love of material things much lower down is perhaps something from which we might learn.

All this, however, shows only that India is *not* materialistic. It does not show that we are! Is the charge true, then, that Western civilization generally, and American civilization in particular, are materialistic? Let us look at some of those features of our civilization from which its basic attitudes and assumptions can be deduced. Consider for example our attitude toward socialism. Whether or not a socialistic organization of society would in the end be wise, its motive at least is humanitarian. It argues that a system of completely free enterprise actually results in an unjust distribution of wealth—in excessive wealth for a few and extreme poverty for the many. Its object is to correct this by a system which, it believes, would insure a juster distribution. Thus its essential aim is social justice. We cannot quarrel with this aim; we can only doubt the wisdom of the means. I am not arguing here either for or against socialism. It is open to doubt whether the measures it proposes, the national ownership of the means of production, actually tend to produce the justice which it desires. I do not propose to discuss that issue. I want to draw attention to another aspect of the matter. One of the great arguments against socialism, perhaps I might say the main argument, is that it would stifle the incentive to produce, and so decrease the total production of wealth in the community. Let us assume that this is correct.

Under socialism the community would produce less wealth than it does under a system of free enterprise. Whether this is true or not I do not know. But for the purposes of argument, let us assume that it is true. Does this show that socialism would be a bad policy to adopt? Not unless you make another assumption, which is that the sole end of the economic system is to amass the greatest possible amount of wealth, regardless of whether it is justly distributed or not. The socialist might quite reasonably reply that he admits that less wealth would be produced, because of loss of incentive, but that there would be greater justice in its distribution. Which do you prefer, he might ask—a society vastly rich but with economic injustice rampant, or a poorer society, having no more than enough for its needs, but with economic justice spread everywhere through it? You see that the question being asked is: Which do you place higher in your scale of values, wealth or justice?

Now I think it would be unfair to say that those who condemn socialism on the ground that it will result in a loss of wealth do not care at all about a just distribution. No doubt they would argue that a system of free enterprise does more to insure justice than a socialistic system would. Such an argument smells rather unpleasantly of a thing that goes by the name of laissez faire. But what I want to draw attention to is not that. It is rather that this whole side of the question is commonly ignored. It tends to be taken for granted that the supreme end of the economic system is the amassing by the society of the vastest possible amount of wealth, other considerations such as those of justice being either forgotten or at best regarded as subsidiary. If I were to urge that it might be better for us if we were a relatively poor nation, say like Sweden, I should be thought hopelessly unpractical. But this emphasis on the mere amount of wealth, with very much less emphasis on its just distribution, is an indication that we in our hearts, whatever words may be on our lips, place wealth above justice in our scale of values.

There are other signs that the mere amassing of vast quantities of wealth, irrespective of the justice of its distribution, is the sole thing most of us think about in our economic reasonings. The total figures of trade, of imports and exports, the total national income—these are the things which always figure in the charts, tables, statistics that are published. And these are the figures that are quoted as being the criterion of our prosperity. Statistics tending to show how *much* we make are blazoned abroad in newspapers, books, government returns; but statistics tending to show how justly the wealth is distributed are not in evidence.

But there are countries in the world which are small and not very rich and not at all powerful, where wealth is not worshiped as the sole end—little, comparatively unimportant countries, one might perhaps say (one might give the Scandinavian countries as examples); where men are content with what we should think small incomes; where very few people have refrigerators, cars, radios, television; where peace, quiet, home life, the thought and reading of leisure hours still form the substance of the life of the people, rather than the feverish rush after money which obtains here, and which leaves no time for the older and simpler and better patterns of living. Our scale of values, I say without hesitation, is inferior to these, because it is more materialistic.

We see the same thing in that phrase which is so constantly on our lips—*the standard of living*. It is assumed by all our newspapers, by our senators and congressmen, by everyone we meet in the street, that the glory of America is its standard of living, which is higher than in any other country in the world. It is assumed that the supreme end of all policy must be to keep up or increase this standard of living at all costs. It is taken for granted that anything which would lower it is ipso facto bad. But what *is* the standard of living? If it meant the genuine standards of a good life, wisdom and knowledge and loving care for human happiness, we should indeed be fortunate if our country had the highest standard of living in the world. We should be right to insist that this must be the supreme end of all our efforts. But nothing of the sort is in our minds. In our national philosophy the "standard of living" means a radio, a car, a refrigerator, a television set for everybody. These material ends are what we mean by "the good life."

And where does this materialistic philosophy lead us? I

think Mr. Vincent Sheean was quite right in saying that it leads us into wars. Plato said more than 2,000 years ago that wars are caused by greed and especially by the desire for luxury. And this is still true. I do not deny that there may be, and indeed frequently are, idealistic motives involved in wars. I do not deny that the late great wars were fought largely on moral issues. But the point is that these moral issues themselves would not arise if it were not for human greed. We take as our sole end the amassing of the greatest amount of wealth. Another nation does the same thing. This leads to a head-on conflict. Of course, one or the other side is the aggressor in the sense that one side is more ready to proceed to actual violence than the other is. Aggression is then denounced and becomes a moral issue. Questions of justice also arise and become genuine moral issues. But the root cause of all this is greed and a materialistic philosophy. It is as if two men, each seeking nothing but his own aggrandizement, should both covet the same thing. Conflict arises. The one is a more violent and aggressive character than the other, more selfish perhaps, more ready to trample on the other's rights, more ready to trample on justice. There will be moral issues here too mixed up with the basic issue as to who is to get the coveted wealth.

Plato notes in particular that it is the desire for luxury which causes wars. Men, of course, must have their material needs satisfied. They must have food and clothing and houses and other simple necessities. These are what Plato calls "necessary wants." And so long as men are content with these there need be no wars. Under the head of luxuries, or what he calls "unnecessary wants," Plato lists couches and tables and viands and fragrant oils and perfumes and courtesans and the damsels of Corinth. That is no doubt rather amusing. And there is no reason why we should limit our desires to the barest necessities, the simplest food, a suit of rough clothes, and a roof. We might want to delete some items from Plato's list of luxuries and add others. I should say that we must add refrigerators, cars, radios, and television, and that your insistence and mine that we must have these things is a powerful cause of war. We may differ as to where we should draw the line between a reasonably comfortable life and a luxurious one, between necessary and unnecessary wants. British courts of law used to draw distinctions, saying, for example, that though one pair of trousers would do for most of us, ten pairs of trousers were to be regarded as necessary for an Oxford man. But the higher we draw the line between reasonable needs and luxuries, the greater our peril. For Plato is right in his basic insight that it is the desire for luxury which is a prime cause of war. And this means that our insatiable desires for automobiles and television and radios and fine houses and the latest electrical gadgets, in short everything we include in our national worship of what we call the highest standard of living in the world, is a prime cause of war. We think that we shall be able to abolish or control wars if we invent a suitable organization of the nations of the world, the League of Nations, the United Nations, or perhaps a world government. I do not wish to underestimate the value of such institutions. I am all in favor of them. But I do not believe that we shall get rid of war by mechanical arrangements of this sort, so long as the basic cause of wars, our materialistic philosophy, remains.

Let us now look at another remarkable phenomenon of our societies which is symptomatic of our materialism—I mean the enormous growth of advertising. Advertisement has a legitimate place and value in the social organism. Its value consists in the fact that it provides information as to what products are available on the market and where they can be got. If I wanted a razor or a can of soup and did not know who made and sold these things, I should be much at a loss. But this is the sole legitimate function of advertising. When it goes beyond this, it becomes parasitic on society, a useless, valueless, and positively harmful activity, a sign of disease, a cancer in the social body.

That the business of advertising as it actually exists in our midst is largely the art of skillful lying, I think it hardly necessary to insist. I do not deny that there is some more or less honest advertising, and it may be a fact that some of our best business firms try to keep their advertisements within the bounds of truth. But I believe that this sense of truth in advertising, though it exists, is very much the lesser portion. Most advertisers care nothing about it. You advertise a summer resort. You exaggerate its charms, and you say nothing about its disadvantages. That is, you lie. You include pictures or photographs skillfully done so as to make the gardens or the buildings look larger or more splendid than they are. You lie again. Or you advertise a toothpaste and say that it is the best on the market, that it whitens your teeth better than any other. This must be a lie, because you have not tried all other toothpastes and formed an impartial judgment as to which is the best. Possibly this does not mislead anyone very much, so that it may be said that no harm is done. But that it does not mislead only means that you are such a notorious liar that no one believes you. And as to its doing no harm, that is quite untrue. The harm of it is not only that you have become a liar, but that the sense of truthfulness and honesty in the whole community is undermined and largely destroyed. The result is a low standard of business ethics.

Am I demanding an absurdly high and impracticable standard of truth and honesty? By no means. For there are plenty of people still who live by the old standards of honor. Sometimes they are called "gentlemen," though unfortunately this word has become mixed up with low ideas of snobbishness. But a gentleman once meant, and still means for many, a man who will not stoop to low moral standards, who is proud that his fathers before him never did a shady or dishonorable thing, who is determined to pass on that tradition to his sons. There are plenty of people still who would rather their sons were poor than that they should make money by helping in the business of concocting dishonest advertisements.

But it is not in fact this matter of the untruthfulness of most advertising that is the worst thing about it. There is a much worse evil connected with it. It is that advertising creates wants in people which did not exist before, perfectly unnecessary wants. This is, in fact, one of the main purposes of advertising. You invent a gadget or a new food product. Sometimes, of course, you may have invented something for which there is a real need, and then you are a public benefactor. But in a vast majority of cases there is no real benefit to society in your product. There may be in fact no desire for it. So you get to work to create a demand by an advertising campaign, by dinning into the ears of the public how much better it will be if it uses your product. Then when people get accustomed to using it, an artificially fostered desire for it grows up. In this way the number and variety of human wants is constantly being increased. In this way the demand for luxurious living grows. And since the demand for luxuries is a main cause of war, it follows that the art of advertisement has its own measure of responsibility for war.

And the chief evil of all this is that, whereas the best receipt for human happiness lies in keeping the number of your wants small, so that you are easily satisfied, this advertising process does the exact opposite. It constantly increases the number of your wants, makes it constantly harder for you to be satisfied, and harder for you to be happy. Happiness lies in the adjustment of what you have to what you want, the equilibrium between the two. So long as you have few wants, equilibrium is easy and men can be happy. But in our age, our civilization, the monstrous accumulation of human wants, largely caused by advertising, is a destroyer of happiness.

I will cite one other evidence of our materialism. When we wanted to know what the Greeks valued most, what their philosophy of life, their scale of values, was, we looked at the writings of their philosophers. In the great philosophers of a people can always be found an expression of the soul of that people. The same fundamental attitudes to the world and to life appear in different forms in the art, the literature, and the philosophical systems of a culture. In art and literature they appear in concrete sensuous forms; in philosophy they appear in the form of abstract thought. Thus for instance the philosophy of Plato is the Greek spirit, the Greek sense of life, put in abstract form.

Where then are the great philosophies or philosophers of America? Undoubtedly America's characteristic philosophy is pragmatism, and its greatest representative was John Dewey. What does this philosophy tell us about the values of life? We know what Plato thought. He ranged human values in an order—wisdom and knowledge, honor or prestige, money or material goods, pleasure. In general it was his essential message that the things of the spirit are higher than material things, the things of the body. And this has always been the burden of the teaching of all the great prophets, saints, and sages of the world. What then is pragmatism's scale of values? I do not want to make a charge of materialism against those academic philosophers, such as John Dewey, who are the professional exponents of pragmatism. It is very difficult to say whether such an accusation would be true.[1] But I will simply ask the question: Why is it that pragmatism makes the enormous appeal to the people of America which it undoubtedly does make? Why has it become, in some sense, *the* popular philosophy of America? I have myself no doubt of the answer. It is because, rightly or wrongly, the public sees in pragmatism a justification of its own materialistic values. Pragmatism, or instrumentalism, as Professor Dewey called it, teaches that all thinking—and this will include science, philosophy, and, in general, the things of the mind—is in the end only instrumental to, and justified by, its practical utility. Science and

[1] Professor Warner Fite wrote, "American pragmatism is disposed to . . . hold that spiritual needs are only bread and butter needs disguised" (*The Living Mind*, p. 97).

philosophy, and the things of the mind generally, are not ends in themselves, as the Greeks thought, but means to practical utility. You can see at once how this can be interpreted (I will say "twisted," if my professional philosophical friends prefer it) as justifying materialism. For practical utility means for most people the acquisition of material goods, material comforts, the things of the body. If pragmatism is interpreted in this way, it means in the end that spiritual and intellectual things are of no value in themselves, but only as they minister to material ends. This means that material ends are placed higher in the scale of values than spiritual ends. And this is the definition of materialism. Thus the vast popularity of pragmatism becomes evidence of a fundamental materialism in the minds of the American people.

We in America pride ourselves on being what we call "practical." As a philosophy of life, pragmatism is nothing but the apotheosis of the practical. But what is meant in the popular mind by being "practical"? (We will not ask what professional pragmatists mean by it.) Nothing, I think, is meant except being materialistic, valuing above everything material things and the satisfaction of purely material needs. When the ideals of the Sermon on the Mount are called unpractical, as they sometimes are, what is meant except that they exalt spiritual things and set wealth and worldly power low in the scale of values? When an artist, driven on by his vision of beauty and content to live on crusts of bread, is called an unpractical person, what is meant except that he values his vision above material comfort? I am persuaded that the word *practical*, as it is commonly used among us, simply means materialistic. And the mere fact that we in America regard ourselves as especially practical people simply indicates that we are materialistic people. The businessman is the practical man par excellence because it is his essential function to cater to material wants. The artist, the thinker, the philosopher, the saint, and the man of learning are not practical. They are tolerated by the practical man partly because they provide what are in his view unimportant but harmless activities to occupy men's leisure time, forms of amusement, and partly because he sees that, in various indirect ways, they can be made to minister to what he regards as the important, that is the material, things. Science, above all, he values in this way. It aids industry and provides material comforts. But for science itself simply as a form of knowledge, as ministering to the hunger of the mind, he has no use at all. Science, art, and philosophy are really so much nonsense, except in so far as they help in various ways to subserve material ends. And if he does not say that the love of God is nonsense too, that is only because he is too cowardly.

For these reasons when I see it written or hear it said that ours is the greatest civilization in the history of the world, that we are the most wonderful people, when I hear of modern progress and the progressive character of Western culture, I cannot help but wondering. I think not only of ancient Greece but even of poor benighted India, with all its poverty and bodily disease and its so-called stagnation, but with its heart set on God. And the words of the poet keep ringing in my ears:

> *For frantic boast and foolish word*
> *Thy mercy on thy people, Lord!*

All that I have been saying is, of course, very unpractical. But then I am by profession an unpractical man. It may be that these things of which I have spoken are in some sense inevitable, that we cannot now turn back along the road of materialism down which we long ago started—although I refuse to believe that it is too late. But I know that it is the road which leads to war rather than to peace, to darkness rather than to light.

III

Imagery and Thought in Poetry

Imagery and Thought in Poetry

I WANT to discuss here the roles of imagery and of thought in poetry, and especially their relation to the element of what we may rather vaguely call feeling or emotion. There is no doubt that every poem, and indeed every work of art, must be intended to evoke in those to whom it is addressed some kind of feelings or emotions. These may range all the way from the quiet feelings of pleasure which can be aroused by a blend of colors or a musical-sounding pattern of words to the violent emotions of pity and terror excited by a tragedy.

In addition to feelings, most poems also contain imagery and thoughts or ideas. I think that everyone knows what is meant by imagery. It means mental images seen by the mind's eye. But I ought to give a word of explanation about what I mean by the words *thought* and *idea*, which I am using here synonymously with one another. I use them to mean abstract or conceptual ideas or thoughts. Thoughts in this sense are usually expressed in propositions. If someone says, "It is a good thing to be well educated," or "Life is not worth living," these sentences express thoughts or ideas of one kind or another. In what are called philosophical poems, the philosophy they express is the thought content. Some poems have expounded scientific ideas; for instance, Lucretius explained the atomic theory of matter in his famous poem.

The main contention of this essay will be that imagery and thought should never appear in poetry for their own sakes; that they can properly exist in a poem only because they minister to the excitement of feelings or emotions. Their function is to be carriers of emotion or feeling. They are only means to that end, not ends in themselves.

Let us, by looking at an example, see how imagery works as a carrier of feelings. Consider the following line taken from one of the poems of James Elroy Flecker, who is now perhaps hardly read at all, and belongs to that lost generation of poets who flourished about the time of the first world war. Here is the line: "The dragon-green, the luminous, the dark, the serpent-haunted sea." It does not matter what the context of this line is. We may simply consider the mental picture which it calls up. Possibly a luminous dragon-green is a beautiful shade of color. But it is not for that reason alone that the poet paints this picture in the imagination. The imagery is not introduced for its own sake, for its beauty of color, but because it evokes dim feelings of the eerie and uncanny. It seems to stir in us vague half-conscious race memories of the fears and forebodings of our prehistoric ancestors who peopled the world with ghosts and monsters. This is done by the deft use of verbal and mental associations. For instance, the epithet "serpent-haunted" suggests something akin to the ghostly, because of the association of the word "haunted" with ghosts. It is true that we may say of a drunkard that he haunts the tavern, but hauntings are more usually carried out by ghosts, so that an association has been set up. If the poet had used the prosaic epithet "serpent-inhabited," the vague fear of the supernatural would not have been activated.

Notice also the cunning use of the expression "dragon-green." Ostensibly it is nothing but the name of a color, a particular shade of green. But if the poet only wished to indulge, like the abstract painter, in the beauty of a pure color, he might just as well have introduced some other shade, for instance, "emerald-green." But, of course, "emerald-green" would have ruined the effect of this line. For, as the poet has written it, the mention of dragons has the effect of depositing

in our consciousness a faint penumbral image of those creatures, which reinforces the feelings of the eerie and uncanny
which the line as a whole evokes.

In this case the feelings were simple and easy to analyze,
and we could even give them labels, such as "eerie" feelings
and feelings of the "uncanny." But this is seldom true. Poets,
instead of harping on old and familiar feelings, which already
have ready-made labels in our language, more often create
new feelings for which there are no words. And these feelings
may be so subtle and evasive as to elude altogether the clumsy
machinery of conceptual analysis. Who, for example, can analyze or name the feeling-tones evoked by the tremendously
powerful image in W. B. Yeats's line which reads: "That
dolphin-torn, that gong-tormented sea." If one is asked *what*
feeling this line evokes, one can only repeat over again the
line itself, and say: "*That* feeling."

I turn now from the consideration of imagery to the discussion of the function of thought or ideas in poetry. And
first of all, one should notice that a poem need not necessarily contain any thought at all—in the sense in which I am
using the word *thought*, namely, as meaning abstract or general ideas. And much of the best poetry contains only imagery
and no thought. For the essence of the poem is its emotional
effect. And imagery alone can produce emotion, without the
aid of thought. Here, for instance, are some lines of a poem
by Ezra Pound under the title "Taking Leave of a Friend."

> *Blue mountains to the north of the walls,*
> *White river winding about them;*
> *Here we must make separation*
> *And go through a thousand miles of dead grass . . .*
>
> . . .
>
> *Our horses neigh to each other as we are departing.*

There is no abstract or general idea here embodied in this
imagery. There is simply the vivid picture, and the human

episode of the parting of friends. And it is moving and beautiful.

But although thought is not a necessary element in poetry, as a matter of fact, much poetry does contain thought. And therefore we now have to ask the question: What is the place and function of thought in those poems which contain it?

We find that just as imagery does not appear in poetry for its own sake, but only as a carrier of emotions, so also the same holds true of thought. Thought per se has no place and no right in poetry. The function of thought in poetry is to excite feelings, and it is a means to that end. The intellectual interest in ideas as such is foreign to art, though it is the life-blood of science and philosophy. It is only the emotional interest of ideas, their moving character, if they have any, which can be the substance of poetry. The question for us therefore is how thought evokes emotion. There are, I think, two main principles which govern this matter.

The first principle is that thought cannot appear naked in a poem. It has to be clothed in imagery, and it only produces its emotional effect indirectly by means of the imagery. To say this is the same as to say that thought, which in its own nature is abstract, cannot appear in poetry as abstract but has to be individualized and concretized by imagery. It is the nature of every work of art to be individual, concrete, and sensuous. Abstractions as such cannot be made the subject of art because they do not excite emotions. Emotion apparently precipitates itself only on the particular or individual. Abstractions are, by their nature, arid and lacking in warmth. Mathematical propositions are perhaps the most abstract of all possible thoughts, and ordinary mortals cannot become emotional about a quadratic equation—although I cannot venture to be sure that the same is true of pure mathematicians. Likewise purely scientific or philosophical statements are abstract and cannot, as such, make poetry. However great a poet Lucretius may have been, it is difficult to believe that those parts of his poem which merely expound the atomic theory of matter, and the different shapes and sizes of atoms, can be genuine poetry.

The first few lines of T. S. Eliot's poem *Burnt Norton*— the first of the *Four Quartets*—read as follows:

> *Time present and time past*
> *Are both perhaps present in time future,*
> *And time future contained in time past.*
> *If all time is eternally present,*
> *All time is unredeemable.*
> *What might have been is an abstraction*
> *Remaining a perpetual possibility*
> *Only in a world of speculation.*

I do not think this is poetry at all. It is an abstract philosophical statement about abstract time. It is nothing but versified philosophy. If it were not written in meter, or rather in rhythmical lines, it might have been taken from a chapter on the problem of time in a philosophy textbook.

But I will quote the very next lines in the poem, those immediately following the ones above. You will notice that there comes a sudden change in them.

> *Footfalls echo in the memory*
> *Down the passage which we did not take*
> *Towards the door we never opened*
> *Into the rose-garden.*

This is genuine poetry, because the thought here is not presented in the abstract, but clothed in imagery. The images of the footfalls echoing in memory, the passage we never took, the door we never opened, the rose-garden grip us and move us. And from then on there are no more thin and pale abstractions in this poem, but it moves confidently in the concrete world of images, with the result that in spite of the poor beginning we have a noble poem.

There is another passage in the *Four Quartets* which embodies thoughts about time. But fine poetry is achieved because this thought content, these ideas about time, are embedded in a mental picture of a fog at sea and the sound of a bell buoy.

> *Under the oppression of the silent fog*
> *The tolling bell*
> *Measures time, not our time, rung by the unhurried*
> *Ground swell, a time*
> *Older than the time of chronometers, older*
> *Than the time counted by anxious worried women*
> *Lying awake, calculating the future . . .*

Philosophy, like science and mathematics, is, of course, concerned with abstract ideas and theories. Therefore a philosophical theory as such cannot be made into a poem, unless it is presented in the guise of sensuous imagery. Could one, for example, make poetry out of what philosophers know as the theory of absolute idealism, which was preached by metaphysicians like Hegel and Bradley? Consider the following sentence which I have invented although it might have been written by Hegel or Bradley: "The Absolute Reality is a concrete, timeless, changeless unity which, however, appears as a flux of multiple events in the phenomenal world of space and time." That is a piece of detestable jargon, of course. But could the thought content of it be put into poetry? Well, Shelley managed something very like it, in some famous, indeed hackneyed, lines. This is his version:

> *The One remains, the many change and pass;*
> *Heaven's light forever shines, earth's shadows fly;*
> *Life, like a dome of many-colored glass*
> *Stains the white radiance of Eternity.*

What the metaphysician calls the Absolute Reality appears here as "the white radiance of Eternity." And what the philosopher calls "the multiplicity of the phenomenal world of space and time" becomes in Shelley "a dome of many-colored glass." The abstract thought is imbedded in imagery, and the whole is suffused with exalted emotion.

The second principle regarding thought in poetry arises from the fact that the thought contents of a good poem do not necessarily have to be true, and do not even have to be believed to be true either by the poet or his audience. For a poem aims at evoking feelings, and the thought content is only subsidiary and is a carrier of feelings. What is essential to the thought of a poem is not that it should be true but that it should be moving. And it is a fact that an idea can be moving, or evocative of feelings, whether it is true or false, believed or not believed. Some thoughts are pleasant, others unpleasant, whether true or not. We can be transported by imaginary delights, saddened by imaginary woes. The thought content of Shelley's lines just quoted is the philosophy, or at least a part of the philosophy, of absolute idealism. Most philosophers now think that philosophy to be false, and perhaps it is. But Shelley's lines are just as moving whether it is true or false. And he would be a very dull critic who should say, "I think Shelley's lines are poor poetry because I disagree with its ideas." In the same way we do not have to believe in the idea of Fate in the ancient Greek tragedians to be profoundly moved by their tragedies.

A prize was once awarded to Ezra Pound for some poems of his which were said to be an expression of fascist ideas. There was quite an outcry. I pass no judgment upon the aesthetic merit of these particular poems, and I do not know whether on aesthetic grounds they deserved the prize or not. But I think the judges were quite right to act upon the principle that although the fascist ideas of the poetry might be judged by us to be false, and even detestable, that would not alter the fact that the poetry was great poetry—if on aesthetic grounds it was so.

Let me quote a couple of stanzas from Swinburne's poem "The Garden of Proserpine."

> *From too much love of living,*
>   *From hope and fear set free,*
> *We thank with brief thanksgiving*
>   *Whatever gods may be*
> *That no life lives forever;*
> *That dead men rise up never;*
> *That even the weariest river*
>   *Winds somewhere safe to sea.*
>
> *Then star nor sun shall waken*
>   *Nor any change of light:*
> *Nor sound of waters shaken,*
>   *Nor any sound or sight:*
> *Nor wintry leaves nor vernal*
> *Nor days nor things diurnal;*
> *Only the sleep eternal*
>   *In an eternal night.*

The thought content of this is very simple. It is merely the denial of any life after death. Let us suppose that you and I are firm believers in a future life, and consequently we believe that what this poem is saying is false. Yet we can recognize this as fine poetry and can take delight in it. And we show ourselves to be mere philistines if we criticize it adversely because we disagree with its philosophical beliefs.

Fitzgerald's Omar Khayyam is a perfect gold mine of examples of what I am saying. Nearly every quatrain in it expresses ideas which probably a majority of us would reject as false. But notwithstanding this, we think it admirable poetry. In general its thought content may be roughly described as the philosophy of materialistic hedonism. Idealism and religion are frauds. There is nothing but the dead world of matter, mechanism, and force. Consequently, the only values of life are the ephemeral pleasures of the senses, of wine and women and song. The chief message of this poem is summed up in the line "Drink, for once dead you never shall return."

Probably none of us believes this philosophy of life to be true. But the stupidest thing you can say about a poem is that you disagree with its ideas. Nor should the fact that you may perhaps be a firm believer in the efficacy of prayer make any the less moving to you Omar's cry:

> *And that inverted bowl we call the sky,*
> *Whereunder crawling cooped we live and die,*
> *Lift not thy hands to it for help—for it*
> *Rolls impotently on as thou or I.*

Nor if you happen to be a firm believer in free will should you for that reason think any the less highly of the poetry of this quatrain:

> *With Earth's first clay they did the Last Man's knead,*
> *And then of the last harvest sowed the seed:*
> *Yea, the first morning of creation wrote*
> *What the last dawn of reckoning shall read.*

—in which the philosophy of determinism and the absolute denial of free will are asserted.

But what I have just been saying—that the thought content of a poem need not be true, or even believed to be true—will now have to be toned down and modified somewhat. For you may well object that if there is *no* sense in which poetry yields truth, if it is not in any way an expression of any insight about the nature of things, if it is indifferent whether it expresses wisdom or folly—does this not reduce it to an idle plaything, at most a mere decoration of life, not to be considered seriously? And such an objection must give us pause, for it seems to indicate that something has been left out in what we have been saying. And this, I think, is really true. Something *has* been left out, and we must try to say what it is that is lacking in our account so far.

Poetry, I shall say, *is* always revelatory of truth. But the truth it reveals is indirect. The poem may make statements about the universe, about the non-human world, about mountains or stars or trees, or about God, or about free will, or about anything else whatever. These statements need not be true about mountains or trees or God. But they should always reveal some truth about human nature, about what people call "the secrets of the human heart." If Wordsworth writes about the mountains, his poem does not really tell us anything about mountains—we had better go to the geologist if that is what we want—but it tells us, in the first instance, about his own *feeling* for mountains; but secondarily, and more importantly, about feelings which we, as human beings, can all share in if we are sensitive enough, and which the poem can communicate to us even if we never felt those feelings before. Perhaps it may be true that Wordsworth created a new feeling about mountains. But he nevertheless succeeded in evoking this feeling in his readers. This he could not have done if they had not already possessed the potentiality of these feelings. In this sense the feeling which Wordsworth created was a universal human feeling, even if no one ever had that feeling before him; and he was revealing a truth not merely about his own heart, but about the *human* heart.

This will not only be true of the older poetry but also of the poetry of the twentieth century. There is much talk nowadays about the private meanings of poetry, about the private languages, words, images, metaphors, which a poet may use and which are supposed to be comprehensible only to himself. But there is a great deal of confusion about this whole notion of privacy. It is no more than a matter of degree. Does it mean private to one person only, namely the poet? Or does it perhaps mean private to a very small élite? If the thought, the feeling, the imagery, of a poem were private in the absolute sense that no other human being could ever possibly be taught to share them, then the poet would be, to that extent, not a human being at all, but some sort of a monster;

and no one could be induced to publish or read his poems. At least it must be possible to communicate with an élite. And I should say that what can be communicated to an élite must be something which it would be possible for all human beings to share if their sensitivities could be developed in the highest degree. And, in this sense, even the poet who most prides himself on the privacy of his poems is in fact revealing some truth about human nature in general, or, as we said, about the human heart, and not only about his own heart.

Ezra Pound wrote a poem in which he said:

> *Go, my songs, seek your praise from the young,*
> *and from the intolerant,*
> *Move among the lovers of perfection alone.*
> *Seek ever to stand in the hard Sophoclean light*
> *And take your wounds from it gladly.*

This appeal for an élite, and for poetry written for an élite, is perfectly legitimate, and is, in fact, admirable. It is, after all, nothing but a demand that poetry should appeal to the highest possible aesthetic sensitivity, and that it reach the highest possible poetic standards. But this does not prevent it from being an appeal to universal human nature in the sense which I have explained. The ideal that poetry should appeal to an élite and the demand that it be universally human are not incompatible.

I said that poetry reveals truth about the human spirit, even though it purports to tell us about mountains or stars. How does this apply to Omar's quatrain about the uselessness of lifting your hands in prayer to the impotently rolling sky; or to Swinburne's lines about the eternal night which follows on death? What truths about human nature do these poems reveal? For certainly, just as Wordsworth is not revealing truth about mountains, but rather about human feelings, so Omar and Swinburne are not giving information about whether prayer is efficacious or whether there is a life after death; but rather about the feelings of human beings. The point is that, whether or not prayer is efficacious, it is at any rate a human thing that a man should look up at the sky and wonder whether after all there is anyone who hears and listens to his cries. And it is a human thing that men should question whether after all there is anything but darkness beyond the grave. And there may come from one who is either torn and tormented by these thoughts, or who is gladly receptive of them, or who entertains any other feeling-attitude towards them—there may come perhaps a cry of despair, perhaps an expression of bitterness, perhaps of bravado, perhaps of resignation, perhaps of serenity, calmness, and peace in the face of the inevitable, or perhaps of thankfulness and relief that the troubles of life will someday have an end and that

> *Even the weariest river*
> *Winds somewhere safe to sea.*

My point is that these are universal possibilities of human feeling, in which we ought all to be able to share, whether we happen to believe in the efficacy of prayer and the survival of the soul after death or not. If you are so completely imprisoned in your own beliefs that you are incapable of entertaining, even in imagination, the opposite beliefs, incapable of sympathetically entering into the feelings which they engender in those who hold them, then there is something not completely human about you; and there is something about the human spirit which you have not understood. And it is this something which these particular poets are revealing to us, if we are capable of receiving their revelation. The converse of this case is also true. If you should happen to be a religious skeptic, an agnostic shall we say, and if, being that, you are so narrow in your denials, so imprisoned in your skeptical dogmas, that you cannot imaginatively entertain and sympathetically represent to yourself that hunger for God which is the life of the mystic and the saint, then there is about you, too, something not fully human, and there are secrets of the human heart which you also have not understood. Thus the old adage "Nothing that is human will I consider foreign to me" is an important principle for poetry and for art generally. The proper study of poetry is man, not mountains, or theology, or any other non-human thing.

The kind of poetry of which this is most obviously true is, of course, drama. Hamlet and Polonius, Lear and Cordelia and Regan, Macbeth and Macduff, Othello and Iago and Desdemona, may, in the course of their speeches, tell us a good deal about their beliefs and their ideas and their philosophies of life. It is of no importance to us whether these beliefs and ideas are true or not. If Shakespeare is revealing truths to us, it is only truths about human nature.

But it may be thought that this is not true of lyric poetry. Here, it is often implied, the poet is only telling us about his own personal ideas and feelings. This is a mistake, a mistake which is part of the cause of the confused talk about privacy in poetry to which I referred earlier. Of course the lyric poet *is* telling us, in the first instance, about his own inner thoughts and images and feelings. And in this sense, what he says is private. But if he has any audience at all, even if it is an élite which is limited to a mutual admiration society of two or three persons, then it must be that the poet is revealing truths about the feelings and images and thoughts of these other two or three persons. And this will be true even if the poet has to create, or rather evoke, in those two or three individuals, feelings and thoughts which they never actually entertained before, but which had merely lain dormant in them. And, if you admit this, then in the end you will not be able to deny that even this most exclusive lyric poet, who thinks he is confining himself to an audience of two or three, has in reality the whole human race for his possible audience and for his subject matter. He is expressing feelings which are possibilities for all men if they can be brought to a sufficiently high level of sensitivity, and which are therefore in some sense or other latent in all men, waiting to be evoked. And therefore, the lyric poet too, and not only the dramatic poet, is revealing truths, not merely about himself, but about the whole of humanity.

IV

The Snobbishness of the Learned

The Snobbishness of the Learned

THERE is a story told of a very well-known living writer who produced a popular book on a branch of modern science—one of the best books of its kind now in print. He is said to have submitted his manuscript for criticism to a fellow expert, who, having read it, tossed it back contemptuously, saying, "You understand thoroughly the subject on which you are writing, and I have no adverse criticisms to offer. But why do you waste your time writing stuff of this sort?" The story is quite possibly apocryphal. But that such a story can be passed round, and gain credence, illustrates very forcibly the fact that there is among learned men a widespread tendency to look down upon popular writing as something not worthy of their serious consideration, as something to be despised and discouraged.

On the face of it, this would seem to be an extraordinary attitude. That the discoveries made by men of science and the world conceptions of philosophers should be made as widely known as possible would be, one might expect, their especial desire. And how else can this be done, if not by translating their thought from the technical jargon in which it is apt to be expressed into plain English which the world can understand? How else can it be done, in fact, if not by the labors of the popular writer? It would seem obvious that the widespread dissemination of knowledge already attained is of at least equal importance with the discovery of new knowledge.

For what, in the end, is the value of knowledge? His acquisition of knowledge is, to the expert, often an end in itself. He may be uninterested in its subsequent influence on the world. And it is quite right, and even necessary, that there should be men who take this point of view. The advance of knowledge mostly depends upon such men. But the matter, after all, cannot end there. To many others, discovery is of value because of the practical benefits which it confers upon mankind, as when pure science is applied to the extermination of disease or the invention of useful implements. But I would suggest that the supreme value of knowledge lies not in the thrill which its discovery gives to the small band of experts, nor even in its practical usefulness, but in the enlargement and ennoblement of the human mind in general of which it is the cause.

Of the human mind *in general*. That means the minds, not of a few experts, but of the multitudes of civilized humanity. This has certainly been the case with the greatest discoveries of science. They have revolutionized human conceptions of the universe, given men at large a vaster sweep of mind; and it is this which has constituted their chief importance. The greatness of the Copernican hypothesis lay neither in its purely theoretical value for the scientist nor in the better application of astronomy to navigation or other practical affairs to which it may have contributed, but in the fact that it gave to mankind some conception of the immensity of the universe in which we live, and that it destroyed forever the petty views, the insolence, the self-conceit inevitably connected with the belief that the whole creation exists for, and revolves around, man.

This is why the Copernican theory constituted a revolution in human thought. This is why it is so vastly more important than, shall we say, the discovery of a new variety of ant, or of a new theorem in mathematics. Exactly similar remarks might be made about the theory of evolution. That too obtains its importance neither from its theoretical nor from its immediately practical bearings, but from its influence upon man's general conceptions of the world. Thus what makes the difference between an important and a trivial scientific or philosophical discovery is precisely the influence which it exerts upon mankind in general, not upon the minds of a few learned men. And that is why, in philosophy, however interesting such a subject as symbolic logic may be to a few experts, it sinks into triviality beside the world conceptions of a Plato or a Kant. It is in itself a mere intellectual plaything, nothing of real importance, though it may become of importance if it can be applied to the solution of the great problems of philosophy. And it will be noted that it is precisely this trivial kind of subject which *cannot* be popularized.

In truth it matters little what the doctors of science or the doctors of philosophy think, believe, or say among themselves in their cloisters. What humanity thinks and believes—that is what matters. And the true function of the cloistered few is precisely to be the intellectual leaders of humanity and to guide the thought of mankind to higher levels. This function can only be carried out if *someone*, either they themselves or others, will translate their thought from technical language into the language of the market place. The best and the ablest discoverers and thinkers often possess both the ability and the desire to do this themselves. (It is worth noting that Einstein wrote a *popular* book on relativity.) Or if their talents are not of the kind required for successful popular writing, it can be done by men who make a special business of spreading the best knowledge of their age. This type of popularizer is the liaison officer between the world's thinkers and mankind at large. Thus it appears that the function of the popular writer is profoundly important and responsible.

It is related that the soul of a dead man was conducted by Saint Peter on a tour of inspection of the Heavenly City. After seeing all the marvelous glories of the Lord, and the millions of white-clad worshiping souls, he was shown by his guide a little curtained-off enclosure in which half a dozen people were praying, cut off from all the rest of the multitude. These, he was told, were the Plymouth Brethren, who believed themselves to be the only people in Heaven. Those experts who look down upon popularization, and who would, if they could, make all knowledge the exclusive property of a little coterie of intellectuals, show a spirit identical with that of the poor souls in the story.

But, it will be said, much, if not most, of what learned men think and discover *cannot* be made intelligible to the masses. This is, on the whole, untrue. The big conceptions, the important results of science and philosophy, *can* be communicated to the layman. What cannot be communicated is, as a rule, the detailed processes of discovery and argumentation which have led to those results. Every educated person now understands the main conceptions involved in the Copernican and Darwinian hypotheses, although the proofs and details may be a sealed book to the majority.

In a tube of anti-typhoid serum there are so many millions of dead bacteria. The methods by which the number is counted or calculated may remain a mystery to the layman. But the fact that there *are* these many can be understood by a child. The same principle holds true even in those sciences which seem to most of us too hopelessly mathematical. The *results* reached can usually be disentangled from their mathematical formulation and set forth by themselves. This is not true, of course, of pure mathematics itself, but only of those physical sciences which use mathematics as a mere instrument to reach their conclusions. And this is, after all, what one would expect. For mathematics is not itself knowledge at all. It is an instrument for obtaining knowledge. The actuary makes use of higher mathematics which no one except the expert can follow. But the resulting knowledge which he obtains is intelligible to everyone. The astronomer uses mathematics to calculate an eclipse, but none is required to understand his final prediction. And it is not fundamentally different with relativity. To think otherwise is like supposing that one cannot appreciate the scenery of Niagara Falls without understanding the mechanism of the railway locomotive which conveys one there.

Mathematics, said a famous writer, is a science of which the meanest intellect is capable. The statement by no means reflects, as one might be inclined to think, the mere partisan prejudice of a one-sided and narrow intelligence. There is a real truth in it. It is obviously false if it is understood to mean that a stupid man can be a good mathematician. For plainly it is only a very clever man indeed who can be first-class in this, as in any other, subject. But his intellect may nevertheless be, and indeed is, mean if he is incapable of doing anything with it except juggling with symbols—however cleverly he may do this. For mathematics, as I said before, is not knowledge, but only an instrument for obtaining knowledge. A Newton or an Einstein uses mathematics to help him reach out to great and grand conceptions of the universe. This employment of mathematics as an instrument of general culture is the work of noble, and not of mean, intellects. But in so far as it cares for nothing save its own internal affairs, is without effect upon general culture, is a mere manipulation of symbols for their own sakes, it certainly can be cultivated, and successfully cultivated, by mean minds—that is, by minds which know nothing of, and care nothing for, what is really great in human culture.

It is because mathematics is a *means*, and not an *end*, that a purely mathematical education is a bad education—or, rather, no education at all. For the true purpose of education is to teach men what things in life are genuinely valuable. That is, it is concerned with ends. Therefore education ought not to concentrate upon means. They are a secondary matter. The true order is to learn first what to aim at, and then only what are the instrumentalities by which we may attain our ends. Mathematics, accordingly, should be part of a subsequent technical training. Thus the now old-fashioned preference for a classical—which really meant a humanistic—over a mathematical education, although it may have degenerated into a prejudice or even a pig-headed obscurantism, was originally rooted in a true insight.

The impression that philosophical and scientific ideas cannot be explained in plain language to plain people is also in large measure due to the fact that philosophers and men of science have not, as a rule, the wit to do it. It is due, in plain terms, to the stupidity of the learned men, not to the stupidity of humanity. They lack the mental flexibility and adroitness which are required if they are to come out of their hiding places in the laboratory and the library and make themselves intelligible in the big world of men. They can speak only one language, the language of cast-iron technical formulas. Change the language, take away from them their technical terms and symbols, and they no longer know where they are. They are like those inferior boxers who can only box according to the rules and are nonplused by anyone who disregards them and fights as the light of nature teaches him. They lack too that human sympathy with simple people which is also essential if the teachings of science and philosophy are to be made available to the many. They cannot move with ease in the world of men. And these too are the reasons why erudite men, great figures in their own secluded world, are so often observed to behave like buffaloes in society.

The contemptuous attitude toward popular writing so often affected by learned men is, then, nothing but an unwarranted prejudice. And it may not be uninteresting to inquire into its psychological motivation. May I be allowed to recommend to the reader that, whenever in this human world he finds a totally unreasonable opinion adopted by large bodies of people, he make a practice of looking, not for *reasons*, but for *motives*. He will thus save himself much time which might otherwise be wasted in searching for rationality where none exists.

Why, then, do so many workers in intellectual fields look askance at any attempt to make the results of their labors intelligible to the world at large? It is true that some apparently plausible reasons may be urged. Popular writers tend to develop certain characteristic faults. Cheap cleverness not infrequently mars their writings. And they are apt to slur over difficult and profound conceptions, and to substitute superficialities—because they have not the gift of being both simple and profound at the same time. Thus a writer on Aristotle, who wished to make easy for his readers that philosopher's teleological conception of the cause of motion, wrote that in Aristotle's view "'tis love, 'tis love that makes the world go round." But a moment's thought should be sufficient to convince one that these facts afford no basis whatever for a general contempt of popular writing. Popular writers may often be cheap and shallow. But to entertain a prejudice against popular writing because some popular writers are bad is like condemning all books because of the existence of certain inferior authors.

The real ground for the disfavor in which popular writing is held among experts is to be found elsewhere. It is rooted in class prejudice. The learned think themselves superior to the common herd. They are a priestly caste imbued with the snobbishness that is characteristic of caste systems. Their learning is the mark of their superiority. It must be kept within the limits of their own class. And the means by which this is accomplished consists in a learned language of long words and technical terms. Anyone who translates knowledge from the technical into the popular language is disregarding the rules of caste, and is thus taboo. Technical terms, long words, learned-sounding phrases are the means by which second-rate intellectuals "inflate their egos" and feed their sense of superiority to the multitude. If an idea can be expressed in two ways, one of which involves a barbarous technical jargon while the other needs nothing but a few simple words of one syllable which everyone can understand, this kind of person definitely prefers the barbarous technical jargon. He wishes to be thought, and above all to think himself, a person who understands profound and difficult things which common folk cannot comprehend. He wishes to feel himself cleverer than other people. The long words and clumsy phrases with which he encumbers the simplest thought are the badges of his class superiority. And as this kind of person is always in a majority in any large assembly of intellectuals, a definite prejudice against popular writing is engendered.

The poorer a man's intellectual equipment, the more does he revel in technicalities. A man with a wealth of valuable ideas is anxious to communicate those ideas and will naturally tend to choose for that purpose the simplest language he can find. But a man whose intellectuality is a sham, and who has in truth nothing to communicate, endeavors to conceal his emptiness by an outward show of learning. The more unintelligible his language, the more profound will he appear to himself and (he hopes) to others. He fails to see that the love of long words and technical terms is in fact nothing but a symptom of his mental infirmity. It is a kind of intellectual disease. And perhaps those who suffer from this disease would like to have a technical term for their own malady. I will therefore make them a present of a new long word. I will christen their disease *macronomatamania*.

It is true that a few really great men, such as Immanuel Kant, have seemed to revel unnecessarily in technicalities. But let not all the macronomatamaniacs of the world attempt to shelter themselves under Kant's umbrella. Kant was great in spite of his obscure language, not because of it. And one does not become great by aping the weaknesses of a great man.

It is true, too, that technical terms are a necessity. In many branches of knowledge one cannot do without them. This is especially true in science. And it is true (but in a much lesser degree) in philosophy. About their use in science I will say nothing at all. Even regarding their use in philosophy I will not attempt in this place to say *what* their legitimate functions are, nor legislate as to where they should be used and where avoided. For that would be itself a technical inquiry, not suitable to this essay. I will, however, set down what I regard as an elementary first principle of a good style in philosophical writing. It is this: *Never use a technical term when a simple non-technical word or phrase will equally well express your meaning.* And I would add as a gloss: *Cultivate in yourself a dislike and suspicion of all learned-sounding words and technical terms, a habit of regarding them not as fine things, but at best as necessary evils.* This will come easily to anyone naturally endowed with a hatred of humbug, and also to anyone with an artistic sense of the beauty and value of words; and the result of it will be that, whenever a technical term springs to the writer's mind, he will instinctively cast about to see whether he cannot replace it by plain English. Sometimes it will happen that he cannot do so without prejudice to his meaning. But often it will happen that he can.

I think that these principles should be applied not only to popular writing in the usual sense, but to *all* philosophical writing of whatever sort, even that which is written by experts for experts. For the use of a good style and of plain decent English will always facilitate the communication of meaning, to whomsoever it is addressed. And if anyone asks for an example of a good philosophical style, of the kind I have in mind, I would point to the writings of Bertrand Russell as showing the best philosophical style of recent times. Russell, of course, uses technical terms, plenty of them; but never, I think, where they could reasonably have been avoided.

A technical term as such is, anywhere and everywhere, a barbarism, an eyesore, an offense to the soul, a thing to be shuddered at and avoided. Macronomatamaniacs, therefore, are not only to be suspected of emptiness, but also to be accused of lack of taste. When a man uses a hideous jumble of technical terms where he could use plain English words, he writes himself down as a person without the sense of the beauty and dignity of langauge. After all, the issue is a simple one. Do you wish to communicate thought? Or are you impelled by some other motive—to appear clever, to boost yourself up as a highbrow, to impress the simple-minded with your superiority, or what not? If you write an article or a book, your sole motive *ought* to be to communicate what you conceive to be truth to as many people as possible. If a writer is governed by this motive, it is inevitable that he will express himself in the simplest language which he can possibly find. And if, in addition to this sincerity, he has also some sense of the beauty of language, he will choose short, sharp, simple, expressive words in preference to long, uncouth, and clumsy ones. He will not, for example, write "ratiocination" when all he means is "reasoning," nor "dianoetic" when the word "intellectual" would do just as well.

Unfortunately, however, to communicate ideas is by no means the most usual motive for writing books. And if a man writes because he thinks himself a superior person, and wishes to impose this same delusion upon other people, he tends to make his style as obscure and difficult as possible. He hopes that his obscurity will be mistaken for profundity. He will write, if he can, in a learned language instead of a simple one. He will prefer big words to little ones, and a barbarous technical jargon to plain English. And the American custom of forcing university professors to "produce" (that is, to write books), and of practically making their promotion in their profession depend upon their doing so, is responsible for no little evil in this matter. Not only does it result in the publication of floods of inferior books, which the world would be much better without; not only does it compel men who have no taste for writing, and no gift for it, to waste their time writing bad books when, if left alone, they might have made admirable and even great teachers; but it also demoralizes style, and develops macronomatamaniacs. For the man who has nothing to say worthy of publication is encouraged, almost compelled, to conceal his lack under a smoke screen of technicalities and obscure verbiage. He has to convince his university superiors of his intellectuality; and since he cannot do this by the inner worth of his thought, he must do it by putting out a spurious and pretentious conglomeration of learned-sounding words.

How easily this succeeds, how easily the world (including the learned world) is gulled by long words, the following incident may serve to illustrate. Years ago, in a certain university, there flourished a "Philosophical Society," in which the tendency to read papers couched in obscure and unintelligible language became rampant. A brilliant Irishman, wishing to prick the bubble, read before the society a paper called "The Spirit of the Age." In this paper there was not a single paragraph, not a single sentence even, which possessed, or was intended by the author to possess, the faintest glimmer of meaning. It was full of long words, of loud-mouthed phrases, of swelling periods. It *sounded* magnificent; it *meant* nothing. The society listened to it in rapt attention. Not one of the members perceived that the society was being fooled; and a long and learned discussion followed, in which not one of the members admitted that he had not understood the paper. A man may write whole books of what is either totally meaningless or palpably false, and may secure by doing so a wide reputation, provided only that he uses long enough words. For example, the thought that there is no such thing as thought is self-contradictory nonsense. But if a man wraps up this same nonsense in a learned-sounding hocus-pocus about reflex arcs and conditioned reflexes, if he talks enough about neurons and the neural processes, and if he interlards his whole discourse with the technical terms of physiology, he may become the founder of a school of psychology, and stands a good chance of earning an enormous salary.

But to come back to popular writing and its place in the

world of learning. I would contend for two positions. First, the works of the pure popularizer—the man who has nothing of his own to say but who popularizes other people's thoughts —is of the utmost importance. So far from being despised, he ought to be regarded as performing an absolutely vital function in the intellectual progress of mankind. And it is perfectly possible for him to be popular without being either shallow or cheap. Secondly, I would urge that, in a sense, *all* writing, even of the most original, learned, and abstruse kinds, should aim at being popular *as far as possible*. That such writing can always be made entirely suitable for the general reader is not for a moment contended. But the writer can at least aim at using technical terms as sparingly as possible, at avoiding unnecessary jargon, at expressing himself as simply and clearly as he can—even as beautifully as the nature of his subject permits. He can surely avoid giving the reader the feeling that he positively likes ugly words, that he revels in unintelligibilities, that he dotes on gibberish. Most readers will be grateful to him if they feel that he is at least trying to make some meaning clear to them, and not merely to stun, intimidate, and befuddle them with his cleverness. His writing will be popular in the only sense—and in the best sense— in which this can be demanded of him.

Nearly all the great philosophers of the English tradition have been in this sense popular writers, though I am afraid that the same cannot be said of the Germans. The style of Locke is lucid, if pedestrian; of both Berkeley and Hume beautiful in the extreme; of Mill clear and simple, though undistinguished and marred by some affectations; of Spencer perfectly lucid in spite of the "hurdy-gurdy monotony of him." William James, the greatest of American philosophers, had an absolute genius for graphic, telling, and brilliant English phrases. And of living writers, as I have already said, Russell's style is the best, and is a standing example of the fact that philosophy, and original philosophy too, can be written in plain English with an absolute minimum of technical terms.

V

Political and International

Have Nations Any Morals?

INTERNATIONAL morality may seem a figment of the imagination. It is bad enough to talk morals to the individual man in connection with his individual affairs. Tell the businessman that he ought to behave with Christian unselfishness towards his competitors and you are likely to appear intolerably smug or perhaps merely irrelevant and absurd. There is a story—perhaps it is quite apocryphal—that Carl Frederick Taeusch, Professor of Business Ethics at Harvard, was introduced to Samuel Alexander, the English philosopher, who was very deaf. The introducer said, "This is Professor Taeusch, Professor of Business Ethics at Harvard." Alexander said, "What?" The introducer shouted, "Professor of Business Ethics at Harvard." "It's no use," said Alexander. "I can't hear. It sounds to me just like 'Professor of Business Ethics at Harvard.'" Alexander thought, evidently, that "business ethics" is a contradiction in terms.

Well, if talking morals at the private individual often seems irrelevant or smug, how much more would this seem to be true if one were to talk morals at the nations. Would there be any sense in saying to the nations: "You ought to behave to one another like Christian saints?" How childishly unrealistic that sounds. Is it not an axiom that nations, in their dealings with one another, are guided and must be guided solely by considerations of national self-interest? And if so, what room is there here for talk about moral principles? Now it has always struck me that there is a curious contradiction at this point in our international thinking. On the one hand, we keep repeating glibly this saying that states in their international actions are and must be governed exclusively by national self-interest. This idea is not only popular: it reaches the highest circles of our government. Once—a long time ago—a British Minister, Oliver Lyttelton, actually had the effrontery to accuse America of entering the second world war not wholly out of self-interest, but partly out of a generous feeling of sympathy for those nations, including the British, who had been attacked by the Nazis! He suggested that this American attitude and the actions which resulted from it had been partly responsible for Japan's decision to attack America. Secretary Cordell Hull was furious. He thundered from Washington that America had no such motives. American action and the American attitude had been entirely correct; that is, America had been motivated exclusively by considerations of self-defense—which is to say, self-interest. The British government, pursuing its policy of appeasing America, thereupon compelled Oliver Lyttelton abjectly to apologize. Thus this slogan about national self-interest is a fixed part of our international thinking.

But, on the other hand, we also talk loudly about morals in international affairs. Did we not say that there were moral issues involved in the war? Did we not claim that we were fighting for justice? Do we not say that Nazism was the repudiation of international justice, of international morals? Do we not say that we want to establish an international order based on law and justice, and not on the law of the jungle? Also we high-mindedly disapprove of imperialism, and we used to lecture the British about keeping their promises to the Indians in India or to the Jews in Palestine. But why in the world should we disapprove of imperialism? And why in the world should the British keep their promises? There is implied in these attitudes a belief that moral principles ought to have some place in national actions.

Again, there actually exists a body of rules and principles called "international law," and *some* nations *sometimes* observe *some* of its provisions. But this international law is hardly law at all in the sense in which acts of Congress are laws. For acts of Congress are enforceable by sanctions. Congress does not merely exhort you to pay your income tax. It tells you that if you don't, something extremely unpleasant will happen to you. The existence of a sanction, of some way of enforcing a law, is part of the essence of law. But there is no way of enforcing international law except the crude way of reprisals. Therefore, international law is not in the full sense law, although it is true that courts adjudicate on it. What is it, then? It is mainly moral exhortation. It is a body of *moral* principles which civilized nations have agreed that they ought to follow, and which some of them do follow in some respects.

The theory that nations must act exclusively from national self-interest is identical with the theory that in international affairs the law of the jungle should prevail. It was, incidentally, Hitler's theory. That does not necessarily make it wrong, but what I am pointing out is the utter muddle-headedness of our American thinking, which believes two flatly contradictory principles.

The atomic bomb, besides having exploded Japanese cities, may possibly explode some of our incredibly foolish notions. We think that nations ought not to be moral—for this is the plain meaning of our chatter about self-interest as the only proper motive of nations. Well, we had better change our opinion and change it fast. Otherwise there may be no nations left to have any self-interest. I propose to show that this opinion is false—that not only *ought* nations to be moved by moral forces, but in point of fact they *are* moved by them already.

Let us take first what would seem to be the hardest case, that of the Germans in the two world wars. Moral forces, we might say did not operate in their international actions in any way. But I think this is a mistaken view. Hitler in *Mein Kampf* says repeatedly that force of arms will succeed only if it is inspired by some ideal. People will not fight, he says—or at least will not fight successfully—unless they believe that they are fighting for some great idea, for some ideal, for some just cause. They will not fight for merely selfish and material ends. Hitler was a much better psychologist that some of our statesmen. He knew that he could not make the German people fight simply out of self-interest. If he had said to them simply, "By means of a vast spilling of our blood we can conquer the earth and make everyone on earth slave for us. And then we shall all be twice as rich as we are now. We shall all eat twice as much. And those who now can drink only beer will all be able to drink champagne," not a German would have followed him. He had, on the contrary, to impregnate the German mind with a moral, ideal, and even mystical creed. He had to invent something like a new *Weltanschauung*, even a new religion. He had to persuade the German people that they were called on to sacrifice their blood for a *noble* cause.

You will say, of course, that Hitler's ideas were in fact not moral but diabolical, that his *Weltanschauung* was false, that the ideals he fostered were in fact profoundly immoral. But I do not think this is correct. It may have been a false morality that animated the German people, but it was a morality. It was certainly not mere self-interest. It contained the ideas of nobility and heroism—and these, however distorted their application, are moral ideas. The point is that Hitler had to make the Germans believe they were struggling towards a higher world morality—however hideously false that morality may in fact have been.

Now let us take another case, that of England during the first world war. In 1914 when the Germans invaded Belgium, British national self-interest was involved. It was contrary to British interests that the powerful German nation should control the Channel ports and the Continental shores opposite Britain. Also it would destroy the balance of power. But Sir

Edward Grey put the matter to the British nation mainly (though not exclusively) as a moral issue. Germany was breaking her solemn promises and was oppressing a little nation whose neutrality Britain as well as Germany was pledged to defend. Why did Sir Edward Grey put it thus? Because he knew, as Hitler knew later, that a nation will not be moved to the supreme effort of war by mere material self-interest, but only when the people feel themselves inspired by a moral purpose. At this point the cynic, who knows all the answers, will say, "It is evident that the real cause of Britain's going to war in 1914 was self-interest, and Sir Edward Grey knew this, but had to delude the British into believing they had a moral cause, just as later Hitler had to delude the Germans." I think this is cheap cynicism for two reasons.

In the first place it is an open question how far the leaders of a self-respecting nation ever deliberately delude the nation and invent moral issues in which they do not believe. I should say that Sir Edward Grey probably himself believed both that it was Britain's self-interest to go to war and that it was her moral duty to do so, but that he was a good enough psychologist to know that he must play up the moral issue rather than the self-interest. I think he believed in the moral justice of the British cause as much as anyone else and that he was perfectly sincere in his insistence upon this. And even Hitler, I should say, at the time he wrote *Mein Kampf*, believed in his so-called higher German morality. In the second place, even if I am wrong about this, even if we represent the leaders of nations, including Sir Edward Grey, and Hitler, and perhaps Wilson and Franklin D. Roosevelt, as a pack of cynical hypocrites who in their hearts believed in nothing but selfishness between nations, but deluded their people with talk of moral ideas—even if we believe this, I say, it does not in any way lessen the force of my argument. Rather, it strengthens it. For it is an admission that the nations, the *peoples* of the world, are moved by moral ideas and moral forces, that moral ideals do enter into the motivation of their actions in regard to each other. It is therefore utterly false to say that the motives of international action are purely those of self-interest. And this assertion will remain true even if we hold that the moral forces acting in these peoples are merely used by their leaders to steer the nations into those courses which the leaders think they should, from their national self-interest, follow. Moral ideas are not only relevant to the international scene but are profoundly powerful in it.

There used to be, among economists, an absurd abstraction called "the economic man." The economic man was governed solely by considerations of profit and loss—that is, by self-interest. His mind was nothing but a calculating machine. It added up the probable profits and losses of a proposed action, and if the calculation showed a balance of profit to himself, he acted. If not, not. And no consideration other than profit and loss moved him in the slightest degree. Economists have now given up the idea of the economic man. It involved a fantastic oversimplification of human nature. Human beings are simply not like that. No businessman, even the most hardheaded, is a mere calculating machine of profit and loss. All sorts of other motives, some generous, some ungenerous, some indifferent, irrelevant, or merely whimsical, enter in. Even if he allows his liking for a friend to deflect his action by a hair's breadth—to make him contented, for example, with a profit of only a thousand dollars where he might have made a thousand dollars and fifty cents by ruining his friend—even this trivial deflection of his action by a slight feeling of generosity to a friend takes him out of the class of purely economic men, since it means that his action is in some degree motivated by moral impulses—for generosity and friendship are moral impulses.

Now this absurd abstraction of the economic man, long out of date in economics, pops up again in our international thinking in the form of the doctrine that foreign policy is and ought to be governed only by national self-interest. This is just as much an oversimplification of the psychology of nations as the economic man was of the psychology of individuals, and it is the same oversimplification. The motives of nations, as of individual men, are extraordinarily mixed and complicated, and somewhere in the mixture you will always find moral ideas working. The element of truth in the current belief that nations have no morals seems to me to be this: the level of morals as practiced by individual human beings between themselves is relatively high; the level of morals as practiced by nations between themselves is deplorably low. There *is* such a thing as international morality. That is to say, moral forces do operate on the international plane. But the *standard* of morals as between nations is much lower than the *standard* of morals practiced by decent people towards each other in the sphere of individual action. It is this fact which gives rise to statements that moral ideas do not apply to nations at all, and that nations act purely from self-interest. These statements are to be explained simply as exaggerations. We see the deplorably low level of international morality, and then we make wild statements denying altogether its existence or even its possibility.

Why is there this vast difference between the ethical standards of individuals and the ethical standards of states? There are several reasons. One is the mere fact that other nations are at a distance from us. We cannot easily wrong a person on our doorstep, where we see the results of what we do, but we can more easily act with indifference, or even brutality, when the victims are thousands of miles away and we do not see the results of our actions. But the reason which is more relevant to my topic is the following: Individuals act within a community of individuals, the state; but nations do not act within a community of nations. There is no world-state or super-state. The morality of individuals is embodied in institutions, of which the chief is the state, but which also include all sorts of other institutions, such as the family, the churches, the universities, schools, unions, societies of all kinds, even social clubs. The morality of the individual is at every point created for him, upheld, inspired, supported by the whole social organism of which he forms a part. His morality is objectified in these institutions. But there is no nation of nations, no state of states, no institution in which international morality can organize and objectify itself. Therefore, international morality inevitably remains at a low level, because it lacks the necessary organs and instruments by which to realize itself.

Several consequences follow. First, the low level of international morals is not due to any inherent non-moral character of the nation or the state as such. It is not because in the nature of things the state is super-moral or sub-moral or outside morality, or that morality does not apply to it. Men collected into a nation have the same moral feelings and moral natures as do the individuals who compose the collection. But as nations they lack the institutions, especially the institution of a great overall state, in which their moral natures can express and objectify themselves. Second, you cannot have a very high level of international morality until you do have a world-state. And in the peace after a war it is foolish to expect ideal solutions. But the general problem of the control and government of human beings everywhere, even within an organized community, is to leaven the vast inert bulk of human indifference and even wickedness with that bare modicum of morality and justice which it will stand. That is why the law of a country always lags behind the moral sense of its best citizens. It cannot enforce the highest standards of its best citizens, but only the much lower standards which practically all its citizens, even those who are most undeveloped morally, will support. If it tries to aim higher than that, the law is flouted and breaks down. How much more true will this be in the international sphere, where there is no government to enforce any law. To be more specific, if you try to force on a country like Russia some law or principle which that country is not ready to accept, then that country will flout your law and your principle. And the result will be not merely that law breaks down in that instance, but that all respect for law is gone, and that it breaks down everywhere all over the world. And then your entire peace breaks down.

As to the world-state, without which I say you can never get a high level of international morality, I have no doubt that it will someday come. It is in the direct line of human evolution. Smaller wholes coalesce into larger wholes. There are unicellular organisms. Then single cells coalesce into multicellular organisms. Individual multicellular organisms coalesce into families, families into tribes, tribes into nations. The evolutionary process would not naturally stop till it ends in the organization of all men into a single society. But that is a long way off. Perhaps in five hundred years, perhaps even in a hundred years, we might have a world-state. At any rate, it is no use writing of what may happen in a remote future. Let us consider merely the decade or so which lies directly in front of us.

The problem of the immediate future is: Admitting that we cannot yet have a world-state, and that a very high level of international morals is impossible without it, how, in these circumstances, can we gradually raise the level of international morals? I think that there are just three principles we should try to apply.

The first principle is that we should, as a nation, place ourselves always on the side of justice, in every dispute, and endeavor by our example to influence others to do the same. In general, the American people already instinctively do this. The practical difficulty, of course, is to know which *is* the side of justice. And here we are often likely, through ignorance of complicated sets of facts about remote countries, to go astray. But even if in the particular case we may be partly ignorant or even mistaken about a situation, the fact that we

167

stand for just solutions in general will exercise a great weight. For instance, in the matter of India. We placed ourselves on the side of freedom for the Indians. The British replied that they were as anxious for Indian freedom as we were, but that we did not understand the complexity of the problem. This charge was in general true. We are most of us woefully ignorant of even the most elementary facts of the extraordinarily complex Indian situation. But even though we underestimated the immense problem which India presented to the British, and thereby in our words and thoughts often did some injustice to our British friends, yet the fact that we stood for Indian freedom put the pressure in the right direction. It tended to force the British to solve those problems which otherwise they, even if we grant their good intentions, might have given up as insoluble. Keeping up this pressure, even sometimes in rather an ignorant way, helped towards solution of these problems.

The second principle is that we should try to persuade nations that national self-interest is in the long run best served by international justice and morality rather than by the law of the jungle. Perhaps we need to preach this more to ourselves than to other people, certainly as much. It is the failure to understand this principle which produces isolationism. I do not mean to suggest that one can attain the highest standard of morals by basing morality on self-interest. It is not true that they always coincide. The world's moral giants and teachers, the saints, the martyrs, the moral heroes, to whom we look up as the best of our kind, were never made merely by taking a long view of their own interests. The cynical opinion that the good man is merely more clever at advancing his own interests than the bad man, but that they both aim exclusively at their own interests, is psychologically false. But, then, we are not hoping at present to produce a world of heroically moral nations. We are trying to inject a bare minimum of morality into the international chaos. And at that low level of morals at which we are compelled to operate, it is roughly true that intelligent self-interest and decent behavior coincide. For example, you do produce a relatively decent level of business ethics by getting businessmen to see that honesty is the best policy. The same will be true in the international sphere.

The third principle is that we should support all international organizations which tend towards common action and the submergence of individual national interests in a larger whole. But here we find ourselves involved in a difficulty which is something like a vicious circle. The reason we cannot attain a high level of international morality is that there is no world-state. But, then, the reason we cannot at present achieve a world-state is that our level of international morality is so low. This is the first half of the circle. I will say a word about the second. Why can we not have a world-state now? The League of Nations was not a world-state, but it was a move in that direction. The reason why the League of Nations broke down was not that its instrument or its machinery was faulty. It was a very good instrument; it was very good machinery. It broke down partly because it was not supported by the great powers, and partly because even those powers which did join it were not willing to back it to the extent of risking what they believed to be their individual national interests for the sake of the interests of the community of nations, To be specific, they would not enforce the necessary sanctions in the cases of Manchuria and Ethiopia because they did not see that their own interests were immediately involved. But morality, if it means anything, means the merging of your individual interests in the interests of the community. So it comes to this: the League broke down because the level of international morals was so low.

What, then, are we to do to get out of this circle? We can't have a high level of morals until we get a world-state. And we can't have a world-state till we get a higher level of morals.

There is nothing we can do in these circumstances except try to get rid of old habits of thought. We are still, all of us, everywhere in the world, in the grip of old habits of thought, carried over from the day when the nations were relatively independent or self-dependent, into an age in which they have become, whether they like it or not, interdependent. Our habit is to think in national terms only, whereas we have to learn to think in international terms. The practical problem is, not to explain this idea—any child can understand it; it is not even to get people to believe the idea—most of us believe it now; it is to get our own people, and the peoples of the world, so soaked with this idea that they naturally and instinctively act from it—that acting from it goes with the grain of their minds, not against the grain. The achievement of this result almost involves implanting a new instinct, and is a problem of education, of conditioning.

Immediately after the first use of the atomic bomb, President Truman warned the Japanese that they had still time to save themselves, but that the time was short. He might as well have addressed these words to the American, or any other, nation. How long have we been living in a fool's paradise, imagining that we can shape our world policy by nothing save our own narrow interests conceived as independent of the interests of other nations? In the next war, if we allow one to come, we may be "vaporized" en masse by rockets fired from a distance of thousands of miles, almost before we know that we are at war. There is only one way out. We have to learn the lesson that nations, deserting their petty ideas of sovereignty, prestige, national self-interest, must combine to act together for the common good of humanity—which is the meaning of acting morally. There is still time to learn this lesson. *But the time is short.*

British Colonialism

On the wall in the office of a certain British administrator in the tropics there used to hang a notice to the public which read: "There's no reason for it. It's just our policy." What a brilliant summation of the absence of any political philosophy in the British—and also of British arrogance! It may be true that in some sense the British are past masters in the arts of diplomacy and government. But they are so by instinct, and not by any rational understanding. As D. W. Brogan has said, they do not, like the French and the Americans, regard politics as a rational science.

Ceylon, which was formerly an autocratically governed crown colony and has now evolved, after a series of remarkable political experiments covering a quarter of a century, into an independent, self-governing dominion within the commonwealth, provides an interesting case history of British colonial methods. While methods and policies have naturally differed in details in different colonies, there is a certain characteristic and common British stamp and pattern to them all. Ceylon was always considered the leading crown colony. There British methods had been worked out to their highest development, and an examination of them will disclose in its greatest clearness the main tendencies of British colonial rule. To find these characteristic marks of the British brand of colonialism we have to look, not at the recent developments which culminated in independence, but at how things were done there before those developments began, that is to say, before about 1920. We have to examine how the British acted when they ruled the colony autocratically.

In 1796 the maritime provinces of the island were taken from the Dutch, and in 1815 the mountainous interior, still ruled by Sinhalese kings, was by treaty ceded to the British. The first fact to note is that they exercised an absolute rule for a century thereafter, and that during that century no political advance whatever was recorded. The details of the constitution of the government changed from time to time, but the general autocratic pattern was always the same. In 1910 when I landed there as a junior civil servant the setup was as follows: The country was ruled by a British governor. He had as cabinet an executive council whose function was purely advisory. It was composed of British civil servants who, of course, drew their salaries from the governor's treasury and were in no way independent. There was also a small legislative council to pass the necessary statutes. A majority of its members were British officials who were bound always to vote according to the governor's orders. A minority of the members were not officials, usually natives of the country, who were supposed to represent the various native communities. They were appointed by the governor, but could vote as they liked. But even if the unofficial minority voted solidly against a government measure—a rare circumstance because they were divided by mutual jealousies—it was always automatically outvoted by the official majority. Thus the governor completely controlled the legislature and could pass any measure he wished. He was, of course, subject to the orders of the Secretary of State for the Colonies in London, who would no doubt stop any legislation he considered unwise or unjust.

This government, though autocratic, was not otherwise evil or oppressive. On the contrary, it was well intentioned and its spirit was benevolent. The governor himself, and the army of British civil servants who worked the actual machinery of government, were usually good men—according to their lights. They were highly educated, among the best that Oxford and Cambridge and the other British universities could produce. They were just, and as humane as such men usually are. They were incorruptible. They were impelled nearly always by a remarkably high sense of duty, and they conceived their first duty to be the safeguarding of the interests of the native inhabitants, not those of the British businessmen, traders, and tea or rubber planters who made their living in the island. Not infrequently they found themselves called upon to protect their native subjects against the rapacity of some of the less enlightened of the British business communities. And they did so unostentatiously and as a matter of course. These were some of their virtues. Of their defects I shall speak later, remarking here only that they sprang mainly from narrowness and lack of imagination.

It should throw light on the spirit of British governmental methods, both in the colonies and in the home country, to consider what type of men were selected for the civil services, how they were selected, and especially what kind of education or training they were expected to have. Entrance to the senior civil services, that is to say those of Britain itself, India, Ceylon, Malaya, and Hong Kong, was exclusively by competitive examination. The examination was so stiff that none below the highest grades of university honors men, or men of equivalent intellectual caliber, could hope to be selected. Thus first-class brains and a first-class education were insisted upon.

What was most remarkable about this examination was that it was quite unnecessary for a candidate to have made any study of political theory, of government, or of any subject which could have the slightest direct bearing on his future career. He could include political science among his subjects for the examination if he were so minded, but it was not a compulsory subject. In fact there were no compulsory subjects at all. There was a long list of subjects, about thirty if I remember rightly, and the candidate could select at his pleasure any of these up to a certain total of possible marks. They included Latin, Greek, various modern languages, half a dozen natural sciences, mathematics, history, literature, the arts, philosophy, political science, economics, English law, Roman law, and so on. These subjects were not all equally weighted. For instance, in my time, both classics and mathematics counted four times as heavily as either political science or economics. Philosophy counted twice as heavily as either of the latter. This shows what little importance was attached to directly vocational studies in government or connected subjects. So long as the candidates were of first-class intellectual ability and were highly educated, it did not matter what they were educated in. As a rule, and unless they happened to have chosen political science as one of their subjects of examination, they began their lifework of governing men with no knowledge whatever, either theoretical or practical, of the art or science of government. There was some exception to this in the case of men going to India who, after they had passed the examination, were given some months' training in Indian affairs before they took ship. No such training was given to men going to Ceylon, Malaya, and Hong Kong. They were shipped to their colonies to begin work immediately after passing the examination.

How would these men learn the principles of government? They would learn them on the job itself, working themselves into the daily routine of the government offices to which they were assigned, watching their superiors work—they would themselves be given almost no responsibility to start with—picking things up as they went along. As my own case was, I believe, quite typical, I will recount it. My education had been in philosophy and literature. I landed in Ceylon, my head full of the Absolute, with occasional thoughts about Shelley and Keats. Thus equipped I was dropped suddenly and unceremoniously into the main administrative office of the government agent (provincial governor) of one of the nine provinces of Ceylon. I was ordered to check the account books daily—though I had no previous knowledge of what account books looked like, or even what they were for. I was given hundreds of gun licenses, cart licenses, opium licenses to sign. The licensees had been approved by a junior slightly higher up than myself. I had likewise to sign routine letters which had been drafted by my superiors. I was supposed to read the letters and learn from them. They were about drains, taxes, irrigation channels, rice fields, harbor dues, sales of land, land disputes, rents, building permits, licenses of various kinds, waterworks, the town electric lights, burial grounds, appointments of headmen, the building and maintenance of roads and bridges, sanitation, prosecutions of offenders, police matters, civil service discipline—the list could be prolonged indefinitely. No one in the office had time to explain to me any of these mysteries, and I could find nothing about them in Shelley or the books on the Absolute. I learned the hard way, picking up tiny crumbs of knowledge here and there. But one did, of course, learn in the end.

These British methods are by no means as foolish as they perhaps sound. Mr. George Kennan, in the pages of *The Atlantic*, once insisted that as a preparation for statesmanship and diplomatic work college courses in the techniques of government are of no great value. What is above all needed in those who are to engage in political or diplomatic work is that sympathetic understanding of human beings and human values which is nourished by the study of history, literature, art, music, religion—in short, by a broad humanistic education. Political techniques are only tools. Skill in the use of these tools can be learned afterwards, or at any time. They require nothing more than a certain mental dexterity. What matters is the humane and understanding spirit of the man who uses them. And to produce this should be the aim of the prior education of the statesman. With all this I agree most heartily. And one may perhaps claim that it is the English theory of how to educate statesmen. In saying this, I am far from meaning to attribute to my countrymen any abstract theorizing on the matter. As usual they have reached their procedures by instinct and practical experience. But Mr. Kennan's theory is the one by which they *could* justify their procedures if they were interested in a theoretical basis for them—which, characteristically, they are not.

What sort of government, then, was handed out in the colonies by these civil servants trained—or, if you prefer it, untrained—in the manner described? I have said that it was of good intention, benevolent, just, incorruptible, and ruled by a high sense of duty to the native populations. But what more? What actual benefits did they confer? What good did they do? And wherein did they fail? It may be taken for granted that they provided for material progress. They made roads and railways. They built hospitals and trained doctors to man them. They introduced improved methods of agriculture. We may pass over these things with a bare mention, and ask what they did in the sphere of the more intangible values. Above all, what did they do, here in their colonies, to advance human freedom and human spiritual rights?

The brief answer is that they gave to the subject peoples no political freedom at all (until after the first world war), but that of personal freedom they gave generously and up to the maximum. By political freedom I mean self-government, and by personal freedom I mean freedom of thought, speech, assembly, the press, and religion. If we think in terms of political abstractions and clichés, without keeping the concrete evidence in view, we are too apt to suppose that freedom is one and undivided, and that where there is no political freedom there can be no personal freedom either. British colonial practice provides a striking and complete refutation of any such airy generalization. Though the government of Ceylon was wholly autocratic, the personal freedoms were as absolute and complete under it as they are in England or the United States. Freedom of the press was established in India in 1835. And in Ceylon newspapers owned and edited by members of the indigenous population could and did criticize the government as severely, even as abusively, as they pleased. No one thought of raising a finger against them, and censorship was unheard of—except, of course, during the war. Meetings could be held to denounce anybody or anything—though I do not remember that this was often done because there was no occasion for it. That there was, for Christians, Buddhists, Hindus, Muslims, complete freedom of worship goes without saying. And the rights of each religion were scrupulously protected by the government. On one occasion the congregation of a Roman Catholic church threatened violence if a projected Hindu procession, carrying their god to the temple, should pass along the highroad on which the Catholic church fronted. The governor at the time, Sir Hugh Clifford, was himself a Catholic. But he sent troops to the scene to enforce the right of the King's Hindu subjects to use the King's highway for their lawful procession.

How far the right of free speech was carried may be judged from the following incident. A disgruntled Englishman, out of work and perhaps half out of his mind, appeared suddenly on a rubber estate and began preaching some brand of communism to the hundreds of ignorant and illiterate estate laborers. The white superintendent of the estate, fearing serious trouble from his labor force, had the man apprehended by the police; and the Governor, purporting to act under emergency regulations still in force after the war, ordered his deportation from the colony. But on a writ of habeas corpus the Chief Justice ruled that his arrest and deportation were illegal—he having done nothing but exercise his right of free speech—and ordered his release. The man, as it happened, was an Englishman. But the court's ruling would certainly have been the same if he had been a native of the country. It is at least arguable that the rights of free thought and speech were more respected—that citizens had less to fear from speaking their minds—under that autocratic government than is the case in the democratic United States of today.

The fact that the British, in the last decades of their Indian empire, imprisoned so many fighters for independence and political freedom cannot be quoted as evidence that they failed to respect the personal freedoms of thought and speech. For as the title "civil disobedience" which Gandhi adopted for his movement itself attests, these imprisonments were for the intentional breaking of positive laws—for example, the law against private persons' distilling salt out of sea water—and not at all for criticizing the government or expressing opinions which the government did not like. Private persons possessed the right of free speech and were not imprisoned for exercising it. This is not to say that the British acted wisely or well in imprisoning all these people, but that is another question which it is not necessary to discuss here.

Lord Acton's famous observation that all power tends to corrupt and absolute power tends to corrupt absolutely, though, of course, it has its truth and its value, has become a cliché. I cannot see that the absolute power of the British in Ceylon for a century, or in their other crown colonies for longer or shorter periods, ever corrupted their belief in the personal freedoms, not only for themselves, but also for those whom they governed; nor can I see that it corrupted their colonial governments in any other way, although those governments had their serious faults, some account of which I shall shortly give. The British no doubt committed the original sin of subjecting other peoples to their rule. But it is surely a remarkable thing that they carried their Magna Carta with them to the ends of the earth, planting and watering the seeds of personal freedom in places, all over the world, where they had never existed before.

Wherein did the British mainly fail? That they subjected

foreign peoples to their rule was, we should now all hold, an evil thing, though it is thoughtless not to remember that the strong moral objections which now move us against colonialism hardly existed in world opinion during the periods when most of the British Empire was built up. It is only as of yesterday that ideals of national self-determination have come to be generally recognized and to operate powerfully in world affairs. And it is idle to judge actions of a century ago by standards which were not recognized when they were performed.

On the other hand, I cannot join in the common chorus of praise of the British for their supposed generous withdrawal from India and their other possessions. It would be hopelessly sentimental to suppose that as soon as it came to be realized that the subjection of foreign peoples is a moral evil, the British immediately repented and out of sheer righteousness gave up India and Ceylon. The history of the last half-century shows plainly that the British government never gives anything up out of mere generosity, but that, on the contrary, it hangs grimly on to whatever it holds, deaf to all entreaties, until forced out. The treatment of the Irish in the twenties of this century shows this, and so does the long battle against Gandhi and the other Indian aspirants to freedom. I do not mean that the British people are, or have been in the recent past, unmoved by ethical considerations in regard to their empire. But it is only very slowly that an international conscience is aroused, especially in the governments as distinguished from the peoples; and power politics are still far more powerful in the world than moral scruples. And this is true not only of the British, but also of other great nations.

But apart from the fundamental wrong of colonialism, wherein, we must ask, did the British mainly fail in their colonial governments? Ceylon again may be taken as a typical case. Their main faults there were lack of vision and arrogance. Of arrogance we need say little. The facts are too well known. Arrogant behavior in the colonies was, of course, mixed up with the color bar, a phenomenon not peculiar to the British, as we in America know only too well. It showed itself in social rather than political relations. Officially and legally in Ceylon the colored subjects and the white rulers were on a par. Equality before the law was rigidly enforced. And even in official receptions, so far as these could be viewed as social rather than political occasions, equality was respected. Thus at a state dinner party given by the Governor, prominent native inhabitants would be invited and would sit side by side with the white guests, and social amenities as between colored and whites would be in general respected. But it was quite otherwise in private homes and clubs. In private relations the British—apart from missionaries, theosophists, cranks, and occasional individuals who had "gone native"—never mixed with their subject peoples. They behaved always as a ruling race openly contemptuous of the people they governed.

I turn to the other, less well-known fault of British colonial rule: its lack of imaginative vision. While they pressed forward in all matters of material progress, engineering projects, agriculture, and the like, they did not aim at political progress, but always only at preserving the status quo. They had no sense of mission. It is true that statesmen in England had, even in the early decades of the nineteenth century, expressed liberal views as to the ultimate aims of British rule in India. There is no reason to doubt their sincerity. And they had behind them a large body of British public opinion. But the words they uttered had little effect on the practical goings-on in the subject territories. They never actually inspired the day-to-day work of the Indian or colonial governors, or of the civil servants who worked under them. In practice the "gradualness" of the process of political education meant that the achievement of its nominal goal of self-government would never come. Going slowly meant never moving at all. These colored peoples, it was said, were not yet fit for self-government. When would they be fit? "Some day, but not for quite a long time" might have been the official answer. "Never" was the answer which worked practically in the actions of the rulers. Every demand for the littlest step forward was resisted and fought to the last ditch, or granted in the most niggardly and ungenerous fashion only when it became practically impossible to hold out against it any longer.

The civil services worked only in a blind routine. Precedent, what had been done before, became the binding rule for what was to be done now or in the future. The ideal was only "efficiency." Efficiency means doing the same things over and over again but doing them with great skill. It does not mean advance. It simply keeps the old machinery running smoothly and without jolts. That the British colonial civil services were enormously efficient, far more efficient than their native successors are ever likely to be, is past all doubt.

I have spoken of the manner in which young civil servants, at the beginning of their careers, were taught their jobs— dumped into government offices, told to sign papers, to watch their superiors at work, to pick up the know-how of government as best they could. But this "picking it up" only meant learning the precedents, acquiring the routine skills. The sheer quantity of activity, of things going on, in these offices was immense. But what it all aimed at, what higher policy was supposed to direct it—of such things we never heard. Why were we Britishers here at all, ruling a foreign people? That question, of course, no one ever asked. Our being here was just a fact, handed down from the past, a fact which had to be accepted like the existence of the sun and the moon. But anyhow, being here, what were we supposed to be accomplishing, either for ourselves, the British rulers, or for our subjects? At what star were we to aim? Efficiency, of course. That meant going round in circles without wobbling and without tripping up. Beyond that, what? Was there any goal, any policy, any directing vision of future ends? Certainly if any young man just beginning his lifework had raised such questions in the office, had asked them of his superiors, he would have been quickly squelched, taught his manners, and put in his place. It may be said that youngsters have to learn first only to obey, leaving the higher wisdom to their betters. But did these betters ever give thought to these questions, or attempt genuinely to give a real forward direction to our activities? If they did, they kept it very darkly to themselves.

Why have the British civil services acquired, as they certainly have, so high a reputation, in America and perhaps elsewhere in the world? I think mainly because of their three virtues—efficiency, incorruptibility, and justice. What efficiency means has just been explained; and about incorruptibility nothing need be said. But a word about justice. In Ceylon in my time "British justice" was proverbial. The phrase was constantly on the lips of the lawyers, nearly all of whom were natives of the country, who frequented the law courts. And outside the courts, in the political arena, too, the words were often reiterated. If the government did anything unpopular, or contrary to what the people thought to be right, the cry would be "this is not British justice." Thus the belief that British rule was fundamentally a reign of justice was no legend invented by the British themselves. They would have taken it for granted as something hardly worth mentioning. It was put into circulation by the subject peoples themselves, who knew well enough that they had never experienced anything like it under their own rulers before the British came.

In itself this was something fine and noble. And I should be the last to wish to depreciate it. But it must be pointed out that justice, like efficiency, is quite consistent with standing still, making no advance, having no goal, no policy, no imagination, and no vision. For justice—unless the word is used in some very wide sense as practically equivalent to all virtue—means only administering the existing laws and institutions with strict impartiality and without respect of persons. It does not include the effort to make better laws and institutions. It does not imply the aspiration for a better future, the leading upwards and onwards to self-government, or greater freedom, or any other higher goal. Thus it is a virtue which a government that thinks only of routine and the status quo may perfectly well possess. And it was thus that the British colonial administrations possessed it.

Perhaps it will be said that all this is inconsistent with the theory stated earlier in this paper that the public servant should be given a broad humanistic education in preference to a vocational training in political technique. For the evidence—it will be suggested—shows that such an education does not in fact produce the sympathetic understanding and breadth of vision which the theory says it should produce. But to argue thus would be something like the error of those Athenians who blamed the faults of Alcibiades on the education he had received from Socrates. Education can only make the best of whatever human material it has to act on. No education could hope to impart high wisdom and imaginative vision to the hundreds and thousands of more or less average —though doubtless clever and highly educated—human beings who must necessarily compose the civil service of a large country or empire. In any case it would be absurd to claim that a vocational training in political techniques would do better in this respect.

But neither is anything I have said meant to suggest that some other colonial administration—say the French, the German, or the Dutch—has been more enlightened, sympathetic, or imaginative than the British. The opposite may well be true. Very likely the defects of British colonial rule were defects which appear wherever one race autocratically rules another. They sprang neither from wrong education nor from any special deficiency of British character, but from the universal human fact that no one people can ever understand a foreign people well enough to govern them in a truly enlightened way. The lesson to be learned is not that the British are especially lacking in vision, nor yet that their educational theory is mistaken, but simply that the most enlightened colonialism is always and necessarily unenlightened.

I have described British colonialism as it was when it was at its zenith. At the present time it is dying and, indeed, nearly dead. The beginning of its more or less rapid decline may be dated about 1918, the year in which the first world war ended. There was some growth of the national spirit in subject peoples before that. But the ideal yearning for the self-determination of all peoples, the recognition of the moral rights of small nations, were born out of the agonies of that war. They caused a ferment which, beginning in the West, rapidly spread all over the world. The Asian peoples caught the infection. The "awakening of the East" began. The independence of countries like India and Ceylon did not, of course, come suddenly, even then—but very slowly and step by painful step. We need not trace those steps here. Enough that those countries are now independent, and that others, still under the yoke, seem likely in the near future to achieve the same goal.

VI

Philosophy and Science

The Place of Philosophy
in Human Culture

I THINK there is scarcely any academic subject regarding which there exists so much general misapprehension as philosophy. If I were to introduce myself to the readers of almost any newspaper as a professor of chemistry, or of classics, or of music, most of them would have a fairly good general idea of the nature of my subject. But if I were to introduce myself as a professor of philosophy, I suspect that many of them would vaguely associate my subject with theosophy, or palmistry, or occultism. Very few would have any notion of what philosophy really is. Even in a university, even among the learned themselves, it would be true to say, I think, that while the nature of such subjects as mathematics, classics, geology, is pretty well understood in a general way even by those who are not specialists in them, the nature of philosophy is not. If highly educated people do not mix it up with palmistry or occultism, they are at any rate apt to regard philosophy as hazy, high-flown talk, or as a kind of quibbling disputatiousness, or as the asking of vast, vague, and probably unanswerable questions about the universe.

So long as one does not trouble oneself about precisely accurate definitions, there is no great difficulty in describing, roughly at least, most other subjects; in saying at any rate what they are *about*. Biology is about living organisms. Astronomy is about the heavenly bodies. Physics is about light, heat, sound, and so on. The universe, man's total environment, has been cut up, more or less arbitrarily, into sections; and each science takes one section for its province. Botanists take the plants, zoologists the animals, astronomers the stars. Thus it comes about that, in spite of difficulties here and there about boundaries, these sciences are on the whole fairly easy to describe, at least in a popular way.

But the difficulty in describing the nature of philosophy arises precisely from the fact that there is no one section of the universe which is more especially its province than any other. This is not indeed true of "linguistic" developments. But here I shall be discussing the place of philosophy over the ages, not merely at the present day. It does not, as most of the other sciences do, peg out a claim to some comparatively small area and leave all the rest untouched. It is true, in a sense, that there is nothing anywhere in the universe with which philosophy is not concerned, and that the whole universe is its subject. Yet it has its own special content. And this is a kind of paradox. On the one hand, philosophy is clearly distinguished, by its own special content, from all other subjects. On the other hand, it overlaps them all. Clearly, then, philosophy is in some way peculiar as regards its relation to other branches of knowledge. What is this relation? What is the place of philosophy in the general scheme of human knowledge? I think it is obvious that this question will have to be answered before one can say what is the place of philosophy in education or in culture generally. Therefore I make no apology for beginning by considering the relation of philosophy to other branches of knowledge.

One theory on this subject is that the special function of philosophy is to co-ordinate the other branches of knowledge, to knit together the sciences into a single whole; to treat them in much the same way as a central government treats the several departments which come under it—except, of course, that philosophy has no special authority. This, I think, or something like it, was Herbert Spencer's conception of the business of philosophy.

I do not think this at all a satisfactory view. It is out of date now, and no living philosopher would be likely to accept it. So I do not propose to discuss it at length. I will give only *one* reason for rejecting it—one among many which might be given—namely that it finds no place for many of the problems which have always been regarded as essentially philosophical. Take, for example, the problem whether the material world is in any way dependent for its existence upon mind. That it is so dependent has often been asserted in the past by idealistic philosophers, and has, during this century, been asserted by some astronomers and scientists who were also amateur philosophers. This problem, which is certainly one of the most central and important of all philosophical problems, has no connection at all with the question how the sciences ought to be co-ordinated. It would therefore be excluded from philosophy by the suggested definition. This definition, therefore, cannot be satisfactory.

Another idea, more common in recent times, is this. It is said that philosophy has for its subject matter all those problems which have not *yet* been appropriated by any of the special sciences. Human knowledge is like a tree, with a trunk and many branches. The trunk, the parent stem, is, or was, philosophy. The branches are the special sciences. All knowledge was originally included in philosophy. But as knowledge has grown, it has differentiated itself. When the knowledge of any particular section of the universe became sufficiently advanced to stand alone, it separated itself from the parent stem and became a separate subject. There are still a certain number of subjects and problems regarding which our knowledge is so vague and rudimentary that they have not yet organized themselves into special sciences. This residue of problems not yet taken over by any science is what we call philosophy at the present day. I will call this view of the nature of philosophy the "trunk-and-branch view."

The evidence for this view is as follows. It is an historical fact that knowledge has grown much in the way described. Modern science has its roots historically in ancient Greece. The Greeks were the first people in the world to develop the scientific attitude. They were the first people to ask such questions as: What are the sun and the stars made of? What size are they? How far away are they from the earth? You may remember, as a picturesque piece of early astronomy, the assertion of Anaxagoras that the sun is a red-hot stone, larger than the Peloponnese—a statement which got Anaxagoras into serious trouble with the orthodox Greeks, who regarded the sun as a god. The Greeks were also the first people who studied animals and plants in at all a scientific way. They were the first genuinely theoretical mathematicians. They were the first people to speculate as to whether the many different kinds of matter may not be ultimately reducible to a single kind of matter. They were the originators of the atomic theory, the theory that matter is ultimately composed of minute, hard, indivisible particles without color, taste, or smell.

But the Greeks, or at any rate the early Greeks, did not distinguish between science and philosophy. The problems of the constitution of matter, the nature of the sun and stars, the properties of the triangle, were regarded by them as *philosophical* problems, and were not separated from such purely metaphysical problems as that concerning the nature of God. The scientist and the philosopher were in those days one and the same person. Aristotle, the philosopher, was the founder of the science of biology. Pure mathematics was mostly studied and advanced in the philosophical schools of such men as Pythagoras and Plato. Thus philosophy in those days was practically synonymous with all human culture. Consequently, it was the parent stem out of which grew all branches of knowledge. It was only later, when the body of knowledge increased beyond the point at which one man could master it all, that specialization took place. The study of the stars broke off from the parent stem and became the special science of astronomy. And so with the other sciences.

It is commonly added that we can to some extent see the same sort of process going on even now. It is only in the last fifty or sixty years that psychology has established itself as an independent science. It was, until then, included in philosophy. And following out this idea, I understand that Professor Samuel Alexander thought there are signs that aesthetics is shortly about to separate itself from philosophy and become an independent science.

Now of course no one can dispute the historical facts just referred to. But for my part I do not think that this trunk-and-branch theory of the nature of philosophy and of its relation to other subjects is any more satisfactory than the view which we previously rejected. It implies that philosophy has no real content of its own. Philosophy is merely that which is one day going to be science, but which is not yet scientific enough. It is rudimentary science. And philosophy therefore has no real content distinct from what is, or ought to be, science. But in my view philosophy has a content of its own, quite distinct from anything that is, or ever could be, science.

I do not doubt that many problems, which were never properly speaking philosophical problems at all, have in the past been wrongly jumbled up with philosophy, and that these have gradually been sorted out and assigned to their proper spheres. That is all that the supposed historical evidence really proves. And no doubt psychology is a case in point. But I believe that there is a certain *core* of philosophical problems which are in their nature philosophical, and *not* scientific, and which will therefore never be handed over to the special sciences, and will always remain what they are—philosophy proper.

As examples I would give all problems regarding the nature

of what we call *values*—moral values, artistic values, and so on. I think that these can never, however far knowledge advances, become the subject matter of science, or be dealt with by the methods which science adopts in other fields. I cannot here enter into a full justification of this statement, because it depends essentially upon the view one takes of the function of science and the nature of scientific methods. But I will say that, as I see it, the sole business of science is to describe facts and events, to tell us what happens, what has happened, what will happen. I do not think it is at all the business of science to estimate the *value* of what happens, to say what *ought* to happen, or to say that one event is *better* than another. All such questions of value fall, in my opinion, within the sphere of philosophy.

The biologist, for example, tells us that organic species have evolved. Man is descended from ape-like ancestors, and originally from creatures which can scarcely be distinguished from little lumps of moving slime. That is an account of actual facts and events, of what has actually *happened* on the planet. It is the business of the evolutionary biologist to discover and piece together these facts and events, and to give, if possible, a complete description of them. And when he has done that, his task is finished.

But now suppose I begin to ask, as regards evolution, such questions as the following: Is the change from protozoon to man a change for the *better*? Is it an *advance*? Is a man in any way a *higher* being than a protozoon, or a higher being than a dog? Or has the process of change, traced out by the biologist, been merely a process of change from one indifferent thing to another? Or—another possibility—is this whole conception of better and worse, of higher and lower, as applied to evolution, a misconception, an illusion? Are these merely *human* values, which have no application to affairs outside human society, no application at any rate to events on the cosmic scale? Is it altogether false, or meaningless, to apply conceptions of value to the non-human universe? Or what is the truth of this matter?

Such questions of value, I say, fall outside the sphere of biology. They belong to philosophy. And they will always belong to philosophy, and will never, at any time in the future, come to belong to biology, or to any other science, as the trunk-and-branch theory would have us believe. Or at least this must be so if what I said just now about the function and nature of science is true, namely that the sole function of science is to describe what *happens*, and that it is in no way concerned with the valuation of what happens.

Of course an individual biologist may very well have opinions on these questions. And his opinions may very well be interesting and important, although he must, if his opinion is to be of any real value, take into account many considerations besides his bare biological facts, considerations with which biology cannot supply him, but with which philosophy can. But however that may be, the important point is that, in having such opinions, he has really ceased to be a pure biologist and has become a philosopher.

I have given the problem of values as an example of a problem which belongs, and must always belong, to philosophy, in order to show that the trunk-and-branch theory of philosophy, which implies that philosophy has no content of its own, cannot be true. But I do not mean to imply that the problem of values is the sole content of philosophy. I do not mean to say that the relation between philosophy and the sciences is that science deals with what happens, philosophy with the valuation of what happens. That would be far too simple a division of labor. And philosophy has many problems of its own, which are not scientific, yet which are not in any sense problems of valuation. And I will try now to indicate what, in my opinion, the special nature of philosophy is, and what its relations to the sciences are.

The view which I advocate may best be described by saying that, in my opinion, philosophy is concerned with the search for *ultimate* principles, the attempt to push all knowledge back to its *ultimate* grounds, to answer *ultimate* questions; and that it is distinguished both from the sciences and from all other branches of knowledge by this fact. I would, in short, define philosophy as the knowledge of ultimate principles.

Of course you will say, and quite rightly, that this is a very vague definition. For what is the meaning of the word *ultimate* here? I certainly think it ought to be defined. And I think perhaps it could be defined by a process of careful logical analysis. But I think I can better convey to you something of what I mean when I speak of ultimate principles and questions if I give you a few examples than if I attempt the difficult logical feat of defining *ultimate*.

You will find, if you take almost any subject of human discourse—whether it is a scientific subject or any other—that it leads *back*, upon reflection, to problems and questionings of a very fundamental character, problems and questionings which are not usually considered at all by those who specialize in that subject. These problems constitute, I should say, the special content of philosophy.

Suppose you take what are generally considered the first principles of any branch of knowledge. If you work *forward* from those principles, taking them as ultimate, you will find yourself moving among the particular details of that branch of knowledge. For example, if you take the axioms of geometry (any geometry) as your first principles and work forward from them, you will find yourself among the detailed theorems of that geometry. But if you reflect upon these so-called first principles of any subject, you will generally find that they are not really ultimate at all, that it is possible to go *backward* from them, instead of forward, and to ask upon what more ultimate principles they themselves rest. You may, for example, ask yourself what is the basis of the axioms of geometry.

Are they a priori laws of the human mind? Or are they laws gathered by observation from experience like most of the ordinary laws of nature? Or are they arbitrary assumptions based upon nothing but convenience? Or what are they, and on what depends their right to *be* the first principles of geometry? When you proceed backward in that way from what you had hitherto considered to be first principles, and when you search for the more ultimate principles on which these depend, then you are in the realm of philosophy.

What I have just said is not only true of mathematics. I say that it is true of *any* branch of human knowledge. And I will take as further examples the specific spheres of morality, art, and science. In the sphere of morality, we commonly say that some actions are right, others wrong. Most people take it for granted that there is *some* distinction between right and wrong, and that they know pretty well what is meant by those words. And if they discuss moral problems, it is usually some detailed question about the particular *application* of moral principles which they discuss. Was a man, in a given set of circumstances, right or wrong in what he did? Is suicide ever justifiable? Would a doctor ever be right to administer a deadly drug to a patient suffering from an incurable disease and undergoing ceaseless physical torture? These are the kinds of questions which practical moralists generally discuss, and if we had good answers to them all it might be said that we possessed a complete body of moral knowledge.

But now suppose that instead of working forward from moral principles to their detailed application in life, I try to work backward. Suppose I raise questions about the foundation of these principles themselves. Suppose I ask: What is the foundation of moral principles? Is it true, for example, that right actions are merely those which tend to produce among human beings generally a balance of pleasure and happiness over pain and unhappiness? Or is morality founded upon biological considerations, so that right actions are simply those which tend towards the preservation of the species? Or have moral principles some profounder, less obvious basis than these ideas would suggest? These, I think, would be questions of that very fundamental and ultimate kind which I should call philosophical.

Exactly similar questions arise from reflection upon the sphere of art. In the moral world we have the antithesis of the good and the evil. In the artistic world we have the antithesis of the beautiful and the ugly, or perhaps, of the artistic and inartistic. These conceptions are commonly taken for granted, just as are the conceptions of right and wrong. What are usually discussed are questions of their detailed *application*. Is this picture genuinely artistic or not? Or is it more artistic than that picture? Is this poem successful or not? Is a certain musical composer justified in introducing into his work discords and other innovations which would have shocked his predecessors? The attempts to answer questions of this kind constitute the branch of knowledge that we call criticism.

But now suppose that, instead of moving forward from the principles of art to their detailed application, we move backward towards their more ultimate foundations. Suppose we raise questions about the nature and validity of the conceptions of the artistic and the inartistic themselves. Suppose we ask; what is the nature of the artistic as such? What is that quality which may be shared in common by a picture, a statue, or a poem, and which makes each of them what we call artistic? What *is* art? What are its ultimate criteria and foundations? These again would be questions of that fundamental and ultimate kind which no art critic or artist as such ever asks, and which I should call philosophical.

Turning now to the sphere of science, there are, I think, all sorts of ultimate questions to which science leads back, but which the scientist as such does not usually consider at all. There is, for example, the question of the nature and justification of mathematical axioms, to which I have already referred. Again, science is, or has been in the past, very largely concerned with the *causes* of phenomena. What is the cause of the movements of the planets, of the evolution of species, of ocean tides, of eclipses, of the pointing of a comet's tail away from the sun? And so on.

These are all questions of the detailed application of the principle of causality. But suppose I ask about the principle of causality itself? What, in the first place, is its proper analysis and definition? And then, upon what grounds have I the right to assume that the same causes must always necessarily give rise to the same effects? In that case, it seems to me, I am asking very fundamental and ultimate questions, and I should call these questions philosophical.

Or, to take a very different example, Professor P. W. Bridgman, in his book on *The Logic of Modern Physics*, wrote regarding science, "The nature of our thinking mechanism essentially colours any picture we can form of nature." There is nothing new in the suggestion that the world as we know it is to a greater or less extent determined by the structure of our own minds. That is an opinion which has frequently been held by many philosophers. The only novelty is perhaps that it should now be a physicist who makes the suggestion. But obviously this raises very fundamental and ultimate questions regarding the relation of our minds and our knowing processes to the world. The sciences profess to give us *knowledge* of the world. But we may raise the more ultimate question: What *is* knowledge? Is our knowledge of the world a sort of photograph, or mirror image, or picture, of the world as it actually is? This is what most people used to think. But if all our knowledge is colored by the structure of our minds, it seems obvious that it is not a true picture of the world at all. And it becomes a profoundly difficult question what the relation of our knowledge to reality actually is. And that, I should say, is a very fundamental and ultimate question which belongs to philosophy, and which no specialized science ever considers.

Some of the central problems of philosophy, too, are reached by going backward, not from science, art, morals, or mathematics, but from the everyday knowledge of common sense. But I think I have now given enough examples to illustrate my general contention, which is that philosophy has for its subject matter the ultimate principles upon which all other branches of knowledge are based; and that all other branches of knowledge necessarily lead back to, and end in, philosophy, if one reflects upon their grounds. No matter what subject you study, no matter through what gateway you enter the kingdom of knowledge, philosophy looms in the background. If this view is accepted, you will see that it explains the paradox which I mentioned at the beginning of this lecture. Philosophy has its own special content, these ultimate problems. And yet it is concerned with the whole universe and is entwined with every other subject, because whatever section of the universe your special science takes as its province, that section, and the knowledge of it, give rise to philosophical problems.

Now that we have decided what place philosophy holds in the general scheme of human knowledge, it ought not to be difficult to discover its proper place in education. But first of all, let me deal shortly with a preliminary criticism which is sometimes made. Philosophy, it is said, is an unpractical study. Science yields practical, tangible, results—the telephone, the steam engine, the electric motor. Philosophy yields none, and it has no influence on life. It is, so to speak, all talk.

Perhaps I need hardly point out that, as is obvious, university subjects fall roughly into two classes, those which are of immediate practical utility, such as chemistry and geology, and those which are not. These latter, which have no immediate cash value, include not only philosophy, but also all literature, the classical languages, and the fine arts, not to mention such a subject as religion. These so-called unpractical subjects contain most of what is finest and noblest in human life, because they are concerned not with the production of material wealth but with the advancement of the wealth of the mind.

Nor is it true that philosophy has no influence on life. It would be easy to show that, even as a preparation for practical life, philosophy has its value, since it sharpens the wits, exercises the reasoning powers, destroys prejudices, and develops the habit of considering all questions with an open mind. I have seen it stated in print (by a so-called practical person, not a philosopher) that the second world war was ultimately traceable to the pernicious influence of the philosophy of Hegel. I do not myself agree with that opinion. It is, I think, an absurd caricature of the truth. But it shows that men do dimly perceive what an immense practical influence the philosophical conceptions of a people, or even of an individual, may exert. And it would be a fascinating study to follow out this line of thought, to show to what extent the wise and the foolish actions of mankind have ultimately depended upon what are, in the last analysis, philosophical opinions. But I must leave that field of discussion untouched. I must return to my proper subject, which is the place of philosophy in education.

By education here I do not mean the special training required to make a man a competent doctor, engineer, or lawyer, however important that may be. By education I mean the process of raising human personality to the highest level which it is capable of attaining, the process of developing all that is finest and noblest in it, the process of turning out first-class human beings.

And if education is taken in this sense, it is not difficult to show that philosophy is an essential part of it, and that without some tincture of philosophy a man is an imperfect human being. For it follows from what I have already said that philosophy is an essential part of all human culture. If philosophy is, as I have tried to show, nothing more than an attempt to throw knowledge back upon its ultimate principles; to think out the most fundamental and ultimate problems which are raised by morals, by religion, by science, by art, and by common sense; is it not obvious that any perfect human culture

cannot exclude it? Philosophy is nothing but the most fundamental kind of thinking which a man can do in any branch
of study. It lies at the basis of every other subject. It is bound
up with all human culture and is therefore an integral part
of any complete education.

It is a mistake to think of the different branches of knowledge and culture as if they existed in watertight compartments, completely independent and isolated from one another.
They are, after all, products of one and the same human spirit,
and a sufficiently keen insight will detect one and the same
human life unfolding itself in them all. Every age has its own
peculiar attitude towards the problems which man's environment presents, its own peculiar attitude towards the world.
This attitude of any age is sometimes called the spirit of the
age. The spirit of an age expresses itself in a diversity of different forms, in the forms of its art, its literature, its religion,
its science, its politics, and finally its philosophy. These different forms will usually be found to have the same essential
content. That is to say, the philosophy of an age will be found
to express in philosophical form the same attitude towards the
world which is expressed in other forms in its literature, its
art, its science. It is one and the same life which, in a plant,
puts itself forth in the different flowers and branches. And
literature, art, science, religion, philosophy are the flowers
of the human spirit. Consequently I would say that the philosophy of an age crystallizes in its most abstract form the essential thought and culture of that age, and is therefore a key
to the understanding of that age. Let us give a few examples
of this.

It is almost a platitude to say that in Greece the philosophy
of the Sophists merely crystallized in abstract terms the same
tendencies of thought as were everywhere making themselves
apparent in the political life of the time, in the dramas of
Euripides, and elsewhere. What, again, is the famous *Republic* of Plato but an expression in abstract philosophical form
of that ideal of a balanced and harmonious personality which

contained the essence of the Greek attitude towards life? Another example is to be found in the American philosophy known as pragmatism. The essence of this philosophy consists in its subordination of all the higher human activities, such as knowledge, art, and religion, to purely practical ends. It judges them all by their cash value. Thus it perfectly reflects the predominantly commercial spirit and civilization of the American people.

Turning to modern Europe, I would draw your attention to the fact that during the nineteenth century the essential content of philosophy was identical with the essential content of literature and poetry. In philosophy it took the form of idealism, in poetry of romanticism. At the beginning of the nineteenth century there came in literature that great outburst of romantic poetry which is connected with such names as Wordsworth, Byron, Shelley, Keats. At the very same moment there dawned in Germany the great age of philosophical idealism, and this idealism rose to its greatest heights in the system of Hegel. Hegelian idealism expressed in general the same human attitude to the world as did the romantic poets. The system of Hegel was nothing but a vast elaboration of the idea that the finite world in space and time, the world of nature, is not ultimately real, is but a shadow, an appearance, beneath which lies a deeper, a divine, reality. But this idea is also the very indwelling life of poetic romanticism. The spirit of romanticism is epitomized in Wordsworth's famous lines in which he speaks of

> *a sense sublime*
> *Of something far more deeply interfused*
> *Whose dwelling is the light of setting suns,*
> *And the round ocean and the living air,*
> *And the blue sky, and in the mind of man.*

Wordsworth's reverence for nature is no sentimental vaporing about crocuses and cowslips, but is based upon this belief that nature is at once the veil and the revealer of a deeper divine reality. His vision of the world is the same as Hegel's vision. And this vision Wordsworth transmitted throughout the poetry of the nineteenth century. It inspires in varying degrees the work of all the romantic poets, Shelley, Keats, Tennyson, Browning, and even such an apparently positivistic and anti-religious poet as Swinburne. It finally dies out, I should say, in the early work of the Irish poet, W. B. Yeats, and has now been replaced by a very different attitude.

Parallel, in the nineteenth century, to the stream of romanticism which takes its departure from Wordsworth, there flows the stream of philosophical idealism which has its source in Hegel. It passes over from Germany to England, inspiring the work of such men as Green, Bradley, and Bosanquet. It passes over to America in the work of Royce and many others. And in them, I should say, it finally dies out as an original and creative force—notwithstanding that it still finds admirers and imitators—to be replaced, once more, by a very different spirit.

What is this very different spirit which has now made its appearance both in literature and philosophy? Well, the present age is neither idealistic nor romanticist. There has been a violent rebellion against all that. Romanticism is now set down as sentimentalism. And the present age is above all anti-sentimental. The repudiation of romanticism arises ultimately from the fact that the vision of a deeper reality behind the appearance of the world has been lost. The finite things in time and space, the moving masses of matter, the life of animals and plants and men on the planet, these things, which for Wordsworth and Hegel were mere appearances, are now proclaimed as the only realities. There is nothing behind them, supporting them. They are real in their own right. This is the essential message which is proclaimed by the most characteristic philosophical school of the present day, or perhaps I should say, of the recent past, the school of the realists. The universe of the realist can be obtained by taking the universe of the idealist, cutting away the inner spiritual essence which lies behind it, and leaving only the outward appearance, a sort of lifeless mask, which is now declared to be the only reality. There is no "something far more deeply interfused, whose dwelling is the light of setting suns." There are merely the setting suns and the clouds, and these are composed of oxygen, hydrogen, and what not.

And is it not exactly the same spirit which informs a great deal of current literature? It is no longer the business of literary art to reveal "the light which never was on sea or land." It is now an affair of surfaces and externals. Its message is that a man's life consists of an endless procession of externalities—of smoke and grime, of the streets and the mud in the streets, of offices and houses and money and clothes and hats, of sights and sounds, of pleasures and pains—succeeding each other in a kind of bewildering nightmare. These are the realities, the millions of disconnected experiences of a drab and uninspired life. There is, beneath and beyond them, no indwelling spirit to transform them from the sordid to the sublime. So says the literary realist. And this is what his brother the philosophical realist is saying too.

In this contention between the spirit of the last age and the spirit of the more recent past I am not now taking sides. The realist may be right for all I know. My point is not that the romantic spirit was better than the anti-romantic, or vice versa. I am only concerned to point out that the philosophy of an age on the one hand, and the literature and art of the age on the other, usually express in different forms the essential attitude of that age towards the world, and therefore that their content is the same. And my thesis is, you see, simply that philosophy is an organic part of human culture, one of the natural modes of expression of the human spirit, not something utterly remote and cut off from other branches of knowledge and from the affairs of ordinary life, the idle plaything of a few pedants and recluses.

For not only does the essential thought of each age express

itself in philosophy. It expresses itself there, I should say, in its purest form. For whereas in literature and in art you will find the tendencies of the age expressed diffusely, mixed up with all sorts of unessentials, in a chaotic jumble, in philosophy you will find it crystallized out, reduced to its fundamental principles. It is hardly too much to say that philosophy is the master key to human culture; and that in the last resort no full understanding of the great movements of the human spirit—that is to say, no full understanding of life itself—is possible without philosophy. And if that is so, can it be any longer doubted the the rôle of philosophy in education is vital?

But there occurs a doubt to one's mind. It is a common reproach against philosophy that it is nothing but an arena of disagreements. Compare philosophy, it is said, with any of the well-established sciences. Among scientists, of course, there are disagreements. But each of the sciences nevertheless presents us with a large and growing body of established truths. The sciences, moreover, do not remain stationary. They advance triumphantly from discovery to discovery.

Now if you turn your eyes from science to philosophy, what a pitiful spectacle meets your gaze! Philosophers cannot agree even upon the most elementary principles of their subject. They are divided into numerous hostile camps. Philosophy is nothing but a haphazard jumble of contradictory opinions. There must be something wrong with a subject which has always been, and still is, in such a pass. That is the sort of onslaught which the unhappy philosopher has to meet from his friends the scientists. What reply can he make? I cannot, in the brief space now left to me, deal as fully with this subject as I should like to. I can, in fact, give only the bare headings of what I think would be the adequate reply.

One might, of course, point out that the disagreements of philosophers are often greatly exaggerated; that if one were to draw up a list of matters on which practically all philosophers agree, the list would probably be surprisingly long; that the development of philosophy, as of other branches of knowledge, has not been chaotic, but orderly, a well-defined evolution; and that philosophers themselves naturally discuss the points on which they disagree, and are silent on those upon which they agree, thus giving an appearance of greater disagreement than actually exists. There would be some truth in all these contentions. But such a line of defense would, I think, be rather a case of special pleading. One has to admit roundly that there *is* far more disagreement among philosophers than there is among the men of science. What other reply can we make?

Firstly, it is somewhat oddly overlooked by those who make this criticism of philosophy that philosophy is not alone in this matter. It is true that there is a remarkably large measure of agreement in the purely physical sciences. But in the spheres of art, religion, morals, politics, economics, there is, I should say, as much disagreement as there is in philosophy. If philosophers are divided into idealists and realists, into rationalists and empiricists, are not political thinkers divided into conservatives and revolutionaries, communists and fascists, republicans and monarchists? Do they not dispute regarding every possible political principle in theory, and every possible political decision in practice? Are not American economists divided into various schools? Is not the religious world divided into Christians, Muslims, Buddhists? In moral questions is there not constant and violent dispute as to whether a man in given circumstances ought to have done this or that?

Now what would you think of anyone who should argue that, because there is so much disagreement in the spheres of politics, art, religion, economics, morals, therefore politics, art, religion, economics, morals are unimportant subjects the study of which ought not to be encouraged? Is it not obvious that, in spite of the disagreements, perhaps *because of* the disagreements, these are just the most important subjects in the world, the subjects which ought above all to be studied by a man who wishes to be a first-class human being? Why, then, should philosophy be selected for special reprimand because of its disagreements?

But that answer, perhaps, does not satisfy. It consists, you may say, only in the blackening of other subjects, not in the whitening of philosophy. And it does not go to the root of the matter. Let us leave politics, economics, and so on, to fight their own battles. Let us speak of philosophy alone, and face the issue. Why *should* there be so many disagreements among philosophers, if their subject is really in a sound and healthy condition? I suggest that the answer is, in essence, as follows. There is a special reason why physical scientists are able to present a more or less united front. They are dealing always with *ponderables*, with crass matter, in other words with things which can be measured and weighed. Moreover, they are dealing nearly always with the quantitative aspects of matter, and the questions regarding matter which they seek to answer are mostly questions which can be definitely settled by operations of measuring and weighing. These operations can be fairly easily and accurately performed. And the result is that scientific problems can for the most part be definitely solved.

But philosophy deals mostly with *imponderables*, which cannot be measured and weighed, and the questions which philosophers ask cannot be settled by yardsticks and balances. Take any of the great questions with which philosophers have been concerned. Is the world ultimately a product of mind, or is it mindless mechanism? Is there a cosmic purpose, or is there not? Is the world finally rational, or is there an irreducible element of irrationality in it? What is the significance of the presence of evil in the universe? What is the essence of morality? Is there a single absolute moral law or is there not? What is the ultimate nature and foundation of art, and of the sense of the beautiful? Can any reasonable person expect slick answers to these questions as if they were sums in arithmetic? Can they be answered by means of operations with foot-rules and chemical retorts? Is it not obvious that there will always be room for differences of opinion on such matters? And can we expect more than that we should know what the best minds, who have given their lives to these problems, think, notwithstanding that, among them too, there may, and indeed must be, different views?

Philosophy is deeply rooted in human life. It reflects, as I have tried to show, the essential attitudes of ages and of civilizations to the world. And it is little short of idiotic to expect that these attitudes will not show wide cleavages and divergencies. But this does mean that men's attitudes to the world, and the philosophies which express them, are not among the deepest concerns of human culture.

Therefore I cannot hold out the hope that tomorrow, or in five years, or in fifty years, all philosophers will agree. Only a simpleton will entertain such a hope. And only a shallow understanding will condemn philosophy because of this.

In any case, all this about the disagreements of philosophers is, for me, merely a side issue. My main contention is that philosophy is an integral part of human culture, and whether that culture is divided within itself or not, the study of it necessitates philosophy. Whether we like it or not, we cannot escape philosophy; because, on whatever road of knowledge we travel, philosophy lies in wait for us with its questions.

Science and the Physical World

So far as I know scientists still talk about electrons, protons, neutrons, and so on. We never directly perceive these, hence if we ask how we know of their existence the only possible answer seems to be that they are an inference from what we do directly perceive. What sort of an inference? Apparently a causal inference. The atomic entities in some way impinge upon the sense of the animal organism and cause that organism to perceive the familiar world of tables, chairs, and the rest.

But is it not clear that such a concept of causation, however interpreted, is invalid? The only reason we have for believing in the law of causation is that we *observe* certain regularities or sequences. We observe that, in certain conditions, A is always followed by B. We call A the cause, B the effect. And the sequence A-B becomes a causal law. It follows that all *observed* causal sequences are between sensed objects in the familiar world of perception, and that all known causal laws apply solely to the world of sense and not to anything beyond or behind it. And this in turn means that we have not got, and never could have, one jot of evidence for believing that the law of causation can be applied *outside* the realm of perception, or that that realm can have any causes (such as the supposed physical objects) which are not themselves perceived.

Put the same thing in another way. Suppose there is an

observed sequence *A-B-C,* represented by the vertical lines in the diagram below.

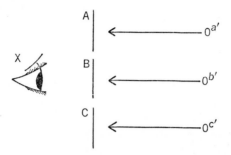

The observer X sees, and can see, nothing except things in the familiar world of perception. What *right* has he, and what *reason* has he, to assert causes of A, B, and C, such as *a', b', c',* which he can never observe, behind the perceived world? He has no *right,* because the law of causation on which he is relying has never been observed to operate outside the series of perceptions, and he can have, therefore, no evidence that it does so. And he has no *reason* because the phenomenon C is *sufficiently* accounted for by the cause B, B by A, and so on. It is unnecessary and superfluous to introduce a *second* cause *b'* for B, *c'* for C, and so forth. To give two causes for each phenomenon, one in one world and one in another, is unnecessary, and perhaps even self-contradictory.

Is it denied, then, it will be asked, that the star causes light waves, that the waves cause retinal changes, that these cause changes in the optic nerve, which in turn causes movements in the brain cells, and so on? No, it is not denied. But the observed causes and effects are all in the world of perception. And no sequences of sense-data can possibly justify going outside that world. If you admit that we never observe anything except sensed objects and their relations, regularities, and sequences, then it is obvious that we are completely shut in by our sensations and can never get outside them. Not only causal relations, but all other observed relations, upon which *any* kind of inferences might be founded, will lead only to further sensible objects and their relations. No inference, therefore, can pass from what is sensible to what is not sensible.

The fact is that atoms are *not* inferences from sensations. No one denies, of course, that a vast amount of perfectly valid inferential reasoning takes place in the physical theory of the atom. But it will not be found to be in any strict logical sense inference *from sense-data to atoms.* An *hypothesis* is set up, and the inferential processes are concerned with the application of the hypothesis, that is, with the prediction by its aid of further possible sensations and with its own internal consistency.

That atoms are not inferences from sensations means, of course, that from the existence of sensations we cannot validly infer the existence of atoms. And this means that we cannot have any reason at all to believe that they exist. And that is why I propose to argue that they do not exist—or at any rate that no one could know it if they did, and that we have absolutely no evidence of their existence.

What status have they, then? Is it meant that they are false and worthless, merely untrue? Certainly not. No one supposes that the entries in the nautical almanac "exist" anywhere except on the pages of that book and in the brains of its compilers and readers. Yet they are "true," inasmuch as they enable us to predict certain sensations, namely, the positions and times of certain perceived objects which we call the stars. And so the formulae of the atomic theory are true in the same sense, and perform a similar function.

I suggest that they are nothing but shorthand formulae, ingeniously worked out by the human mind, to enable it to predict its experience, i.e. to predict what sensations will be given to it. By "predict" here I do not mean to refer solely to the future. To calculate that there was an eclipse of the sun visible in Asia Minor in the year 585 B.C. is, in the sense in which I am using the term, to predict.

In order to see more clearly what is meant, let us apply the same idea to another case, that of gravitation. Newton formulated a law of gravitation in terms of "forces." It was supposed that this law—which was nothing but a mathematical formula —governed the operation of these existent forces. Nowadays it is no longer believed that these forces exist at all. And yet the law can be applied just as well without them to the prediction of astronomical phenomena. It is a matter of no importance to the scientific man whether the forces exist or not. That may be said to be a purely philosophical question. And I think the philosopher should pronounce them fictions. But that would not make the law useless or untrue. If it could still be used to predict phenomena, it would be just as true as it was.

It is true that fault is now found with Newton's law, and that another law, that of Einstein, has been substituted for it. And it is sometimes supposed that the reason for this is that forces are no longer believed in. But this is not the case. Whether forces exist or not simply does not matter. What matters is the discovery that Newton's law does *not* enable us accurately to predict certain astronomical facts such as the exact position of the planet Mercury. Therefore another formula, that of Einstein, has been substituted for it which permits correct predictions. This new law, as it happens, is a formula in terms of geometry. It is pure mathematics and nothing else. It does not contain anything about forces. In its pure form it does not even contain, so I am informed, anything about "humps and hills in space-time." And it does not matter whether any such humps and hills exist. It is truer than Newton's law, not because it substitutes humps and hills for forces, but solely because it is a more accurate formula of prediction.

Not only may it be said that forces do not exist. It may with equal truth be said that "gravitation" does not exist. Gravitation is not a "thing," but a mathematical formula, which exists only in the heads of mathematicians. And as a mathematical formula cannot cause a body to fall, so gravitation cannot cause a body to fall. Ordinary language misleads us here. We speak of the law "of" gravitation, and suppose that this law "applies to" the heavenly bodies. We are thereby misled into supposing that there are *two* things, namely, the gravitation and the heavenly bodies, and that one of these things, the gravitation, causes changes in the other. In reality nothing exists except the moving bodies. And neither Newton's law nor Einstein's law is, strictly speaking, a law of gravitation. They are both laws of moving bodies, that is to say, formulae which tell us how these bodies will move.

Now, just as in the past "forces" were foisted into Newton's law (by himself, be it said), so now certain popularizers of relativity foisted "humps and hills in space-time" into Einstein's law. We hear that the reason why the planets move in curved courses is that they cannot go through these humps and hills, but have to go round them! The planets just get "shoved about," not by forces, but by the humps and hills! But these humps and hills are pure metaphors. And anyone who takes them for "existences" gets asked awkward questions as to what "curved space" is curved "in."

It is not irrelevant to our topic to consider *why* human beings invent these metaphysical monsters of forces and bumps in space-time. The reason is that they have never emancipated themselves from the absurd idea that science "explains" things. They were not content to have laws which merely told them *that* the planets will, as a matter of fact, move in such and such ways. They wanted to know "why" the planets move in those ways. So Newton replied, "Forces." "Oh," said humanity, "that explains it. We understand forces. We feel them every time someone pushes or pulls us." Thus the movements were supposed to be "explained" by entities familiar because analogous to the muscular sensations which human beings feel. The humps and hills were introduced for exactly the same reason. They seem so familiar. If there is a bump in the billiard table, the rolling billiard ball is diverted from a straight to a curved course. Just the same with the planets. "Oh, I see!" says humanity, "that's quite simple. That *explains* everything."

But scientific laws, properly formulated, never "explain" anything. They simply state, in an abbreviated and generalized form, *what happens*. No scientist, and in my opinion no philosopher, knows *why* anything happens, or can "explain" anything. Scientific laws do nothing except state the brute fact that "when *A* happens, *B* always happens too." And laws of this kind obviously enable us to predict. If certain scientists substituted humps and hills for forces, then they have just substituted one superstition for another. For my part I do not believe that *science* has done this, though some *scientists* may have. For scientists, after all, are human beings with the same craving for "explanations" as other people.

I think that atoms are in exactly the same position as forces and the humps and hills of space-time. In reality the mathematical formulae which are the scientific ways of stating the atomic theory are simply formulae for calculating what sensations will appear in given conditions. But just as the weakness of the human mind demanded that there should correspond to the formula of gravitation a real "thing" which could be called "gravitation itself" or "force," so the same weakness demands that there should be a real thing corresponding to the atomic formulae, and this real thing is called the atom. In reality the atoms no more cause sensations than gravitation causes apples to fall. The only causes of sensations are other sensations. And the relation of atoms to sensations to be felt is not the relation of cause to effect, but the relation of a mathematical formula to the facts and happenings which it enables the mathematician to calculate.

Some writers have said that the physical world has no color, no sound, no taste, no smell. It has no spatiality. Probably it has not even number. We must not suppose that it is in any way like our world, or that we can understand it by attributing to it the characters of our world. Why not carry this progress to its logical conclusion? Why not give up the idea that it has even the character of "existence" which our familiar world has? We have given up smell, color, taste. We have given up even space and shape. We have given up number. Surely, after all that, mere existence is but a little thing to give up. No? Then is it that the idea of existence conveys "a sort of halo"? I suspect so. The "existence" of atoms is but the expiring ghost of the pellet and billiard-ball atoms of our forefathers. They, of course, had size, shape, weight, hardness. These have gone. But thinkers still cling to their existence, just as their fathers clung to the existence of forces, and for the same reason. Their reason is not in the slightest that science has any use for the existent atom. But the *imagination* has. It seems somehow to explain things, to make them homely and familiar.

It will not be out of place to give one more example to show how common fictitious existences are in science, and how little it matters whether they really exist or not. This example has no strange and annoying talk of "bent spaces" about it. One of the foundations of physics is, or used to be, the law of the conservation of energy. I do not know how far, if at all, this has been affected by the theory that matter sometimes turns into energy. But that does not affect the lesson it has for us. The law states, or used to state, that the amount of energy in the universe is always constant, that energy is never either created or destroyed. This was highly convenient, but it seemed to have obvious exceptions. If you throw a stone up into the air, you are told that it exerts in its fall the same amount of energy which it took to throw it up. But suppose it does not fall. Suppose it lodges on the roof of your house and stays there. What has happened to the energy which you can nowhere perceive as being exerted? It seems to have disappeared out of the universe. No, says the scientist, it still exists as *potential* energy. Now what does this blessed word "potential"—which is thus brought in to save the situation—mean as applied to energy? It means, of course, that the energy does not exist in any of its regular "forms," heat, light, electricity, etc. But this is merely negative. What positive meaning has the term? Strictly speaking, none whatever. Either the energy exists or it does not exist. There is no realm of the "potential" half-way between existence and non-existence. And the existence of energy can only consist in its being exerted. If the energy is not being exerted, then it is not energy and does not exist. Energy can no more exist without energizing than heat can exist without being hot. The "potential" existence of the energy is, then, a fiction. The actual empirically verifiable facts are that if a certain quantity of energy *e* exists in the universe and then disappears out of the universe (as happens when the stone lodges on the roof), the same amount of energy *e* will always reappear, begin to exist again, in certain known conditions. That is the fact which the law of the conservation of energy actually expresses. And the fiction of potential energy is introduced simply because it is convenient and makes the equations easier to work. They could be worked quite well without it, but would be slightly more complicated. In either case the function of the law is the same. Its object is to apprise us that if in certain conditions we have certain perceptions (throwing up the stone), then in certain other conditions we shall get certain other perceptions (heat, light, stone hitting skull, or other such). But there will always be a temptation to hypostatize the potential energy as an "existence," and to believe that it is a "cause" which "explains" the phenomena.

If the views which I have been expressing are followed out, they will lead to the conclusion that, strictly speaking, *nothing exists except sensations* (and the minds which perceive them). The rest is mental construction or fiction. But this does not mean that the conception of a star or the conception of an electron are worthless or untrue. Their truth and value consist in their capacity for helping us to organize our experience and predict our sensations.

Science and Explanation

My subject here falls within that branch of philosophy which is commonly called the philosophy of science. And it is intended, among other things, to illustrate, by the particular case of science, the suggestion which I made in an earlier chapter that all subjects, scientific, literary, moral, if you examine their first principles, will lead you back into philosophy.

Perhaps I ought to begin, however, by apologizing for talking about science at all. In these days it is a perilous thing for the layman to do. There are some philosophers, I believe, who can claim to possess a fairly expert knowledge of some one or other of the sciences. But I, assuredly, am not one of them. But by way of an excuse I would plead that science, after all, is but one of many forms of human intellectual endeavor, and that as such it must have its special place and its special function in the general economy of human culture. My purpose in this essay is simply to inquire what the special function of science is. And that problem, the problem of the function of science, is not itself, I submit, a scientific problem. For to which of the particular sciences can it possibly belong? It is not a biological problem, or a geographical problem, or a chemical problem. There is no science which claims it. You must stand *outside* science to investigate it. And it is, I should say, a philosophical problem.

I suppose I shall be allowed to say, at any rate, that science deals in some way with nature, with things that happen in nature, with events, with phenomena. Now when anything happens in nature, there are two questions regarding it which human beings are prone to ask. The first is: *What* happened? The second is: *Why* did it happen? We may distinguish these two questions by calling the first the question of the "what," the second the question of the "why." To give a very simple example. Suppose a child who has observed for the first time in his life the freezing of a pond. He may ask, "What has happened?" In reply he will be told that when the thermometer falls to below zero centigrade, the previously liquid water turns solid, its volume increases by roughly one-eighth, and so on. He may also perhaps be told something about the molecular processes involved. But in all such information he is being given simply a *description* of what happens. The answer to the question "what?" is always necessarily a description, and nothing but a description.

But the child may frame his question in a different way. Instead of asking what has happened to the water, he may ask, "*Why* does water freeze?" And if his teacher is a very unsophisticated scientist, he may reply that water freezes *because* the temperature falls below zero centigrade, and *because*, when that happens, the molecules do so and so. Here, apparently, the child is being given, not a mere description of what happens, but a reason *why* it happens, or in other words an *explanation*. Thus the question "what?" asks simply for a *description* of events. The question "why?" asks for an *explanation* of them.

Now the essence of my thesis is simply this—that the function of science is to answer the question "what?" but never the question "why?" In other words, its function is simply to *describe* phenomena, never to *explain* them. But it is also part of my thesis that from the earliest times scientists have as a matter of fact attempted not only to describe phenomena, but also to explain them; and that this false striving after explanations has led science astray in the past, and that it may very possibly lead it astray again in the present and in the future, if the situation is not watched. And what I am going to do is to try to justify these statements.

Science arose in the beginning out of ordinary human curiosity, the curiosity of ordinary, ignorant men. But the two questions, "What happens?" and "Why does it happen?" are the natural questions which ordinary human curiosity always puts. This simple psychological fact has to a large extent governed the development of science. It accounts for the fact that science from the beginning has always attempted to answer both these questions. And although the demand for explanation is, scientifically speaking, an illegitimate demand, science has never quite freed itself from the idea of explanation which it has inherited from its ancestry in naïve human curiosity.

If one leaves out of account certain tentative beginnings in Babylonia and Egypt, science proper may be said to have begun its career in ancient Greece. And the greatest of the Greek scientists was Aristotle. It is extremely instructive to note how Aristotle set about dealing with natural phenomena. When anything came into existence, whether it was an oak tree, or a hen's egg, or a flash of lightning, Aristotle thought that there were four principles which must be used in attempting to understand it. You must ascertain, he said, the material cause of the thing, its efficient cause, its final cause, and its formal cause. With formal causes I am not here concerned, and I will say nothing about them. Roughly speaking, and neglecting fine metaphysical points, the other three principles may be described as follows. The material cause of a thing was the matter of which it was made. The efficient cause was the preceding events or phenomena which brought the thing into being—that is to say, what we should now call simply the cause. The final cause of a thing was the *purpose* which it served in the universe. Thus one might say that in order fully to understand anything one had, for Aristotle, to know three things about it, what it was made of, what its cause was, and what purpose it served in the world.

The first two of these principles, you will see, answered the question "what?" They met the demand for description and nothing else. What is it made of? If you answer that it is made of wood or iron, you are obviously describing it. What is its cause? That is, what other phenomena invariably precede it, or lead up to it? If you answer that question, you are describing not the phenomenon itself, but the one that went before it. You are describing the *series* of phenomena of which this phenomenon is a member.

But the third principle, which Aristotle called the final cause, was intended to answer the question "why?" and to give not a description, but an explanation. What does the word *why* mean? Well, it is ambiguous, and has several meanings. But one of the commonest interprets it in terms of purpose. We say to a man, "What did you do?," which is a form of the question, "What happened?" And when he has told us what he did, we ask, "Why did you do it?" And by that we mean, "What was your purpose?" And Aristotle thought that we could question nature in the same way. After we had ascertained what nature does, we could then go on to ask why nature does it. The answer, in the case of any particular phenomenon, was the final cause of that phenomenon, the purpose which it served in the cosmos. So that in Greece, the country in which science originated, the conception of the function of science which was entertained by its most distinguished representative was that this function included both the description and the explanation of phenomena.

Throughout the Middle Ages, I should say, Aristotle's conception of science held the field more or less unchanged. But when you come to the scientific revolution of the seventeenth century, to the age of Galileo and Newton, you find a sudden change. Most of the conceptions of Aristotle are attacked. And among these the conception of final causes. Aristotle was accused, among other sins, of having introduced into science the futile and fatal idea of final causes, that is to say, the conception of purpose. The modern scientific era began with the firm determination to banish final causes altogether from science. Science was not in the future to probe into the cosmic purpose of anything.

It was not that the seventeenth-century scientists were disposed to deny the existence of purposes in nature. They were most of them religious men who believed that the world is governed by God's purposes. But they supposed that these purposes were beyond the reach of science. They might fall within the sphere of religion, or perhaps of philosophy. But science, in pursuing the will o' the wisp of purpose, had been led into a wilderness, had failed to make useful discoveries, and would continue to do so. Its business was to discover the facts, to describe the facts, and to leave all ulterior questions of purpose out of account. So the point which I am trying to make is this. The seventeenth century in effect rejected the Aristotelian conception of science as concerned both with description and explanation, and declared that the proper function of science is description alone. And it is under this banner that modern science has marched forward ever since.

Scientific laws, I should say, explain nothing. Science never *can* explain even the simplest event. At this statement someone may be inclined to cavil. "Surely," it will be said, "modern science does attempt to explain things, and does, moreover, succeed. Surely the germ theory explains many diseases. Surely the law of gravitation explains the movement of the planets. Surely the theory of evolution explains the appearance of new species on the planet." And so on. It is worthwhile to consider this.

Let us take a very simple case. Suppose that a savage from Central Africa, who has never seen ice, is brought to this country, and is astonished to find water turning solid in the winter. How do you "explain" this to him? You tell him—assuming that he is capable of understanding you—that it is a law of nature that when the temperature falls below zero centigrade, and when certain other conditions are fulfilled, water turns solid. That is your explanation. In consists in reducing this particular event, happening here and now, to an example of a general law of nature. But what is a law of nature? Instead of telling the savage that in this particular case the temperature fell below zero, and that the water then froze, you tell him that in *all* cases, *whenever* the temperature falls below zero, water *always* freezes. You are simply telling him what *always* happens. Your explanation of a particular phenomenon by reducing it to a general law merely consists in saying that this phenomenon, which is happening now, is an example of what always happens. A scientific law, in fact, is nothing but a *description* of what always happens. It does nothing towards explaining *why* it happens.

But, it will be objected, this is merely elementary. The scientist does not merely say that at a certain temperature water freezes. He *explains* the phenomenon by means of molecular processes. He explains that, when the temperature reaches zero, then the molecules do so and so, and the water becomes solid. But what is this, once more, beyond mere description? When the temperature reaches zero, then the molecules do so and so. That just tells us what the molecules do, what happens, not *why* it happens. And however far you go with your molecular, your atomic, or your sub-atomic processess, it will always be just the same. Always you will have description, and never explanation.

Is it different, to take another example, with the law of gravitation? Why does an unsupported stone fall to the ground? On the Newtonian view it is because all particles attract one another with a certain force. But what does this mean? It means only that all particles tend to fall together. This happens here because it always happens everywhere. Newton's law of gravitation, like every other law, simply states what always happens. It gives no reason why. Nor would it make the slightest difference if we substitute Einstein's law for Newton's. We should only be substituting one law for another. And a law, as such, simply states what always happens.

Now I can well imagine that at this point someone may exclaim, "Well, what on earth do you want? The laws of nature tell you what happens. What else do you want to know? You seem to want to know also *why* things happen. What do you *mean* by why?" I hasten to say that I personally do *not* want the scientist to tell me anything except what happens. I do not want him to tell me why it happens. In fact, my whole contention is that he should confine himself strictly to telling me what happens, and that when he tries to tell me why it happens he is deserting the proper function of science. But I will come to that later. Meanwhile let us attend to the last question which was put to me: What do you *mean* by the question "why?"

As we have seen, human curiosity always has asked the question "why?" as well as the question "what?" And now the problem seems to be what is it that ordinary human curiosity wants to know when it asks the question "why?" What kind of information does it expect in reply to this question? Thinking over this problem, I have come to the conclusion that the question "why?" does not really express a desire for information at all. It expresses a *feeling*. It does not proceed from the intellect, but from the emotions. It indicates simply that men want to be made to feel *at home* in the universe. They want to escape from the sense of loneliness, the sense of strangeness and unfamiliarity, the sense even of hostility, which the universe is apt to inspire. For the lonely, the strange, the unfamiliar are terrifying. At this point we tap the psychological source of that desire for explanation which has always haunted the human mind, and which has dogged the footsteps of science. The whole conception of explanation has its roots here. To explain a thing *means*, I believe, to exhibit it as friendly to ourselves, or at least, as not menacing. When a strange, surprising, hitherto unknown phenomenon occurs in nature, when some totally new experience comes upon us, we want to know that this strange new thing is not going to be a menace to us, is not going to be disastrous to us. When by some intellectual process we have become assured of this, we feel that the phenomenon has been *explained*. That, I believe, is the *meaning* of explanation, and of the question "why?"

But historically this demand of our emotional nature has satisfied itself in two quite distinct ways, and this fact has given rise to two quite distinct types of explanation. The first way of satisfaction has lain in developing the belief that the world is rational, purposive. We ourselves are purposive beings. Our actions are governed by purposes. If we could extend this conception to the universe at large, if we could suppose that whatever happens in the universe happens because of some purpose, and especially if the purpose were something to our advantage, we should certainly feel more at home in the world. We should feel that the universe is like ourselves, and perhaps even that it is on our side. It would cease then to be strange, terrifying, and incomprehensible. If we could show the purpose which a phenomenon serves in the universe, the phenomenon would then be explained. This was the significance of Aristotle's final causes. And this is *one* kind of explanation.

Explanation by means of purposes is out of date for science. It was definitely banished from science in the seventeenth century. I do not mean by this to affirm that there is in fact no cosmic purpose in the universe; or that this is the view of science. The universe may, for all I know, be governed by purpose. And any science which *denies* that the world is purposive, is, in my opinion, stupid and dogmatic. But science has long ago decided that the question of purpose lies outside its scope. Perhaps it is a question for philosophy, or perhaps for religion. I do not discuss that here.[1] My only point is that this kind of explanation no longer finds a place in science.

[1] But see the "Note on the Concept of Explanation" at the end of this chapter.

But there is a second type of explanation, which depends psychologically upon another way of making ourselves at home with things. It depends upon the psychological commonplace that familiarity breeds contempt. If anything in the universe appears strange, extraordinary, or menacing, then we try to show that it is after all something quite familiar and ordinary. When an utterly new experience comes upon us, threatening us, we try to show that it is after all only an old friend in a new disguise. It thereupon loses its terrors for us. From this psychological root grows the second type of explanation, which consists simply in reducing the strange to the familiar, the unknown to the known. And my contention will be that, although science has emancipated itself from the first kind of explanation, it has not yet completely emancipated itself from the second.

Is not this what is at the bottom of the common idea that the phenomena of nature are explained by the *laws* of nature? We supposed our African savage to be astonished at the freezing of water. As we saw, you explain this to him by showing that it is nothing unique, but merely an example of what always happens. It is, in other words, nothing strange. It is quite familiar. When you have made him understand this, he feels satisfied that you have explained the matter. And not only the African savage. We all of us feel the same. Which shows that what we *mean* by explanation is simply the showing that the phenomenon in question is not strange, but familiar, that it is something that always happens.

It follows that this idea of explanation is quite arbitrary and unscientific, quite personal and subjective. For what is strange to one person may be quite familiar to another. Hence what explains a phenomenon to me may not explain it to you.[2] And I think you will agree with me that it cannot be the function of science to supply various different individuals with the vari-

2 I owe this point to P. W. Bridgman's *The Logic of Modern Physics.*

ous different kinds of emotions which will make each of them feel at home in the world. In other words, the function of science is not explanation at all.

But evidence that the idea of explanation has not altogether been dropped from the sciences is found in our linguistic habits, in the ordinary turns of phrase used alike by the layman and the scientist. Nothing is commoner than to hear the question, "What is the scientific explanation of this or that phenomenon?" Nothing is commoner than to hear the question "why?" put to the scientist, and answered by him. *Why* do the planets move in ellipses? *Why* has the mammoth become extinct? And wherever the word *why* is used instead of the word *what*, you know that our old mental habit still holds sway, that the old craving for explanation, for making the world seem homely and familiar, instead of strange and alarming, is still alive.

But perhaps you will think that this is a mere verbal matter, a matter of words which does not affect the substance of science. Perhaps it may be a slight terminological inaccuracy to say that the law of gravitation "explains" the movements of the planets. We ought, no doubt, to use some other word. But this is a matter of no importance to anyone except grammatical purists and philosophical hair-splitters. It has never misled science.

I am afraid that such a view cannot be maintained. I am afraid that the false idea of explanation has misled science in the past. And with great deference I venture to suggest that it may possibly be misleading science now, and may continue to do so in the future. I will try to give a few examples to show this.

You will remember the common idea that a thing cannot act, or produce an effect, at a distance from the place where it is. Action at a distance, it used to be said, is an impossibility. That maxim has played a great part in the history of thought, yet it is a pure a priori dogma, without the slightest foundation in evidence. To settle whether it is true or not ought always to have been a matter of observation or experiment, and nothing else. If it were found, as a matter of observed fact, that an event X, happening in one part of the universe, was invariably followed by another event Y at a distance of a million miles, and if there were no empirical evidence of anything happening in between, then it should have been declared, on the basis of such evidence, that X was the cause of Y, or in other words that X acted at a distance.

But what actually happened was that a priori dogmas were allowed to intervene. The question was not settled upon the evidence, but by supposed considerations of pure reason. It was supposed to be *incomprehensible* that anything should act at a distance. And, therefore, it was declared to be impossible.

Now what is this supposed incomprehensibility? Examine it carefully, for it is profoundly instructive in the ways of human thought. You think that if an event *here*, say the blow of a hammer, is followed by another event *here*, say a blue flash, as may happen in an explosion, then this is quite comprehensible, and you will call the two events cause and effect. But suppose it is alleged that the blow of the hammer here is followed by a blue flash a million miles away, with nothing happening in between, then you say this is incomprehensible. I want to know what you *mean* by "incomprehensible."

In the first, you do not mean "logically self-contradictory." For there is no logical contradiction in a blow here being followed by a blue flash a million miles away. The proposition, "a blow occurred here," is obviously not contradicted by the proposition, "a blue flash occurred a million miles away."

I will suggest a second possible meaning. The only way in which science ever understands any phenomenon consists in describing it accurately and in detail. The freezing of water is understood, so far as science can understand it, when all the molecular and other processes involved have been described.

Therefore a thing is "comprehensible" for science if it can be described. And it would be "incomprehensible" if, for some reason, it could not be described. But now, there is nothing difficult to describe in a blow of a hammer here followed by a blue flash a million miles away. It is just as easy to describe as the blow of a hammer here followed by a blue flash here. The only difference between the two cases consists in the intervening distance in the first case. And all you have to do is to insert that fact in your description. The one, therefore, is as scientifically comprehensible as the other. This, therefore, cannot be your meaning. Or, at any rate, action at a distance is not incomprehensible in this, the only scientifically legitimate sense.

By a process of elimination I arrive at the following conclusion. What you really mean by the word *incomprehensible* is simply "unfamiliar." Man in his ordinary avocations of life has been accustomed for hundreds of thousands of years to what we may call action at one place. It is the ordinary type of action. We have seen one thing hitting another and this other thing bouncing off. All man's ordinary, everyday experience has been of action at one place. Such action is absolutely familiar. And it seems to need no explanation. So when man suddenly comes across a case of apparent action at a distance, such as gravitation, it seems astonishing. He declares it to be incomprehensible and impossible. And he demands that the appearance of it be explained. And by explanation of it he *means* that it be shown to be really a case of action at one place after all. Then it will become comprehensible, because it will seem familiar.

As against this it may be urged that gravitational action at a distance, as in the case of the stone falling to the ground, has always been familiar to mankind, quite as familiar as the bumping and hitting of things against one another. I reply that this was not thought of, by prescientific man, as action at a distance. It was not realized that the *earth* causes the stone to fall. The cause of the stone falling was supposed to be its own *weight*, which was a property of the stone itself. It was therefore the stone that acted, and this was an example of action at one place. It was only when science introduced the idea of gravitational *attraction* of one body by a distant body that man for the first time had the experience of action at a distance.

The demand of the average human consciousness for an explanation of gravitation actually set science to work. It resulted in the immense amount of time and labor devoted by scientists of an earlier generation in attempts to explain gravitation, that is, to reduce it to a case of action at one place, by means of such hypotheses as that space is full of flying particles which, by beating upon the unprotected sides of bodies, tended to drive them together.

These attempts, then, and the a priori dogma which led to them, namely, that action at a distance is impossible, were actual examples of how science has been influenced by the false idea that its function is explanation.

The same idea is at the bottom of the view that for the propagation of light through space a medium is necessary. I am not here concerned with the question whether there actually is or is not such a medium as the ether of space. That is a matter for the experts. But what I am concerned to say is that whether there is or is not such a medium is a pure question of evidence. It must not be decided by a priori dogmas. And the suggestion that, apart from any actual empirical evidence of the existence of ether, it must necessarily exist because it is *inconceivable* that light should travel across space without a medium is simply a deduction from the a priori dogma that action at a distance is impossible. There is nothing a priori impossible in the suggestion that certain events in the sun have here on the earth, or on any other distant object, the effects which we attribute to light, without anything, either particles or waves, traveling across the intervening distance.[3] Such a view may, of

[3] This suggestion, too, I owe to Professor Bridgman.

course, be wrong, and I do not say that there is anything to recommend it. But if anyone thinks it a priori *impossible*, it must be because he supposes that cause and effect cannot jump across a distance, but must be propagated from point to point, or in other words that action at a distance is impossible. And this view we have shown to have its roots in the false concept of explanation.

If experts hold, on the basis of positive evidence, that light is propagated through a medium, then that conclusion must be accepted. But if they hold this view merely on the basis of the supposed impossibility of causal action jumping over a distance of space, then we should have a case of science being misled by the false idea that its function is explanation.

All questions of fact ought to be decided solely upon the basis of evidence without the intrusion of a priori dogmas. One might lay down the principle that nothing that is actually observed to happen in nature, nothing for which there is the warrant of experience, ought to be declared impossible on the ground of any supposed a priori law. And I would call this *the principle of radical empiricism*. The phrase *radical empiricism* I have, of course, stolen from William James. But James used it in a different meaning.

But to return to the concept of explanation. One may find, I think, another example of its unfortunate influence in Newton's law of gravitation. Newton introduced into this law the concept of "force." The present tendency, I believe, is to dismiss gravitational force as a fiction. Now quite apart from any questions raised by the work of Einstein, it appears that Newton could perfectly well have stated his law without introducing the concept of force at all. He could have stated it in terms of empirically verifiable factors, such as velocities, masses, and distances. Why then did Newton introduce the concept of force, which was unnecessary even for his own law? What was his motive in so doing?

The motive, I think, was the ordinary human craving for

explanation, for an answer to the question "why?" If Newton had simply stated the relations between the masses, distances, and velocities of moving particles without any mention of forces, he would have given a perfectly good description of what happens and therefore a perfectly good law of gravitation, so far as the data available in his time allowed. But it would have appeared a mystery simply to say that, as a matter of brute fact, particles move in such and such ways and with such and such velocities, and that that was an end of the matter. People would have asked, "*Why* does this happen? *Why* do particles move in this way? *Why* do they move at all?" Newton obviously asked himself these questions, was puzzled by them, and thought he ought to give some reason. And he answered, "Particles move because of forces." And this seemed to explain the mystery because the conception of force is derived from our everyday, familiar sensations of stress and strain in our muscles. The explanation consisted in reducing the strange and unfamiliar motions of the heavenly bodies to the ordinary experiences of pushing and pulling of our daily life. Thus the otiose concept of force was introduced because Newton was not satisfied with a law which should simply describe what happens, but erroneously thought that the law should also explain *why* it happens.

The theory of gravitation, however, has been revolutionized in recent years. The concept of force is no longer the center of it. Einstein's law is not stated in terms of forces, but in terms of geometry. We might suppose, then, that the objectionable features of illusory explanations by means of fictitious entities such as forces would have disappeared. Let us see whether this is so.

I do not profess to understand the mathematics of relativity. But when those who do understand it attempt to enlighten the darkness of us others, we find them using some such language as the following. Space-time, they say, is curved or bent round the sun and other massive bodies. Its geometry is non-Euclidean. One must conceive, then, that space-time has, as it were, hills and valleys in it. Because of these hills and valleys the planets cannot run in straight lines. They have to run round about. This explains the curvature of their orbits.

This, of course, is merely the sort of language used by popularizers, and I dare say it may make some sensitive mathematicians shudder. But it must be remembered that some of these popularizers are themselves experts, and they are presumably responsible for the language they use. It seems a fair conclusion that they suppose that such language, though popular, is not wholly false. They think that, in some sense, space-time really is bent and that this curvature explains the curved motions of the planets.

When the plain man hears such language he is apt, if he is courageous enough to open his mouth at all, to express his puzzled bewilderment somewhat as follows. "I can understand," he may say, "the idea of a bent stick, or a bent material object of any sort. The stick is bent *in* space. But how can space-time itself be bent? What is there to *be* bent? And what is it bent *in*? And if space-time is bent, and so finite, what is outside it?" I do not know what the expert says in reply to this no-doubt crude talk. And I will not pursue the dialogue further. But the whole situation suggests certain reflections to me.

I suspect that there is something wrong here, and that the root of the trouble lies once more in the baneful influence of the false idea that scientific laws ought to explain phenomena. Is not the true position this? Einstein's law, in its strict, that is, its mathematical, form, contains nothing about hills and valleys and bumps in space-time. It contains nothing but mathematical formulae. These formulae are simply a generalized geometrical description of the curves which might be followed by all possible gravitating bodies. They do not explain anything at all. They are simply a description of certain curves.

Suppose you draw on the blackboard a certain curve, say,

an ellipse. A simple geometrical equation will describe that ellipse. Such an equation would not, of course, explain why a particle, which happened to be traveling in that ellipse, was doing so. It would simply describe the curve. Now suppose you draw on the board a number of other ellipses of varying eccentricities. You can get a generalized mathematical formula which will describe not one of the ellipses, but all of them. Once again this formula will not explain why a number of particles which happen to be traveling on these paths, are so traveling. It will be simply a generalized description of all the curves. Suppose, finally, you draw on the board a number of other curves, circles, parabolas, and so on, in addition to the ellipses. You can still get a more generalized formula which will describe them. I believe that Einstein's law of gravitation is nothing but such a formula, only it describes not merely a few ellipses and circles, but every possible path of every possible gravitating body. It does not explain their movements. It merely describes them.

No doubt it is the case that, in order to reach this vastly generalized and complicated description, it has been necessary to introduce time as a fourth co-ordinate, and to make use of non-Euclidean geometry. But that does not alter the principle. The non-Euclidean geometry was not introduced to explain anything, but simply for purposes of description. And it was rendered necessary only because of the variety and complication of the curves which had to be described. You might imagine a universe in which all possible gravitating bodies moved in circles. In such a universe the simple equation of the circle would *be* the law of gravitation, and neither time as a fourth co-ordinate, nor non-Euclidean geometry, would be necessary.

We are usually told that Einstein's law is a description of the curvature of space-time. This, I am convinced, is absolutely meaningless. It is absolutely meaningless to say that space, or space-time, are either curved or straight, that they are either non-Euclidean or Euclidean. A stick may be bent or straight *in* space. But the space in which it lies is neither. It is usually assumed that space had hitherto been regarded as Euclidean, and that this was quite easy to understand, but that with the advent of Einstein we have to think of space as non-Euclidean. Now the essence of my present contention is that it was quite as meaningless to say that space is Euclidean as to say that it is "bent." It is only things *in* space which can be described in either of these ways. Space itself is absolutely amorphous. It has no shape; and therefore no geometry. And if we now ask, "What is it, then, that in Einstein's law is described by the formulae of a four-dimensional non-Euclidean geometry?," I answer that it is the curves followed by gravitating bodies. The law is not a description of space-time, but a generalized description of certain curves.

But the common way of looking at the matter supposes that space-time is itself curved and that this curvature *causes* the planets to move as they do. There are supposed to be, as it were, two distinct facts, first the curvature of space-time, and then, secondly, the resulting orbits of the planets. These two are separated, and the first, the curvature, is then supposed to be the cause of the second, the planetary motions.

Now if I were to say that the cause of this table being square is that it occupies a square piece of space, you would rightly think such a statement nonsense. You cannot separate the space from the table which occupies it, attribute a shape to this pure space, and say that this is the cause of the table being square. You cannot in point of fact attribute any shape at all to pure space. It is tables and chairs, material things *in* space, which have shape. In just the same way, I think, it is nonsense to speak of space-time itself as being either Euclidean or non-Euclidean, *apart* from the things which are in it. And it is just as meaningless to say that the hills and valleys in space-time *cause* the planets to move in curved courses as it would be to say that the square shape of the space which this table occupies *causes* the table to be square. But because this is not realized, the illusory idea of causal explanation slips in. Space-time itself is supposed to have hills and valleys in it, and these are supposed to thrust the planets out of their straight courses. As if the hill or the valley were all there waiting in space-time before the planet comes to it.

What is this but the old idea of pushing and pulling? Only instead of the planets being pulled by forces, as they were for Newton, they are now being pushed by coming up against the sides of hills in space-time, just as the billiard ball is pushed out of the straight by an unevenness in the surface of the table.

What, then, is it which has misled so many writers on relativity? What is the psychological cause of the mental confusion which I have just been trying to clear up. I answer that the root cause of all this confused thinking is *the craving for explanation*, the desire to try to show that Einstein's law, not merely describes, but *explains* the phenomena.

Of course formulae in non-Euclidean geometry may correctly describe the motion of the planets. But I suggest that the curvature of space-time is just as fictitious as the forces of Newton. And it has been foisted into discussions of relativity for precisely the same reason as forces were foisted into Newton's law. Forces were supposed to explain *why* bodies move as they do. They explained these motions by appealing to familiar sensations of muscular strain. And now the hills and bumps in space-time are introduced for an identical reason. They make the phenomena seem familiar by comparing them to what happens when I go round a hill instead of through it. Einstein's law, as a pure mathematical formula, explains nothing. It simply says, "This is what happens. Bodies move in such-and-such curves." But inevitably the human mind asks, "*Why* do they move in these curves?" There is, of course, no answer to this question. It is meaningless. But just as Newton was puzzled by it in regard to his law, and answered, "Oh, it is because of forces," so now modern writers, equally puzzled by the question "why?" in regard to Einstein's law, say, "Oh, it is because the planets are pushed about by the curvature of space-time." This too, like the forces, seems familiar and easy to understand. It seems to explain the phenomena, that is, to make them familiar, until one realizes that the whole idea of scientific explanation is a bogus idea.

And though it is true that this talk about hills and valleys in space-time is a mere popular mode of expression, still I am not convinced that men of science, in their talk of "expanding universes" and "exploding universes," do not take it at least half-seriously, some of them perhaps quite seriously. I am not convinced that their own thought is not infected by it. And if so, I do not know what misguidance of science may not follow. And if there is a misguidance, then it will be due to the fact that science has not *even yet* completely emancipated itself from the belief that its function is to explain phenomena.

I am not suggesting that the scientific theories of expanding and exploding universes are false. That, again, is a matter for the experts, not for the philosophers. No doubt these theories can be *interpreted* so as to be true. And I dare say their pure mathematical expression *is* true, just as is Einstein's law of gravitation. They doubtless describe admirably the known facts about the motions of distant nebulae and other astronomical entities. But if they are interpreted to mean that space itself, or space-time itself, is a sort of round ball which is getting bigger and bigger in the middle of nothingness, with nothing, not even empty space, outside it, then I am certain that it becomes perfectly meaningless. And I do think that there is grave danger that, not only the minds of the general public, but the minds of scientists themselves, may be misled.

I do not know whether I have succeeded in convincing you of anything. But what I have been trying to prove to you is simply this: that such questions as "What are the exact functions of science? What precisely is its business? What is it trying to do? What ought it try to do? What are its boundaries?" are important questions for the scientist himself. Because, if they are wrongly answered, or if, as more often happens, they are not considered at all, then science may be seriously misled *in its own field*. Such questions are usually regarded as belonging to the philosophy of science, and are studied by philosophers to the best of their ability. Perhaps it is a pity that scientists themselves do not usually investigate them, because they might study them so much the more effectually. The important thing, however, is that they should be studied.

Note on the Concept of Explanation

The reader may ask whether explanation, if it is not the business of science, is the business of philosophy. Should we, in other words, admit that there *is* such a thing as explanation, that it is a meaningful concept, even though science is not the place for it? Or should we say, on the contrary, that the whole idea of explanation is illusory, wherever it is found, whether in science or philosophy? Obviously this is much the same as asking whether in the last resort the universe is rational or irrational. If there is no such thing as explanation at all, then all we can say is that the world is as it is, and that things happen as they do, that that is the end of the matter, and that there is in the last analysis no rhyme or reason for anything. Equally obviously, this is the vastest question that the human mind can ask, and one which it is ridiculous to treat in a footnote! Nevertheless, since the question is bound to frame itself in the mind of the reader, I think it is better at least to indicate my personal attitude to it in however brief and unsatisfactory a way.

I have mentioned only two types of explanation. One is teleological explanation, or explanation by means of purposes. The other is explanation by familiarity. There is, however, a third type of explanation which I have not thought it necessary to mention in an essay devoted exclusively to science, because this third type of explanation has never been used in science and has made its appearance only in the writings of philosophers. I will now say something about this.

The question "why?" may mean "for what purpose?" If so

interpreted it gives rise to teleological explanation. Or it may indicate simply a desire to have the unfamiliar reduced to the familiar, and this gives rise to the second type of explanation. But thirdly, the question "why?" may be a request for a *logical reason* or *ground*. Thus the logical reason for any proposition is that prior proposition which implies it and by means of which it is proved. If $A=B$, and $B=C$, then $A=C$. And the facts that $A=B$, and $B=C$, may be given as the logical reason why $A=C$. In this sense, too, the axiom of parallels (in Euclidean geometry) may be given as the reason why the three angles of a triangle are equal to two right angles.

If the question "why?" is interpreted in this sense, then we get the third or *logical* type of explanation. To explain a fact will then mean to give a logical reason for which the fact follows. If the world could be logically deduced from some first principle, if the relation of the ultimate reality to the world could be exhibited, not as the relation of cause to effect, but as the relation of logical antecedent to logical consequent, then the world would be so far, in this sense, "explained."

This idea makes its appearance in the philosophy of Spinoza, in most modern idealism, but most clearly of all in the philosophy of Hegel. Suppose that the universe consists of the things $A, B, C, D, \ldots$ etc. If one could show that A logically implies B, while B logically implies C, and so on throughout the whole universe, then everything in the universe might be said to be explained. B exists *because* A exists, and A is the logical reason for B. The whole universe would be rational, i.e., logical. Hegel attempted to deduce the main features of the universe (categories) from one another in this way.[4] To give an example: He tried to show that the idea of *being* logically implies the idea of *becoming* (change). If this were valid, it would explain why the universe is everywhere characterized by impermanence and flux. For if being logically

---

[4] That this was Hegel's intention has recently been denied by some critics. I cannot discuss this question here.

implies becoming, then any being whatever, from an atom to a nebula, must *necessarily* be in a state of becoming, or flux. And Hegel attempted to carry out this kind of explanation for all the features of the universe.

To this it may be objected that the first term in the series, *A*, must itself be an unexplained mystery, since there is no prior term by which it can be explained. And this means that the whole series is really a mystery, and nothing is, in the end, explained. Hegel attempted to meet this difficulty by thinking of the universe as a closed system, which we may symbolize by a circle. The beginning and the end meet. The first term, *A*, explains all the others until we come to the last term, *Z*. Here the circle returns upon itself, for *Z* logically implies *A*. Thus there is no unexplained term, no ultimate mystery. The universe is a closed system of which every term really implies every other term, so that the whole system is self-explanatory. It is right to mention that Hegel's own philosophy is an attempt to blend together both the teleological and the logical types of explanation.

From the point of view of motivation, logical explanation may be grouped with teleological explanation, since the motive of both is to show that the universe is rational, and therefore like ourselves. For the word "rational" means either logical or purposive. A man is said to be rational if he is logical, and he is also called rational if his conduct is governed by intelligent purpose. Thus the three types of explanation may be arranged as follows:

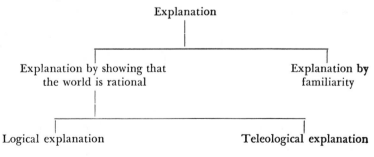

As to the question whether any sort of explanation is ever possible or whether in the last resort all explanation, even in philosophy, is as illusory as we have seen it to be in science, the position seems to me to be as follows. Explanation by familiarity is totally worthless both in science and philosophy for the reasons given above. The other two kinds of explanation fall outside science, and have their place in philosophy, if anywhere. Have they, then, any real place even in philosophy? Opinions differ about this.

(1) *Teleological Explanation.* We may feel vaguely that the universe is driving towards something, and we may envisage this as goodness, beauty, or what not. And there may in all this be a real groping towards some truth. But mere feelings, even though they may vaguely indicate something true, do not constitute knowledge. And as far as any real or definite knowledge regarding the cosmic purpose is concerned, we may well think, with Omar, that

> *The revelations of devout and learned,*
> *Who rose before us and as prophets burned,*
> *Are all but stories which, awoke from sleep,*
> *They told their comrades and to sleep returned.*

And it is not unlikely that philosophy will conclude, as did science in the seventeenth century, that "divine purposes" are beyond human comprehension, and will turn to more profitable fields of study where something can be accomplished. At any rate, no philosophy so far has had the least success in the teleological explanation of anything.

(2) *Logical Explanation.* This position is even more hopeless than in the case of teleological explanation. For all I know, everything in the universe may logically imply everything else. But no one has ever shown that it is so. Hegel's philosophy is the only attempt ever made on the grand scale, and it was, in my opinion, completely unsuccessful. And this is also, I think, the general opinion at the present day.

Hence the prospects of philosophical explanation do not appear to be rosy. Theoretically philosophy might still perhaps, in spite of past failures, aim at explanation. But in practice I should say that the philosopher, like the scientist, has never succeeded in explaining a single solitary fact.

Has philosophy, then, a descriptive function, like science, to which it can turn and do useful work? The answer is that it has. In fact, much of the best philosophical work, both in the past and at the present time, has been purely descriptive. This has always been true, for example, of the British empirical tradition. But philosophy will be descriptive of principles more general in character than those which form the subject matter of science. For example, to give a description of particular causal laws is the business of particular sciences. But to give a description or definition of the principle of causality as such is one part of the business of philosophy. Is the essence of causality properly described as simply invariable sequence? Or should the ideas of necessity, compulsion, force be included in the description?[5] These are the kinds of questions, I think, to which philosophy can attempt an answer with some hope of success, and without condemning itself to that futility which seems always to attend upon its efforts at "explanation." Medieval science stagnated for centuries until the seventeenth-century scientists made an end of attempts to pursue final causes. Is not the stagnation and futility which have always been charged against philosophy probably due to the fact that philosophy still hankers after explanations?

Hence if any philosopher wishes to include explanation among the functions of philosophy, I should not entirely warn him off the ground. There is just the *faint* possibility that he may be right and that he might succeed. For *if* explanation is possible at all, it certainly is the business of philos-

---

[5] This example will make it evident to philosophical readers that what I have here called the "descriptive" function of philosophy is much the same as what many philosophers call "analysis."

ophy and not of science. But I should unquestionably regard his enterprise with the same sorrowful tolerance as that with which one views any other forlorn hope. Thus while making a polite bow to the possibility that there may be such a thing as explanation, I should personally advocate a philosophy which excludes explanation from its objectives. I should advocate a reform in philosophy similar to that which occurred when science in the seventeenth century turned its back upon final causes. Only in such a reform, I believe, lies the possibility of advance.

Science and Ethics

THE relation between modern science and ethics may be treated either systematically, as a presently existing problem which awaits solution, or historically. For the historian of ideas, the questions are: What influence has modern science actually had on ethics, and how, and when? It is these latter problems which I wish to discuss here. We must first decide what we mean by *modern*. When did modern science begin and who were its founders? One possible view is that it had its beginning in what is sometimes called the scientific revolution of the seventeenth century. Newton was born in the same year in which Galileo died, 1642, and everything which has been accomplished since that era may be called modern science. But a physicist to whom I recently posed the question of when modern science began replied that it began with Einstein and Niels Bohr, that is to say, with the theory of relativity and the discovery of electrons and protons. Both answers are, of course, correct. It is only a question of what you choose to mean by the word *modern*. But for my purposes I shall count the seventeenth century as the time of the beginning of modern science. More recent physics, especially Heisenberg's so-called principle of indeterminacy, have indeed raised problems in the sphere of ethics which I shall briefly discuss. But the supremely important, indeed revolutionary, effects of science on ethics came in the earlier time beginning in the seventeenth century.

A word should also be said about what we should take the word *ethics* to stand for here. It may be used either as applying to actual human conduct, as when we inquire whether someone's conduct was ethical or unethical. Or it may mean the philosophical theory of the nature and foundations of morality. And it is in this latter sense that I shall understand it for our purposes in this essay.

Perhaps we can now safely formulate our problem. Let us put it this way: What influence has science had, in the period from the time of Newton and Galileo down to the present day, upon the philosophical theory of ethics? I shall arrange my discussion of this subject under the following three heads: (1) Science and the Subjectivity of Morals, (2) Science and the Relativity of Morals, and (3) Science and the Freedom of the Will.

Science and the Subjectivity of Morals

Before the rise of modern science European thinkers believed, for the most part, in the objectivity of the moral law. The influence of science has been to destroy this theory and to introduce its opposite, the theory of ethical subjectivism. The theory of moral objectivism maintained that moral laws are not a purely human creation, having their seat and origin in the human mind, but that they have a non-human source, either in the mind of God or, according to some versions, in the fundamental structure of the external world, like the laws of gravitation. The influence of science has been to undermine this view and to substitute the view that morals are subjective, having their seat and origin in the human mind and not in the external universe. I do not mean, of course, that this is the official view of science. Pure science, as such, has nothing to say on this question, which is philosophical, and not scientific, in its nature. And individual scientists may take this view or they may not. But in general, intellectuals before the rise of science believed in ethical objectivism, whereas now they generally believe in ethical subjectivism. And it is science which has caused this change.

Historically, there have been two versions of ethical objectivism. There is the theistic version. According to this the moral law originates in the mind of God and is imposed on man by the command of God. This is the view which we find in the two theistic religions which have spread over the Western world, Judaism and Christianity. But there is also a non-theistic version which is found in the religions which originated in India, Hinduism and Buddhism. This Eastern version appears in what is called the law of Karma. This is the law of nature that says every man receives in the long run precisely what he deserves in the way of reward or punishment. This is bound up with belief in reincarnation. Suppose a child is born crippled or diseased. Christianity and Judaism provide no morally acceptable explanation of this. It is an inexplicable injustice. But according to the Indian religions, it is a punishment for some sin committed in a previous incarnation. Usually—though there are exceptions—Oriental thinkers believe that this law of Karma is not imposed by God, or the gods, but is a law of nature, to which indeed the gods themselves may be subject. It is an impersonal part of the structure of the universe.

In many cultures the idea of an objective moral law is connected with the belief in a world-purpose, a plan of things towards which the world-process is working. Right and wrong in human conduct may then be defined in terms of that purpose. That action is right which tends to harmonize with the world-purpose, that action is wrong which works against it. In such a philosophy it may be possible to explain events by reference to their purposes. This leads to the distinction between two kinds of explanation, which philosophers have labeled teleological and mechanical. Teleological explanation means explanation in terms of purpose, mechanical explanation is in terms of causes. Suppose we see a man climbing a hill, and suppose we ask for an *explanation* of this phenomenon. Two quite different kinds of explanation may be given, both of which may be true at the same time. We may say that he is climbing the hill in order to enjoy the view from the top. This would be a teleological explanation, explanation in terms of purpose. But a physiologist might say, with equal truth, that the man's climbing can be explained by its causes. Some external stimulus caused a release of energy stored in the man's nervous system, and this caused muscular movements in the man's legs, and those caused his ascent of the hill. This would be an example of mechanical explanation. Before the rise of modern science, men usually believed that teleological, as well as mechanical, explanations could be given, not only of the movements of men and animals, but of all events and processes in nature. They thought this because they believed in a world-purpose of some kind. Plato for instance, in one of his dialogues, represents Socrates as reproaching the philosopher Anaxagoras on the ground that he denied that the motions of the heavenly bodies, sun, earth, moon, and stars are controlled by mind and purpose and taught that they are the result of nothing but mechanical forces.

In the modern world both of the two connected beliefs, namely the objectivity of the moral law and the purposive character of the world-process, have, except in the minds of a few religious men, ceased to exercise any influence. They are ignored, even if they are not actually denied. And this change in men's minds, it may reasonably be asserted, has been one of the results of the influence of science. There is an often-quoted passage in an essay by Bertrand Russell in which he says:

Such in outline, but even more purposeless, more void of meaning, is the world which *science* presents for our belief. Amid such a world, if anywhere, our ideals must henceforward find a home. That man is the product of causes which had no prevision of the end they were achieving; that his origin, his growth, his hopes and fears, his loves and his beliefs, are but the outcome of accidental collocations of atoms . . . these things . . . are so nearly certain that no philosophy which rejects them can hope to stand.

It is easy to illustrate the emphasis placed by science on mechanical explanation. Newton himself was a highly religious man who certainly believed in divine purposes. Yet the comparison between Newton's solar system and a clock is an obvious example of mechanical explanation. When once a clock is wound up it runs itself, because it is provided with its own force in the spring. The spring which runs the solar system is gravitation. The planets resemble wheels. The solar system is a great cosmic clock, which all man-made clocks imitate. Napoleon asked La Place whether God, as creator, was not required at the beginning, to make and start off the world-clock. Not at all, said La Place, the nebular hypothesis explains the beginning of the world. God seemed to him just an unnecessary hypothesis.

Not only can the world as a whole be thought of as a machine, but all its smaller parts, including human and animal organisms, can be considered machines. According to Thomas Hobbes, who was a contemporary of Galileo, the heart is the spring of the human machine, the nerves are so many strings, the joints are wheels. David Hume, in the eighteenth century, wrote: "Look around the world. You will find it nothing but one great machine, subdivided into an infinite number of lesser machines." This kind of thinking was never heard of before the rise of science and was a direct product of science.

Of course mechanism is not inconsistent with purpose. A clock is a machine but it has the purpose of telling the time. But although science need not deny purposes in nature and, so far as I know, does not deny them, it tends to ignore them, because the conception of them is useless for any scientific purpose. One of the main functions of science is concerned

247

with prediction. But to predict an event a knowledge of its causes is necessary. A knowledge of its purposes will not help. It might be true that in the divine plan of the world the purpose of rain is to make plants and animals live and grow. But this will not enable a meteorologist to predict the weather. It might be true that the purposes of the sun and moon are to enable men to see and find their way in the world by day and by night. But this will not enable an astronomer to predict an eclipse. Only a knowledge of causes makes prediction possible.

The enormous importance thus given by science to the concept of mechanism has simply crowded the concept of teleology from men's minds. The tremendous success of Newtonian science dazzled the human mind. Throughout the middle ages men talked of purposes, gave teleological explanations of eclipses, rainbows, earthquakes, and got scientifically nowhere. The new science came with its mechanical explanations and all seemed to become luminous and clear. No wonder men forgot the idea of purposes in nature, so that we have as an end result the sort of world-view described in the passage I quoted from Russell. The result of this world-view is that the moral law, which is tied up with the idea of purpose, is now conceived as not objective, but subjective, a creation of the human mind.

Science and the Relativity of Morals

The theory that morals are the creation of the human mind tends to lead on to the theory that they are relative to differences in the minds of different human beings. Thus arose the theory of ethical relativity, the view that all moral codes and standards are relative either to individual persons, so that they vary from person to person, or to societies and cultures, so that they vary from culture to culture. Relativity to individual persons was the first view put forward in the mod-

ern period. It was formulated first by Hobbes, who wrote:
"Every man calleth that which pleaseth him good, and that
which displeaseth him evil; insomuch that because every man
differeth from another in constitution, they differ from one
another concerning the common distinctions between good
and evil." This is a very crude kind of moral relativity. It
makes each individual his own standard of what is right and
wrong. A thief or murderer could justify his crimes by saying
simply that since they please him they are good. Since this
obviously will not do, the more sophisticated forms of ethical
relativism which we find advocated in our day make right
and wrong relative not to individual persons, but to civilizations, cultures, or large social groups. The Japanese may
have one moral code, the Chinese another, the Hindus a third,
and Christian nations a fourth. This was the concept put forward by Edward Westermarck in his book *Ethical Relativity*.
It was he, I think, who originally coined this phrase.

There seems to be a popular belief that it was the anthropologists of the present age who originated, or at least proved,
the truth of ethical relativity. This of course is quite absurd.
All that the anthropologists have done is to dig out a large
number of examples of varieties of ethical standards, especially among more or less remote peoples such as the Mela-
nesian islanders. But the general principle has been known
at least since the time of Herodotus, who recorded in his
writings the many different sets of moral beliefs and customs
which he found in his travels even in the restricted area of the
ancient world. Plato, too, knew quite well that the moral
standards of "barbarians" differed from those of the Hellenes.

But I must register a protest against some of the extravagant
conclusions of modern ethical relativists. The proposition
"morals are relative" is systematically ambiguous. It may
mean only that moral *ideas* and *beliefs* vary in different cultures. This is an indisputable fact. Or it may mean that moral
truth varies. This I cannot accept. I am making the distinc-

tion between what is *thought* to be right and what *is* right. I am asserting that moral opinions are variable, but that moral truth is not. I am prepared to admit that the burning alive of witches was *believed* to be ethically right five hundred years ago. But I deny that it *was* right. It was just as cruel and wicked then as it is now. The only difference was that our ancestors did not believe or know this. I am making exactly the same distinction as there is between saying that men long ago *believed* that the earth was flat, but that the truth was then, as now, that the earth was a globe. The earth has not changed its shape from flat to round, nor has burning people alive changed its ethical complexion from right to wrong. On both subjects it is only man's *ideas* that have changed.

The usual reply to this is that the two cases, the shape of the earth and moral values, are not analogous, because statements about the earth's shape can be verified, proved, or disproved, but statements about moral values cannot. Suppose we want to say that Japanese moral ideas are truer and better than those of Australian aborigines. How could we verify this unless we have a common standard by which to measure their relative values? And there is, it is said, no such standard. I cannot accept this view, and I believe that a common standard exists, but before discussing that question it may be worthwhile first to look at some consequences we should have to accept if we deny the existence of any common standard.

First, if there is no common standard then all propositions which purport to compare the ethical codes of different social groups with one another in respect of their relative value, to say that one group's ethical standard is higher or lower, better or worse, than another, will be not false, but meaningless. Most of us would tend to feel that Christian or Jewish moral ideals are higher than those of Australian aborigines, and that the ethics of Confucius are superior to those of the Papuans of New Guinea. Perhaps these examples may be not well chosen. But we do habitually compare one civilization with another and believe the sets of ethical ideas to be found in them to be some better, some worse. The fact that such judgments may often be superficial or erroneous is irrelevant. The question at issue is whether any such judgments have any meaning. We habitually assume that they have. But if there is no common standard all such judgments will be meaningless.

This in turn implies that the whole notion of *progress* as applied to ethical ideals is a delusion. If there is no common standard to judge by, it will make no sense to say, for example, that the teachings of the Sermon on the Mount register an advance on what went before or that the ideal of the love between all men is better than that of a tooth for a tooth and a claw for a claw. Such statements cannot be true or false. They yield no information, but presumably give expression to nothing but our egotism and self-conceit. We think our ideals better than those of savages, simply because they are *ours*. The savage has just as much right to think that his are better, on the ground that they are *his*. And Jesus Christ can only have been led to his quite absurd belief that his gospel of love was better than what went before it by his personal vanity. All he was actually doing was wasting his time by changing Tweedledum to Tweedledee.

I am saying that propositions attributing higher or lower worth to the moral codes of different races or ages are impossible without a common standard which is applicable universally to the whole human race. But now the question arises whether, if we deny such a universal standard, we can even make judgments of better and worse about individual human beings. Does it make any sense to say that President Lincoln was a better man than some criminal or moral imbecile of his own time and country, or that Jesus was a better man than Judas Iscariot? By what standards are we judging? If there is no universal human standard, what smaller areas are to be adopted as the *loci* of different standards? Where are we to draw the lines of demarcation? We can split up humanity, though somewhat arbitrarily, into races, races into nations, nations into tribes, tribes into families, families into individuals. But where do we draw the moral boundaries? Shall we say that each "social group" has its own moral code? But how does one ever fix the boundaries of the group? Does the American nation constitute a single group having a single moral standard? Or does the standard of what I ought to do change continuously as I cross the continent in a railway train and pass from one state into another? Perhaps every town and village has its own peculiar standard. We may go by the saying, "In Rome do as Rome does." But can we stop there? Within the village are numerous cliques, each having its own set of ideas. Why should not each of these claim to be bound only by its own special and peculiar moral standards? And if it comes to that, why should not the gangsters of New York or Chicago claim to constitute a social group having its own morality which can perhaps be defined by Valachi's phrase, "You live by the knife or the gun, and you die by the knife or the gun." Of course we can say that the nation will not tolerate this. But that is irrelevant to the logic of the matter. If there is no common standard these intolerable consequences inevitably follow.

But if we admit the logic of all this, the question is then forced upon us: Where or what *is* the universal standard by which ethical ideals are to be measured? I think we can only say that it is human happiness. I have to plead guilty to being something like an old-fashioned utilitarian. I am suggesting that the ethical ideals of the Sermon on the Mount, if we all actually followed and lived up to them, would lead to a generally higher level of human happiness, while the codes of behavior accepted by cannibals and savage tribes lead to misery or at least to lesser degrees of happiness.

At this point someone may ask: How do you propose to define this vague word *happiness*? Most of the attempts made by philosophers have proved disastrous failures. If you say, as John Stuart Mill suggested, that a man's happiness means the sum of his pleasures, you will have to explain how it comes about that the happiest men are often those who can afford very few pleasures, those who are forced to lead the simple life, while the man of pleasure is often far from happy. I admit this difficulty, but can only say that, within limits and with exceptions, we most of us know when we are happy, and we certainly know when we are unhappy, and that therefore we know well enough in practice what happiness is. It is a delusion to suppose that you do not know the meaning of a word unless you can define it. The test of whether we understand the meaning of a word is whether we use it correctly and do not misapply it.

It may be objected that happiness cannot serve as a common standard because happiness itself is relative and variable. One man's happiness may be another person's misery. To this we must reply that sources of happiness must be divided into two kinds, those which vary with different people and those which are roughly the same for all men. For example, different occupations suit different people. One man is happy as an engineer, another as a politician, and they would be miserable if they had to exchange roles. But there are other conditions of happiness which are the same for most men—for all men except perhaps a few eccentrics. To give a few examples: Good health, the absence of physical pain and mental worry, the possession of at least a certain minimum of worldly goods are, for most men, necessary preconditions of happiness. Those who say that the good man is happy on the rack are, as Aristotle observed, talking nonsense. If a man is in these physical matters sufficiently well situated, it is probable that the next most important essential is that all his powers, both of body and mind, should have opportunity for regular expression and exercise. A reasonable amount of amusement, relaxation, and pleasure is also necessary. And a main source of human happiness lies in the affection of friends and in the love for one another of the members of a family. All these in general are common human goods. True, there are differences between men even in these fundamentals of life. Some men have more need of one thing, others of another. But we must not exaggerate these differences. And if, instead of saying in abstract language that morality is what leads to "the greatest happiness of the greatest number," we say that the supreme end of morality is to see that as many men as possible in the world have health, a sufficiency of material goods, opportunity for the proper exercise of their faculties, a measure of relaxation and leisure, a home, a family, and friends—we shall certainly not be advocating either a false or an ignoble view of morality.

To sum up what has been said under this head of science and ethical relativity:

1. The rise of modern science has caused a general collapse of moral objectivism and a general acceptance of the view that moral rules and ideals have their foundation in human nature and not in the external universe.

2. This led to a widespread belief in the relativity of moral codes.

3. We accepted this as correct provided we admit the distinction between what men *think* right and what really *is* right, and apply the relativity principle only to the former.

4. This implies that there must be a common standard in terms of which ethical codes are to be evaluated, and this common standard we found in the concept of human happiness.

5. To the objection that happiness itself is relative and variable we indicated that there are certain conditions of happiness which are universal, and it is on these that a universal ethical code must be based.

I now pass on to our third heading.

Science and the Freedom of the Will

The third matter for discussion is the charge that science implies determinism, which is inconsistent with free will, and is therefore destructive of the concept of moral responsibility, which rests upon the assumption of free will.

It is natural to suppose that scientific method and the scientific view of the world imply determinism. Science assumes the universality of natural law and especially the law of causation, the law that every event in nature is wholly determined by natural causes and is therefore theoretically predictable in the sense that it could be predicted if we knew all the causes. A human action is an event in nature just as much as an eclipse of the sun is, and it is therefore theoretically predictable beforehand. If so, what room is there for free will, which means that I can choose between two courses of action and am not compelled to adopt either.

Some men of science forty or fifty years ago, for example Eddington, suggested that the solution of this puzzle lay in something like Heisenberg's principle of indeterminacy. The human mind, like the electron, suggested Eddington, may be not wholly subject to determinism and may therefore be free. The difficulty of this—or rather one of its difficulties—seems to be that Heisenberg's principle applies to sub-microscopic entities but not to large objects such as the human body. The principle may imply that the laws of nature are statistical only, but for all practical purposes determinism will still hold in the world of large objects. For instance, though the motions of a single electron may be unpredictable, the motions of large objects such as planets consisting of billions of electrons will be predictable. No astronomer calculating the motions and positions of the planets would consider it a possibility that the earth might suddenly jump out of its orbit into the orbit of Mars owing to the principle of indeterminacy.

If we admit this then we shall have to conclude that the principle of indeterminacy has no real bearing on the problem of free will. Free will should not be analyzed as meaning indeterminacy of the will. We shall have to explain it, I suggest, as meaning determination of the will by motives within the minds of the agents. It will mean psychological determinism. An act is called free if its immediate cause is a psychological state in the mind of the agent. It is called unfree if its immediate causes are all external to the agent. Both free and unfree acts are determined by causes and are theoretically predictable, but they differ in the kinds of causes from which they proceed. The causes of my free actions are my own desires. The causes of my unfree acts lie outside me. Let me illustrate. Suppose a man being tried for murder signs a confession while in police custody. In court the judge asks him whether he signed it of his own free will or because the police tortured him. He replies that he signed it of his own free will because his conscience compelled him to do so. We see here that his act is accounted freely done if it is caused by a state of mind in himself, namely his conscience. But if it had been caused by an external agent, police torture, it would not be considered free. There are no doubt puzzling cases in which it is difficult to apply this criterion of free will. But it may be possible to defend the general principle notwithstanding.

Now suppose that in the case imagined there had been a philosopher, or a philosophically minded scientist, on the jury. He might have argued that the whole question of whether the confession was caused by the prisoner's conscience or by police pressure was irrelevant, because in either case his confession was determined by causes and could not therefore be a case of free will. The judge and the rest of the jury would rightly conclude that the philosopher must be making some sort of a mistake. He must have been using the phrase "free will" in some peculiar way of his own which is not the way in which common-sense people like the judge and the other jurors usually use it. In the English language free will is the phrase we apply to cases where a man acts from his own inner motives. That is what the phrase *free will* means in correct English. The philosopher's mistake simply consists in using bad English, or a jargon of his own.

Moral responsibility is not only compatible with determinism, it actually requires it. The assumption on which punishment and reward are based is that human behavior is causally determined by motives, so that it can be influenced by inflicting pain or its opposite. If there were no determinism of human beings at all, their actions would be unpredictable and capricious, and therefore irresponsible. I think therefore that science can be acquitted of the charge that it makes free will, and therefore moral responsibility, impossible.

Index

Index